SOUL-FORCE:
African Heritage in Afro-American Religion

SOUL-FORCE:
African Heritage
in Afro-American Religion

by LEONARD E. BARRETT

C. Eric Lincoln Series on Black Religion
Anchor Press/Doubleday
Garden City, New York
1974

Published simultaneously in hard and paperback editions by Anchor Press/ Doubleday & Company, Inc., in 1974.

Grateful acknowledgment is made for the use of the following:
"The Boys from Brooklyn." Reprinted by permission of TIME, The Weekly Newsmagazine; Copyright Time Inc. Published July 4, 1960 in TIME. Article by E. Franklin Frazier on Marcus Garvey. Reprinted by permission of *The Nation.*
Portions of *The Philosophy and Opinions of Marcus Garvey,* edited by Amy Jacques Garvey and published by Frank Cass and Co. Ltd., 67 Great Russell Street, London WCIB 3BT.
Excerpts from *The Daily Gleaner,* Kingston, Jamaica. Reprinted by permission of The Gleaner Company Ltd.
"Spirits Unchained" from the book *My Name Is Afrika.* Copyright © 1971 by Keorapetse Kgositsile. Reprinted by permission of Doubleday & Company, Inc.

CONTENTS

FOREWORD

This series of books is about the black religious experience. It is addressed to Blackamericans because the rich heritage that is their history has not been made fully available to them in the usual ways in which a society informs its membership about the significant aspects of its development. Blackamericans want to know—indeed they *must* know—more about who they *were* and who they *are* if they are seriously concerned about whom they intend to become. The black man's religion is a critical component of his American passage from slavery to a freedom which is still to be perfected.

This series is addressed to white America, too. The black experience—religious, social, economic, political—is writ large in the cultural development of the larger society. Understanding it is crucial to an informed perspective of what America is or can become. To a degree not always recognized, America is what it is because the black minority is here, and has been here since long before this nation came into being.

The blacks brought their religion with them. After a time they accepted the white man's religion, but they have not always expressed it in the white man's way. It became the black man's purpose—perhaps it was his *destiny*—to shape, to fashion, to re-create the religion offered him by the Christian slave master, to remold it nearer to his own heart's desire, nearer to his own peculiar needs. The black religious experience is something more than a black patina on a white happening. It is a unique response to a historical occurrence which can never be replicated for any people in America.

The black man's pilgrimage in America was made less onerous because of his religion. His religion was the organizing principle around which his life was structured. His church was his school, his forum, his political arena, his social club, his art gallery, his conservatory of music. It was lyceum and gymnasium as well as *sanctum sanctorum*. His religion was his fellowship with man, his audience with God. It was the peculiar sustaining force which gave him the strength to endure when endurance gave no promise, and the courage to be creative in the face of his own dehumanization.

This is the black religious experience. This is what this book and this series are about.

C. Eric Lincoln
Kumasi Hill
Antioch, Tennessee

ACKNOWLEDGMENTS

The author gratefully acknowledges the contributions of the students in the class "Cult and Cultism" conducted at Temple University, in the Department of Religion over several semesters. Many of the ideas in this book were discussed and analyzed in these class sessions.

The greater part of this book, however, is based on materials gathered in field research in Africa, the West Indies and the United States. To my friends in these countries, the author is deeply grateful. Prudence dictated that names be avoided in fear that some key contributors be omitted.

To my wife, Theodora, whose work it was to type and retype the many drafts of this work, I am more than grateful for her companionship, patience and understanding.

My thanks, too, to Mrs. Karen McCarthy-Brown, who read the manuscript and not only corrected faulty construction, but offered many ideas in the process of its development.

Finally, I am indebted to Professor C. Eric Lincoln, editor and colleague, whose interest and encouragement brought this work to publication. Whatever is wanting, I must attribute to my own deficiencies.

Leonard E. Barrett
Temple University
March 7, 1973

Dedicated to my wife
Theodora J. Barrett

CHAPTER 1

SOUL-FORCE
Introduction

The term "soul" is a popular word in today's Black revolutionary language, but it has also been taken up by the wider American society. "Soul" is a germinal idea, born out of deep social conflict; yet all such ideas seem to spin off into ridiculousness, to take on broad and vague connotations and the term "soul" is no exception. Thus in advertising parlance we now have "soul music," all kinds of jungle rhythms; not necessarily African; and "soul food," a conglomerate of every kind of digestible and indigestible "gumbo" of ill-defined origin. However, in the true world of Black experience the word conveys a potent and very special quality of feeling that is unknown to those who are not Black. However, in order not to appear left out, the wider society uses the word, but only for form's sake and certainly without tuning in on the "peculiar" feeling that properly defines it.

"Soul-force" in "Black talk" describes that quality of life that has enabled Black people to survive the horrors of their "diaspora." The experience of slavery, and its later repercussions still remain to be dealt with; and "Soul" signifies the moral and emotional fiber of the Black man that enables him to see his dilemmas clearly and at the same time encourages and sustains him in his struggles. "Force" connotes strength, power, intense effort and a will to live. The combined words—"soul-force"—describe the racial inheritance of the New World African; it is that which characterizes his life-style, his world view and his endurance under conflict. It is his frame of reference *vis-à-vis* the wider world and his blueprint for the struggle from bondage to freedom. Soul-force is that power of the Black man which turns sorrow into joy, crying into laughter, and defeat into victory. It is patience while suffering, determination while frustrated and hope while in despair. It derives its impetus from the ancestral heritage of Africa, its refinement from the bondage of slavery, and its continuing vitality from the conflict of the present. It expresses itself collectively as well as through charismatic leaders. In addition, it can express itself in states of acquiescence, avoidance and separation. So there is no end to the permutations and combinations of the restless "soul." Soul is visceral rather than intellectual, irrational rather than rational; it is art rather than logic.[1]

Unlike all the other peoples that entered the New World, the Black man was forcibly brought there against his will, to serve other men's material ends. When, in 1619, John Rolfe, the tobacco king of Virginia, spoke of the ship that brought the first Blacks to the shores of America, he declared, "The ship brought not anything but 20 and odd negroes." Little did he know that inside the hold of that vessel were the dynamics that were to change the whole American panorama. In that ship were the seeds of the Spirituals, the Denmark Veseys, Nat Turners, the Frederick Douglasses, the Civil War, the Gettysburg Address, the seeds of the blues and jazz and the spirit of the Harlem Renaissance—in a word—"soul."[2]

The arrival of the Black man in the Americas brought an indirect blessing to a land where materialism and inhumanity were the dominant themes. It was his quality of "soul" that finally leavened the bread of calculated materialism, and his suffering finally evoked guilt in the conscience of his oppressors and brought sanity and humanity to the New World. Due to his original position as slave and his subsequently low social position the Black man has had to fight his way up in this land of his exile. But as he fights, he proves that his soul-force is not just a passive means of survival, but an active instrument of culture formation which has affected every aspect of New World civilization.

In recent times there has been a reassessment of Afro-American participation in history, politics, art, music, literature, sports and religion. The results of this endeavor have not only brought a sudden reawakening for whites to the vast and complex Black participation in American culture, but have also served as an inspiration for the Blacks, who had lost respect for themselves through the corrosive action of prejudice. The revival of pride in Blackness is now being echoed in slogans such as "Black is beautiful," "Black Power," "Black theology," and a return to distinctive Africanisms such as the natural hairdo, African robes, African names and the increasing frequency of Black pilgrimages to the motherland. This period may well be called the "Age of Black Awareness." Historians may come to see it as the age in which Africans in "exile" returned to themselves. In truth, this is an age of Black cultural emancipation from the stigma of Black inferiority and an age of the rediscovery of a new and proud Black identity. This cultural emancipation has been the aim of the struggle of the Black man for over three hundred years.

Torn from his homeland, relatives and friends, the African was reduced to chattel slavery in the New World, and after he had enriched his oppressors with his sweat and blood, he was tossed aside as a disposable and unassimilable waste. As such, he was at the mercy of white society. No more than tolerated by officialdom, he subsisted in a "no-man's-land" of economic deprivation and ignorance. Though highly visible, he became an invisible man in the programs and plannings of his adopted homeland. To survive, he had to acquire the language and customs of his exile environment, so he forgot his past. In order to survive, he was forced to believe that he had no past, or that the one he had was so barbaric that it was not worth knowing. Unable to discount the myth, the Black man accepted what he was told despite the fact that, deep within, he felt the vestigial remains of a dignified heritage which demonstrated itself in covert and overt resistance to enslavement. This persistence of Black dignity is generally overlooked by students of slavery, especially those of the slave-owner class. But the dignity of the Black man and his refusal to remain a slave was the prime factor that destroyed the institution of human servitude. The fact is well known that almost every race experienced some form of slavery in their historical development—either by capture or other accidents of history—but slavery was never accepted by them as their human lot. When, however, the Black race was reduced to slavery, the theory soon developed that this condition was their predestined lot. It was the Black man's persistent denial of this theory by resistance and constant rebellion that brought an end to the institution of chattel slavery in the New World.

Cultural emancipation for the Black, then, is not a recent and sudden accomplishment but the result of that persistent exertion of Black Power, that peculiar *force-vitale,* which Father Tempels saw as an original trait of the African psyche.[3] The pilgrimage from slavery to the present has been an arduous and lengthy one, and the present cannot be appreciated unless one looks at the past. The history of Black struggle from slavery to the present, when fully written, will be one of the greatest records of human heroism of all times! But our aim is more limited. In this book we will attempt to look at the peculiar "soul-force" of our African forefathers through the long struggle in servitude; the forms in which "soul-force" expressed itself; and how their culture has shaped the lives of Black people up to the present.

The interaction of primal societies, in our case Africa and the Africans (both at home and in exile), with the Western world has been so copiously documented by anthropologists, sociologists and historians that one needs only to review this material for directions. Black reaction to white domination has now been established on a broad continuum from xenophobia accompanied by resistance, through imitation. In the latter, a primal society takes on aspects of Western culture, producing periods of nativism, messianism or millenarianism. These reactions may continue for centuries before finally giving way to nationalist revolutionary movements.[4]

Our study concentrates on the period of rejection of white culture in which a vast range of new movements of a religious nature emerge. Such movements reflect the efforts of a primal society to re-establish its traditional life patterns either by repelling the dominant culture by revitalizing its own traditional religion, or by adopting a new faith largely drawn from the West but recast in traditional patterns. Both these types of movements we will call "redemption cults"—a name which suggests that they all have as their goal freedom from intolerable situations. The term "cult" will here be taken to mean any group of people who are organized around an ideology and are committed to this ideology for the purpose of affecting change in their social conditions.

The term *cult* in this respect stands at the far end of the continuum of church and sect. Church in sociological parlance represents the dominant religious institution, with its priests, sacraments and organization catering to the dominant group in society. As such, the church naturally seeks to maintain the status quo. It aims at being the guardian of morals for society at large and the upholder of religious traditions for the group or nation.

The *sect* is generally a collective that has broken off from the church either because of ethnic differences or doctrinal disputes or because they claim unique revelations. It is exclusive to a point, but also seeks to proselytize. A sect generally espouses a very stringent moral code that aims at the purity of the individual and strict group discipline. While the church is outward oriented, the sect is inward oriented. It is generally emotional because it aims at personal experiences and feelings. Although the individual is important, only those who demonstrate unique qualities of holiness in life and character can attain to any measure of status. At the center of the sect is the doctrine and discipline.

The cult, however, represents the extreme of the collective. It generally centers around a set of esoteric beliefs that are considered either dangerous or diabolical by both the church and the sect. Its members are usually the oppressed of society or those who have psychological needs which are not fulfilled by church or sect. The cult emerges with a vision or an ideology that is perceived as the answer to deep psychological needs or as a way out of depraved social situations. This ideology is invariably anti-church, anti-sect and anti-society as a whole, hence dangerous and threatening to the establishment. It may be an ideology that aims at redeeming a repressed racial group. And so the exclusiveness of an ideology such as Black Power becomes threatening to those who are not Black. Or it may work in reverse fashion, as it did in Nazi Germany, where the group in power caused all other races to be threatened. Whatever the ideology around which the cult emerges, it is generally a demonstration of a condition of disquietude and/or of psychological threat to the existence of its followers. Black cults in the New World are the direct result of the threat to Black existence that the Africans have experienced in their four hundred years of contact with the white world. Let us analyze this experience.

A. The Function of Ideology in Black Movements:[5]

Cult ideology may take the form of fantastic myths, without logical consistency or a basis in empirical fact. In some cases the ideology may even abuse all claims to truth and use easily refuted ideas as an effective weapon to urge men into action and to build up sentiments of solidarity. But regardless of its truth-value, once an ideology is established it easily becomes both the spiritual and intellectual foundation of group cohesion.

Speaking generally, Black ideology is the synthesis of the historical experiences of Africans under the institutional constraint of white racism, colonialism and political repression. It therefore has its origin in the repressive and humiliating experience of the Black man's lot in a white man's world. It has as its aim the redemption of that African ethos and the self-determination which were part and parcel of the African heritage.

Black ideology is based on the objective symbol of Blackness, which, although a symbol of rejection in the New World, is the basis for the unity and solidarity of Black civilization. It is the symbol of a unique heritage, the sum total of the economic, political, spiritual, intellectual, artistic and social values of Black peoples. The acceptance and internalization of these values bring about the psychological liberation of Blacks.

As a thought system, Blackness clearly distinguishes itself from that of white society. It serves to reinterpret the past, to understand the present and to plan the future. Specific Black ideologies, be they separatistic, utopian, millenarian or revolutionary, all represent a rejection of the existing order and an effort to restructure social patterns.

The ideology of Blackness has at least three distinguishable characteristics which give it special significance for Black awareness. *First,* it acts as a *prescriptive authority* for people whose existential situation went undefined for over three hundred years. Black awareness re-establishes a sense of history, culture and destiny, and eliminates that sickening sense of insecurity, uprootedness and overdependence on the wider society which the Black man has experienced throughout his sojourn in the New World. In a world dominated by European determinants and a cruel and misapplied Christian ethic, the New World Black inherited a heavy burden of ethical contradiction. His acceptance of his lot was attributed to his docility; and the rejection of slavery to his barbarity. Caught between such contradictory (yet always negative) interpretations of himself, the Black man lived his life as a social schizophrenic.

Another facet of this dilemma was given voice by W. E. B. Du Bois. In 1897 he asked: "What, after all, am I? Am I an American or am I a Negro? Can I be both? Or is it my duty to cease to be a Negro as soon as possible and be an American?"[6] The question "Am I an American or am I a Negro?" is answered by the Black Muslims with an emphatic, "We are *neither* Americans nor Negroes"; by others with the simple statement, "We are Black," or, "We are Afro-Americans." These answers point to the fact that present-day Blacks have resorted to their own self-definition based on their own prescriptive-authority source, and will no more be told by the wider society who they are and what they should be.

This prescriptive authority has been called by various names. In America it is called "Black Power"; in the English-speaking West Indies and Africa—"the African personality"; and in the French-speaking West Indies and Africa—"*Négritude*." By whatever name, it points to the same awareness that liberation of a people, be it psychological, spiritual, economic or political liberation, is not simply handed over; it must be claimed.

The *second* characteristic of Black ideology is that it communicates a strong sense of unity and power. Whereas, before this awakening, the individual Black may have felt himself weak and alone in his life of torments, he now has a new consciousness of shared experience; he sees himself as part of a new community with an unalterable common characteristic, and that is Blackness. Common beliefs held by members of a group generate a sense of strength and power. The single individual is no longer pitted against the world but has comrades who share his beliefs, goals and commitment.

Black awareness is not confined to the Americas; it extends to Africa, Asia and Oceania. The call of Marcus Garvey, which will be discussed in Chapter 6, was a call not only to Black Americans, but to what he called the four hundred millions of Black people the world over.

The *third* characteristic of a Black ideology is its active character. The ideology of Blackness is not merely a passive conceptual fantasy. It is by nature revolutionary. It embodies the *force-vitale* of a vibrant culture. It is dynamic, active and liberating. It expresses itself primarily in movements, even though it may pass through several processual stages before its momentum is actually launched. First comes the *rhetorical stage,* in which the ideology is a mere verbalization of intentions. Then comes the *stage of commitment,* in which the movement absorbs more and more of the time and energy of the followers. Then comes the *encounter,* in which an attempt is made to bring about the fulfillment of the ideology. The concept of Black Power has shattered the security of white America during the present decade because it is clearly only a slight variation on the theme of Black revolution.

The psychological condition of Black people the world over is a product of the stultifying social and economic situation brought about by centuries of exploitation. This legacy of exploitation created distrust and ambivalence and finally a rejection of white values. With this rejection a new power source had to be found either as a means of escape from white oppression or as alternative to white values.

The symbol of power that emerged in the consciousness of the African in "diaspora" is Blackness. This symbol has become sacred—for, as we have seen, it connotes the synthesis of experience of a people under oppression. But some may ask, Why color? Is this not racism? The answer to the question is yes. But this yes must be further explained. Blackness as a symbol is not the creation of the Black man; it is the creation of the whites, who from antiquity imposed a color label on African peoples. Almost all peoples on earth have been known by the lands they inhabit. Thus we have the Greeks, the Romans, the Germans, the English, the Americans and so on. But in the case of the Africans, from antiquity, the color designation became the common referent. Thus we have the Greek *Aithiopes* for the Ethiopians, which means "burnt or black"; and *Melas,* a Greek word for the Melanesians; in Latin, *Niger,* which means black; and from the Arabs, *Sudan,* which also means black. Blackness then became the unique designation of that segment of the human race that was not white. When the Blacks were reduced to slavery the word took on negative connotations. The emergence of Blackness as a symbol, then, is not the creation of African peoples, but a conscious acceptance of an ontological symbol, revolutionary in its implication. As a positive symbol for the Black man, Blackness suggests an "anti-racist" racism; a self-definition based on African referents.

Within the scholarly world a technical vocabulary has been developed to deal with some of these reactions to oppression.

Thus in cultural anthropology we have the term "nativism." A nativistic movement is "any conscious, organized attempt on the part of a society's members to revive or perpetuate selected aspects of its culture."[7] Such movements generally emerge in oppressive culture contact situations, when a subordinate group feels that its existence is threatened by another group which dominates and restricts its indigenous development and denies it a share in the "superior life-style" of the dominant culture. When this occurs, some aspects of the culture of the dominated group may be revived and selected to symbolize that people's identity. In this case the movement is said to be nativistic. It may take one of two forms, either "magical" or "rational." The term "magical" suggests that the movement depends heavily on supernatural means for its redemption, while "rational" suggests that empirical methods are being utilized to achieve its goal. Both aspects of nativism can be found in Black cults of redemption. Generally, the magical element is predominant in the early stages of cult movement, but as it develops, empirical realism emerges and more sophisticated techniques are formulated.

Anthony F. C. Wallace expanded on nativism by incorporating all social movements of a radical type under the heading, "revitalization movements."[8] Closely related to "nativistic movements" are the following: 1) the messianic movement, centering around a savior figure who promises to redeem his people from oppression, 2) millenarian movement, which holds out to its followers a promised land free from present hardships and 3) revival movement, which promises to rid the society of all oppressive alien influences and restore the "golden age."

According to Wallace all these movements emerge in situations of stress, which, when chronic, precipitate action on the part of the oppressed. The function of these movements is to bring about social change, but unlike other social change phenomena, revitalization movements are abrupt reactions of a religious nature. These movements are the breeding grounds of prophets and charismatic leaders, they are also the source of new myths, creeds and rituals, which often are true mirrors of societal distortion.

Examples of revitalization movements are reflected throughout this book. The Back-to-Africa movement is messianic; the Rastafarians are definitely a millenarian movement, while Pukumina and Vodun fall roughly in the revival category. But our main emphasis will be not so much on the trapping of theories relative to these movements, as on the dynamics of "soul-force" as it emerges in various permutations and combinations on the way toward the goal of liberation.

The restless rhythm of the African soul will be the theme of this book. That rhythm was obvious to the white man from the day the Africans came ashore in the Caribbean until the day Emancipation was declared. It surfaced in the drums of the Maroons in the Cockpit Mountains of Jamaica; in the conch shells of the Haitians calling the barefooted soldiers to unite against the elite French regiments "steeled" by the drums of Vodun. It became a movement bound for the African homeland under Marcus Garvey's messianic leadership and later taken up by the Rastafarians. It escalated to a worldwide sound in the sixties in a holocaust of movements, the tremors of which still linger with us. The dynamics of soul-force move in various permutations and combinations as it seeks its way to its ultimate goal of liberation, freedom and the dignity of man.

Keorapetse Kgositsile in his book of poems *My Name Is Afrika* captures the African soul uniquely when, in "Spirits Unchained," he says:

> Rhythm it is we
> walk to against the evil
> of monsters that try to kill the Spirit
> It is the power of this song
> that colors our every act
> as we move from the oppressor-made gutter
> Gut it is will move us from the gutter
> It is the rhythm of guts
> blood black, granite hard
> and flowing like the river or the mountains
> It is the rhythm of unchained Spirit
> will put fire in our hands
> to blaze our way
> to clarity to power
> to the rebirth of real men[9]

This book makes no pretense to being comprehensive on the subject of Black religious cults. In fact it is highly selective, dealing only with a few of the movements in the New World. A comprehensive work would be encyclopedic and that is beyond the ability of the present writer. This little book is designed to make a small contribution to the corpus of literature on Black experience, a literature which is growing at an ever increasing rate.

CHAPTER 2

SOURCE OF SOUL:
Our African Heritage

So much has been written on Africa and so much is being written that a short résumé, such as the one intended here, may seem redundant; yet it is necessary to give a short background in order to provide continuity for our story of the Black man in the New World. This résumé, therefore, will be brief, and uses only a minimum of historical data.

It has been fairly well established that the great majority of New World Blacks came from that part of West Africa which runs roughly from Gambia, along the coast, southward to Angola, an area that includes Senegal, Mali, Sierra Leone, Liberia, the Gold Coast (now Ghana), Dahomey, Nigeria, the Cameroons, the Congo and Angola. Although it is possible that slaves could have come from farther south and from the far interior, not enough of these Blacks were in the "diaspora" to leave extensive cultural marks on the New World. Therefore, the discussion of these peripheral areas is excluded.[1]

Concerning the origin of slaves, it has also been well established that, by the beginning of the eighteenth century, European slavers had selected definite points along the African coast from which they took their human cargo, the allocation of areas being determined by certain charter arrangements. For example, the French dominated Senegal, the coast of Dahomey, the Cameroons and parts of the Congo region; the English dominated Gambia, the Gold Coast and the region now known as Nigeria; the Dutch had a minority position with the Gold Coast, Nigeria and the Congo; while Angola and the remainder of the Congo were allotted to the Portuguese. Europeans also had their own territories in the New World, territories which were theirs by conquest or by fraud, and to which they brought their slaves. The majority of the slaves coming to the French territories were predominantly the Fon-speaking peoples of Dahomey, the Yoruba and Ibos of Nigeria, and a large number from the Congo and the Cameroons. The English territories were dominated by the Akan people, whose main tribes were the Fanti, the Ashanti and related peoples of this complex, with a large sprinkling of Yorubas and Ibos. The Dutch territories were peopled with Yorubas, Ibos and peoples from the Congo, along with some from the Gold Coast. Examples of the latter are the plantation societies in Brazil and Surinam.

Thus the slaves who entered the New World came almost exclusively from the West Coast region of Africa and subsequently almost all were from that segment of people known as the Kwa- and Bantu-speaking peoples. It is rather important to note the homogeneity of the Blacks who came to the New World (despite their differences) in order to understand how they were able to interact effectively in their environment. Much has been made of their differences, but very little has been said of their similarity.

The debasing manner in which African slaves were brought to the New World and the inhumane conditions under which they were forced to work, for centuries provided a climate in which it was unfashionable for scholars to inquire into their cultural, social or political background. The sociology of knowledge of that period naturally forbids any such inquiry. Such scholarship would have been seen as either the work of a depraved person or a would-be conspirator. So the accepted type of scholarship during slavery was that which demonstrated by situational logic that the slaves were inherently inferior. In fact, until the latter half of the twentieth century this was thought to be the acceptable way to deal with Africans in the New World, and the literature of this genre abounds both in Europe and in America. To solve the dilemma of human bondage and especially the bondage of the African slaves, it was necessary to formulate a myth about the inferiority of the African. This myth was reinforced by the Darwinian presupposition that human cultures follow a linear continuum from the lowest to the highest, that there therefore exist in-

ferior and superior races, and that the Blacks of Africa occupy
the lowest strata of the scale of human culture. The image of a
low position on an accepted scale is, however, a bit misleading,
for actually the Europeans thought the Africans had no culture at
all. Thus Black contact with European civilization, under any cir-
cumstance, was to be considered a blessing. The internalization
of this myth by the European slave masters was so thorough that
it became their guiding principle and provided the basis for the
moral code used in dealing with the slaves. The sociology of knowledge during the period of chattel slavery, reinforced this myth in
the pulpit and the press until it became the moral charter on which
the very existence of the slave system depended. This myth is
not yet wholly eradicated from the minds of most modern-day
scholars.

Until recently, scholars both white and Black struggled with
this myth. The Blacks fought it bitterly, some whites questioned
it halfheartedly. It was not until the twentieth century that Blacks
such as Marcus Garvey began to proclaim boldly the glories of the
Black past. The work of Garvey, although powerful in its effect,
was mostly evangelical, having been the result of a passionate
pride in his race. The real research and documentation of the
African past awaited such scholars as W. E. B. Du Bois, a Black
man, and Melville Herskovits, a white. It has happened that Herskovits, because of the anomaly of his situation and the sincerity
with which he took up the study of the Africans, has received
greater attention in white academic circles. Speaking of the "myth
of the Negro past," especially of the idea that Africans came to
the New World without a trace of culture, Herskovits observes
that while mutual borrowing in situations of culture contact is an
accepted sociological fact, anything the white man may have gained
from the Black in the New World is cavalierly ignored. Herskovits
sees this attitude arising out of the nature of chattel slavery, which
deadened all humane feelings. Blacks were seen as property to
be used and/or abused and not as a peoples who could make
valuable cultural and intellectual contributions. "With this in
mind" Herskovits wrote, "we can understand why it is generally
believed that the Africans brought to this country had neither in-
nate capacities nor cultural endowment that they could transmit
to their white masters."[2] Herskovits' observation illuminates
much in the New World slave system. Even in those areas where,

as a result of previous contacts with Africans or because of the restraint of the Church, the attitude of the planters was less harsh toward the African, their prevailing concept of the Black was still that he was less than a human being.

Reflecting on this myth, one cannot but lament the irony of history if it is taken into consideration that those Africans who were brought to the New World as slaves came predominantly from those regions of West Africa where the higher and more complex civilizations were founded and continued to flourish even at the time when the white man made his so-called "discovery" of the continent. If by culture one means that complex whole which includes knowledge, belief, art, law, morals, customs and any other capabilities and habits offered to men as members of society,[3] then West Africa, before and during the slave trade, had a very high culture. To cite a few examples, West Africa was far advanced in the smelting of iron and used iron implements centuries before the slave trade. She had a highly developed music of a polyrhythmic quality, which still baffles the Western world, and had developed a folk philosophy so sophisticated that it has been compared with the wisdom literature of the Hebrews. This wisdom has seeped down to our time in the form of proverbs. Her sculpture has been compared to the finer works of Greece and continues to excite the minds of art experts down to our time. She developed law codes that are still being studied by anthropologists for their intricate perception of equity. Further, African wisdom in the field of medicine, especially the knowledge of herbs, has had no precedent. In turn, African religions have called for rivers of ink to catalogue their belief systems, and the work is merely begun. What is more, all of this is only a "hint" at the cultural complexity from which the Africans were brutally snatched. We can be grateful that their political and social institutions have stood to this day despite the brutal assault of slavery and colonialism.

To understand better the persistent ethos of African culture in the New World, it is necessary to look more closely at the most vital institution of Africa. This is religion. Religion for Africans was, is and ever shall be the source of life and meaning. It is in religion that they live, move and have their being. Given the breadth and depth of this subject, it is impossible, and for our purposes also unnecessary, to look at all of Africa. However, in that the New World Blacks originated in West Africa, there are

certain general beliefs from those tribal areas that can be brought
to light which will reveal a common cultural substructure. It is the
thesis of this section that the religious world view of the Africans
contributed most to their survival in the New World and that unless this world view is well understood, no real perception of the
struggle of the Black man is possible.

A. The Traditional World View:

The world view of African peoples is best described as the vision of a cosmic harmony in which there exists a vital participation
between animate (God, man) and inanimate things. That is to
say, all Africans see a vital relationship of being between each individual and his descendants, his family, his brothers and sisters
in the clan, his antecedents, and also his God—the ultimate source
of being. Thus the world is not just an abstraction; it is a force
field with all things interacting. To put it more clearly, the hierarchy consists of God, the source of all power, at its apex. The
divine power is distributed in descending order, first to the lesser
deities, whose function it is to see that the world of man and things
operates smoothly; second, to the ancestors, whose duty it is to
see that their descendants carry out the moral precepts handed
down to them; third, to the head of the family, the one nearest
to the ancestors; finally to the other members of the family in their
order of age and importance. Animate and inanimate things are
man's to use or abuse and he is answerable to God and to the
ancestors for his stewardship. So important is this world view that
it is necessary to discuss these ideas in more detail in order to
understand their influence on New World Black culture.

To approach the central topics of African religions, a common
creed would be most helpful. It should be understood, however,
that no such creed has ever been attempted by Africans, although
there is a gradual trend toward this. At any rate, we can envision
such a creed and it could read as follows:

I believe in a supreme being who creates all things, and in
lesser deities, spirits and powers who guard and control the universe. I believe in the ancestors, who guard and protect their descendants. I believe in the efficacy of sacrifice and the power of
magic, good and evil; and I believe in the fullness of life here and
now.

Using this as a framework, we shall discuss the important beliefs of those tribes which became dominant in the New World.

1. The supreme being and lesser deities: Among the Akan peoples of Ghana there is a proverb which says: "No man needs to teach a child the knowledge of God." This suggests that, to the African, the knowledge of God is so self-evident that no catechetical instruction is necessary. We now know that every tribe in Africa, before the entrance of the Europeans, had a well-developed pantheon of spiritual beings. The prime example of this may be seen in the missionary translations of the Bible. In every instance, the word used for God, in the translation of the Bible into a tribal language, is the word used for that particular tribe's traditional deity. What else could the missionaries do? How would they, the Africans, know or understand the concept of God if that concept had no relevance to them? The supreme being in African thought, then, was an indigenous concept, similar to the concept of the supreme being in Western Judaeo-Christian tradition. Such titles as creator, begetter, originator, sustainer and orderer of all things, are given to him; he has attributes such as all-powerful, ever present and all-knowing; he is benign and generally considered to be above the affairs of men. Because he is thought to be above the affairs of mundane things, no shrines are specifically dedicated to him, although he is the One who ultimately receives the prayers and supplications of all, through the mediation of the lesser deities and the ancestors. The three most powerful influences on the New World Blacks were those of the Fon-speaking people of Dahomey, the Yoruba of Nigeria and the Akan of Ghana. We will look separately at their notions of deity.

a. The Fon of Dahomey: Those acquainted with the religion of Dahomey are aware of the prominent role it plays in the culture of this segment of African peoples. The highest God is Nana Buluku, who is seldom spoken about, yet is believed to be the creator of all things. This deity has somewhat removed himself from the theology of the Dahomeans and in his place are his two descendants, Mawu and Lisa, and they are generally spoken of as the supreme beings. They are represented in the form of a three-dimensional Janus-like figure, one side of which is female and whose eyes are the moon, and the other side of which is male and whose eyes are the sun. Mawu represents the moon and symbolizes coolness, wisdom and mystery, which is the nature of the aged. Lisa represents the sun, the symbol of strength and energy. Together the divine pair represents the dialectical rhythm of life,

an idea evocative of the Chinese concept of Yin and Yang. Within
such a concept it is the combination of opposites that maintains
the equilibrium of the world. Among the Chinese this interaction
between Yin and Yang is known as the Tao, or the way of the
universe; the power of its manifestation. The idea of Tao in Chinese thought maintains that the universe operates through the interaction of opposites. This interaction of opposites is known as
complementarity; hence there is no night without day, there is no
up without down, there is no east without west, there is no husband without a wife. This masculine-feminine interaction is the
very nature of the universe. The same idea is found among the
Fon. The interaction of Mawu and Lisa is known through the concept Da,[4] which is the manifestation of force or power. This force
and power is represented by the serpent, the symbol of flowing
sinuous movement. The serpentine symbol dominates religious
symbolism in Dahomey to this day and we will meet it again in
Haiti, where aspects of the culture are symbolized by the snake.

The supreme being of Africa is surrounded by lesser deities,
who carry out the will and pleasure of the creator. Their duty is
to see that the supreme will is implemented in the smooth func-
tioning of the world. They are allotted specific dominions within
nature and manifest themselves as gods of rivers, mountains, lakes,
oceans, iron, fire and war or as gods of natural phenomena such
as lightning and epidemics. Below Mawu and Lisa in the Dahomean pantheon are a multiplicity of deities, called by the generic
name vodu, and believed to be the offspring of the twin deity. Their
special function is to control and assist in the affairs of men on
earth. There are two levels of vodu, the greater (the guardians of
land and sea) and the lesser (those involved in man's everyday
domestic pursuits). Each aspect of life is under the direct control
of a vodu, who must be placated by prayers, libations and sacrifices. Shrines are built in their honor and special days are dedicated to their worship. An elaborate system of mythology has also
developed around these deities. In Dahomey we have Gu, the god
of metal and warfare, and in Africa such a god of iron or metal often seems to represent the oldest of the lesser deities. It is he that
made the universe habitable. Then there is Sagbata, the god of
grains and harvest; Fa, the god of divination; and a host of others.
However, the most important of the Dahomean lesser divinities
appears to be Legba. He is the deity called upon most often in

New World Vodun religion. In the New World, he is the god of entrances; he opens the way for the coming of other spirits. In Africa he is the god of communication; he is the one who supervises sacrifices, observing the worship of man and informing Mawu-Lisa of man's morals. He is also known as a trickster, because he has been known to confuse messages from man to God and from God to man. Thus a malfunction in a ritual or in a society is generally blamed on him. It is futile to attempt to go further into the nature and function of specific deities. Let it suffice to say that in Dahomey the gods meet man at every point in life. We shall later observe this religious system of Dahomey and the important place it plays in the life of the descendants of this segment of the African peoples in the Caribbean.

b. The Yoruba of Nigeria: One of the dominant cultural influences from Africa to the New World has been that of the Yoruba peoples, who, today, number many millions of people. The Yorubas are made up of many large clans bound together by language, tradition and religious belief. They have a long history of complex political and artistic achievement, but the keynote to their life and customs is their religion. The supreme being, among the Yorubas, is the almighty Olòdúmaré. He is defined as the one with whom man may enter into covenant or communion in any place and at any time.[5] Among his attributes are such concepts as incomparability, unchangeability, constancy and reliability. Sometimes also called Olorun, he is the ruler of heaven and earth. Olòdúmaré is surrounded by a host of divinities who are known by the generic name of *orishas* and number as many as four hundred. Olòdúmaré, who sits at the pinnacle of the pantheon, as all other supreme beings of Africa do, does not involve himself in the affairs of men—this work he delegates to his lesser deities. The orishas, or lesser deities, are so numerous that only the important ones, especially those that bear upon the beliefs of Africans in the New World, can be dealt with here.

The first of these deities in hierarchical order is Orunmila, who is believed to be the embodiment of wisdom, knowledge and understanding. He is an omnilinguist, speaking every language under heaven; he is the god of oracles and master of destinies; he foresees that which will come to pass and is able to prescribe remedies for any ailment and to ward off any undesired event. Next in importance to Orunmila is Ogun, the god of iron and steel; he is the god of war and warriors, artisans, smiths, engineers and all engines. He also presides over contracts and oaths. He is invoked in traditional courts by the kissing of a piece of iron. Next to Ogun is the great Shango, the god of lightning and thunder (Shango's priests are traditionally called to minister to those struck by lightning). He is by far the greatest hero-god of the Yorubas and there are many legends about him. The most often heard theory is that he was a great prehistoric warrior-king who ascended to heaven. Shango's cult still flourishes in Nigeria and in the New World. The last in our sample of orishas is Esu, a divinity comparable to the Legba of the Fon peoples discussed above. Esu is another trickster god and as such he is the liaison between the supreme being and man. It is he who checks on the piety of man and reports to the great God. He is concerned with the correctness of worship and sacrifice and, like the Satan of the book of Job, tests the sincerity of man by putting obstacles in his way. He is a spoiler and must be placated at all times. Needless to say, this discussion of the orishas could go on for many pages; indeed, a whole chapter, but this is not our goal. We must examine the idea of God in one more important people whose influence was transported to the New World.

c. The Akan of Ghana: Anyone visiting the English-speaking Caribbean will find out, either by prior knowledge of the Akan peoples or by word of mouth, that the dominant African influence there is that of the Ashanti and the Fanti people. In fact, there are many words in common usage in that part of the Caribbean which would be quite intelligible to a man from modern-day Ghana. The name of the supreme being common to all Akan people is Nyame or Onyame,[6] which may be translated, the shining or resplendent one. Other common names which depict his nature are Nyankopon, "he who is the greatest," and Tweaduampon, "he on whom men lean and do not fall." Unlike that of most other West African religions which we have surveyed, the Akan doctrine of God is highly philosophical. There seem to be three levels of deity: first, Nyame or Onyame, who is far away; then Nyankopon or Odomankoma, who is present in the daily life of man and on whom men call for succor and strength; and finally Asase Yaa, the god of earth, who gives life and sustenance to man. It is from Asase Yaa that man is produced and to whom man will return. As we have seen for other African peoples, there exists also in the literature of the Akan a rich source of attributes for the supreme being. He is "the great one," "the dependable one," "the creator of all things," "the powerful one," "the eternal one," "the great spider" —that is, the wise one.

The representatives of the Akan deity on earth are called *abosom,* and they have physical representatives in rivers, lakes and mountains. In some cases, the name of an abosom is given to an actual physical object. An example of this can be seen in the river Tano of Kumasi. Tano is both a particular river and a god around whom many myths are woven. The same holds true of Lake Bosomptwe, which is both a lake and an abosom. The original ancestors of the Akan people, according to mythology, came out of Lake Bosomptwe. In addition, other natural phenomena such as trees and stones may become the dwelling places of abosom. Such places are treated like shrines and generally demand the service of a priest or priestess. There are many of these sacred places all over Ghana and, in addition, there are shrines which are especially built for the abosom who guard the villages and the clans.

From the above discussion it should be clear that a study of the African idea of God is a broad and intricate subject. Many important monographs on it have been published in the last few years;[7] however, our aim, in the above discussion and in what follows, is only to sketch the background of the religious beliefs and practices which was the heritage of New World Blacks. For this is all that is needed to prove conclusively that the African did not enter the New World *tabula rasa.* Also it is our purpose to emphasize that the Blacks had highly developed ideas of God and that these ideas took root in their new environment. Furthermore, it was precisely this traditional belief that enabled them to survive in the New World. It was this world view that they handed down to their descendants and, though greatly modified, it still forms the underpinning of their society to the present time.

2. The ancestors: The second major component of the African religious heritage in the New World is the belief that the ancestors have enormous influence over their descendants. This concept is universal among African peoples. Unlike the Westerner, whose dead "rest from their labor and their deeds do follow them," the deceased of Africa are not dead until the memories of them are lost to the living, and, even then, they are not considered totally

lost.[8] All other deities are respected and reverenced only if they aid man, but the supreme being and the ancestor always receive the highest devotion regardless of the African situation in life. So intense is the African devotion to the ancestors that the concept has been disparagingly called "ancestor worship" by Western writers, and this is especially true in the writings of missionaries, who historically have not seen anything of value in African traditional religion. However, many African scholars have rejected the idea that reverence for the ancestors is the same thing as worship of them. Some say that it is a method of communication and defend the statement by referring to the behavior of the African in dealing with the ancestors.[9] For one thing, there is no sense of self-abasement on the part of the people in ancestor rituals; for another thing, the ancestors are generally well known to those who call upon them, in fact they are part of the family. An argument could be made against this view in respect to the founding ancestors or to hero-ancestors such as Shango, but the deification process which they have undergone is quite different from what happens with the ordinary ancestor. It may be true that the reverence shown to the ancestors is the nearest thing to a worship experience, but such reverence is also a common attitude that all African peoples adopt toward the living ancestors, the ones who have attained a ripe old age.

As long as there are people in the family who remember the departed, they are not dead. Their collective power energizes the living, protects their homes and their belongings and pervades their daily life. Thus the African concept of community includes those who are dead, those who are alive and those yet to be born. However, this should not be understood as a concept of three distinct stages of being, since the line of demarcation between the living and the dead, like that between the living and the not-yet-born, is a flexible one. As a footnote to the concept of the ancestors, it may be added that the ancestors are represented in the numerous varieties of the plastic arts—wooden sculptured human forms are extremely important and rather common all over West Africa.

It should be made clear, at the outset, that when Africans speak of the ancestors they do not speak of all the dead in the family, clan and tribe. They speak more specifically of those whose lives were examples to their descendants: those who were paragons of moral virtue, or had valorous lives on the battlefield or made some specific contribution to the ongoing life of their descendants. After death, these more influential persons are venerated within the cult of the living-dead. They are the root of the race, the guardians of tribal tradition. Having achieved a great old age with its corresponding wisdom, they become spiritual guides for those who must continue to live with the vicissitudes and problems of this life. Theirs were lives of achievement, having successfully negotiated the pitfalls of human existence. They are believed to be able to give spiritual insights to the living in dreams and visions, and when their spirits are reborn in children of the family, such children are named after them. They are consulted in times of crisis and are believed to be diligent in answering the requests of their descendants. They are the spiritual title holders of tribal lands, land that cannot be sold without risking the dire consequences of their wrath.

Since the ancestors are part of the family, there is a certain responsibility among the living members of that family to see that their daily needs are met. Consequently, they are fed at mealtime; libation is poured out to them and prayers are directed to them. In addition, special festivals are held periodically for the sustenance of the ancestors, since as long as they are sustained, their good-will is assured. According to one of the leading scholars of Ghana, this esteem for the ancestors, and the reverence for the supreme being, are the two most important ideals of his people.[10]

3. The belief in spirits and powers: To the African, the world of the spirit is real and self-evident. As we have seen, the spirits of the ancestors continue to take an active part in man's affairs. They can communicate with man, appearing in various forms in dreams and visions; or as animate or inanimate objects and making their wishes known. The idea of the spirit is based on the concept of the soul, a concept that is common to all African religions. An example from the Akan people of Ghana should clarify the point. Among the Akan it is believed that man is the aggregate of these basic components: the *E-su**, the *Sunsum* and the *okara*. The E-su, or man's basic nature, is his biological make-up; while the Sunsum, his personality, consists of his overt expression or the projection of his life-force on the family, the community or the nation. The latter may be described as his acquired disposition; and, in Africa, if one said that such and such a person had

---

* Not to be confused with Esu who is a Yoruba deity.

"personality-plus," he would be referring to the Sunsum. In the Bantu language the expression for this quality is *Muntu,* which simply means man or the manness of a man. The third part of man is his okara, which means the pure spirit of a man. It is the breath of man which returns to God at death. It is the divine part of the soul. Hence we have three important aspects of life: the E-su or the biological make-up, which is the given of all man and animal; the Sunsum, which is the acquired personality of man, his manness; and the okara, or his vital breath or spirit.

It is this vital personality, or Sunsum, which must be guarded at all times. When a man dies, if his Sunsum is not correctly sent off, it may linger as a ghost to haunt the living. This general type of belief is common in West Africa. As long as the departed is remembered and is sustained by the living through offerings and libation, so long will his Sunsum be strong among his descendants.

The belief that the spirits are able to possess those whom they favor is a vital part of African traditional religion. It is believed that both the lesser gods and the spirits of the ancestors can possess a devotee at will. Possession by a spirit or a god generally takes place within a cultic context, yet it is still a unique experience in the lives of African peoples and an experience greatly sought after. Under possession one becomes the mouthpiece of the god or the ancestor, and thus the spirit uses this medium to make its will and wishes known. Possession also has a therapeutic value. The devotee, on recovering from possession, is believed to have undergone personality transformation.

In a later chapter, it will be seen that this element of African traditional religion was directly transplanted into the Black religion of the New World and became a vital means by which the Africans in diaspora were able to keep in touch with their gods and ancestors.

4. Belief in sacrifice:[11] The traditional religion of Africa is sacerdotal religion, that is to say, a religion in which priests and priestesses are the main functionaries. And one of the most important functions of the priest is to offer sacrifice on behalf of the people.

Sacrifice in African religion is a time-honored tradition and varies from the now abandoned human sacrifice of Ashanti, to the offering of kola nuts among the Yoruba in Nigeria. To this day, thousands of sacrifices are offered in Africa daily. They are offered to avert sickness, to aid in recovery from illness, to counteract failure in business and agriculture, or other ill fortunes. An animal such as a fowl may constitute the sacrifice or it may consist of the firstfruits of the garden, eggs or kola nuts. Sacrifice generally accompanies the rites of passage, that is, birth, puberty, marriage and death ceremonies. Each sacrificial occasion calls for certain kinds of sacrificial objects. In the case of animal sacrifice, certain types of sacrifice call for a specific color such as black, white or a mixture of both. In animal offerings the blood is dedicated to the spirits, while the carcass is generally eaten at a feast designed to promote the solidarity of the community. In the case of bloodless offerings, it is the essence that is offered; the object itself is not usually destroyed. In all cases only the best is offered to the spirits.

Sacrifice in Africa is of various types. Dr. Christian Gaba of Ghana suggests that four separate types of offering may be distinguished; they are propitiatory, substitutionary, preventative and purificatory. In the sacrificing of animals, a three-act drama is performed. First, the presentation of the offering to the priest by the officiant. Second, the prayer by the priest that the god may accept the offering and answer the petition of the officiant. The third act is the immolation. The animal is killed and the blood is offered to the spirit—this ends the sacrifice.[12]

The importance of sacrifice in African religion cannot be overlooked. Many African scholars of religion have shied away from discussing this vital topic because of the distorted and sensational propaganda of missionaries about the practice of human sacrifice. But that is hardly reason enough to avoid a topic so close to the African soul. To the contrary, because of the misconception about human sacrifice, the topic should be discussed more often. It should be remembered that human sacrifice did not happen only in Africa; this practice was worldwide. It was well entrenched among the early Hebrews.[13] It also should be stated that human sacrifice was not a practice undertaken for frivolous occasions. It was rather the highest gift of man to God, an offering for great events of state. It was no more gruesome to give a few human lives on these great occasions than it is for civilized states to sacrifice thousands of lives in a war for the so-called defense of freedom and liberty.

5. The belief in magic—good and evil: Any study of African tradi-

tional religion must deal with the subject of magic and witchcraft, because it is on this subject that the greatest amount of distortion has occurred. All trained anthropologists know that magic and witchcraft are a cultural universal, which means that all cultures have practiced both in the evolution of their respective societies. Indeed it can be said that despite the rise of science, magic and witchcraft are two of the most tenacious cultural institutions and continue to hold sway over the minds of both peasant and sophisticated peoples. It is the modern view of anthropologists that religion and magic are two sides of the same coin and that it is difficult to make a neat separation of the two. The reason for this is that both deal with the supernatural. Modern writers on the subject separate religion and magic by defining religion as propitiation of the gods and magic as coercion of them; or by noting that religion serves group ends while magic serves private goals; or by stressing that religion exists in a shepherd/flock relationship, while magic exists in a client/practitioner relationship.[14] This type of interpretation, however, is mere intellectual exercise. Very few of the actual practitioners of a religion have the sophistication to distinguish between these intellectual fineries. In traditional, as in present-day Africa, this line of inquiry is beside the point—the magico-religious ambience still prevails. It is our intention here to deal with the broad subject of magic and witchcraft, and to discuss the functionaries who are a part of it, the medicine man and the sorcerer.

However, before entering into the analysis of magic and witchcraft, two African concepts must be clarified; the first concerns power and the second, illness. The term *force-vitale,* life-force or life power, is a most important concept in all Africa.[15] It is found in every language grouping on the continent and carries the same meaning. The supreme value of life is to live robustly. Anything that diminishes this life-force is considered dangerous to both man and community. A man's health and vitality rest on his ability to continue to fulfill the duties of his particular clan, because it is only when he is dutifully serving the gods and ancestors that they will protect him from all things that would reduce his vital energy. This vital force is, however, constantly threatened by the spirit world as well as by the malice of other men. In the first case, a man must, through prayer and sacrifice, placate the spirit and set things right. In the second case, a man has to seek the aid of a sorcerer

stronger than the one his enemy uses against him. Life, then, is
an existential battle, of force against force. If a man is overcome
by a force from the outside, it is invariably said that his vital force
has been diminished by some action of the gods, the ancestors or
other men.

Illness, most Africans believe, is unnatural. It is either caused
by the breaking of some ritual taboo or, again, by the malevolence
of another human being. Since sickness can bring on diminution
of the vital force, it is never viewed as a natural thing, and the
African always looks for causes. This must be done on two levels.
The first level asks the question, what is the ailment? The second
asks the question, why am I sick in this way? The first is the physical dimension and the second the spiritual dimension. To the
Western mind this is naïve thinking, but to the African, it makes
situations more manageable. To counteract illness, the African,
like the Westerner, turns to the traditional specialists in his society,
the medicine men or traditional doctors. These men are not only
specialists in administering herbs and other medical practices, but
are also well acquainted with the spiritual beliefs of the people.
Thus they are not only prepared to treat the physical malady but
also the spiritual sickness thought to be at the root of the illness.
To the sick, African specialists are part doctor and part pastor.[16]
The traditional doctor generally prescribes herbs, powders, roots,
leaves and a host of other time-tested medicines. While different
from his Western counterpart, he is not necessarily inferior. His
techniques may call for bleeding, massaging or pricking the patient
with needles; but he will also perform sacrifices of fowl or goat,
and he may prescribe a taboo. In Africa, there is an involvement
between the doctor and patient; they participate in a ritual dialogue. Healing in this sense is not a profession but an art. The
art of restoring a man not only to physical well-being but to his
well-being in the community. Healing is both herbal and ritual.
This is a totally different dimension of healing from that which is
known in the West, where a prescription, a piece of paper, is considered sufficient for the cure.

Most important is the incantation or the exorcising of the illness; this is considered the central part of the cure. The incantation is important in the analysis of African healing art because
medicine, of all types, is secondary to it. Incantation is that which
energizes; the power primarily of healing in it, and only second-

arily in the medicine. Leaves and roots are inert things empowered by the force-vitale of the medicine man.

A medicine man in Africa is not a "Johnny-come-lately." He
undergoes a long period of formal training. At the outset of his or
her call to become a traditional doctor, he is scrutinized by men of
the profession, or by his would-be teachers, to ascertain the sincerity of his wishes and the fitness of his personality. His initial
training may last from three to ten years. During this time he must
study the lore of the society, and learn to know the herbs, which
sometimes necessitates that he test them upon himself. At the end
of this period of training he is put to a rigorous test and if he has
satisfied his peers he is then initiated into the fraternity. John S.
Mbiti in his *African Religions and Philosophy* forcefully came to
the defense of the African medicine man when he wrote:

> To the African societies the medicine-men are the greatest
> gift, and the most useful source of help. . . . Every vil-
> lage in Africa has a medicine-man within reach, and he is a
> friend of the community.[17]

Here we have an African of superior mind, supporting an institution which has been greatly disparaged by Western scholars. Not
only is Mbiti a scholar but he is a university professor of worth
and an ordained minister of the Church of England. At present
there are many Western-trained Africans who are coming to the
defense of their ancient traditions.

Magic, as it is called by the West, needs further discussion. To
call African healing art "magic" is a gross insult to the specialist
who, for centuries past, has been of such great help to his community. It cannot be denied that Western medical technique is
more scientific and percentage-wise more effective, but is this a
reason to throw out all the good that has been done by these herbalists? The answer is no, because each culture demands its own
technique. The premise upon which Western medicine operates
is as follows: first, the remedy must be effective only for a strictly
defined malady; second, the effect of the remedy is so reliable
that its success is predictable and its failure leads to doubt of the
diagnosis; third, given the same malady, the result is repeatable by
all doctors all over the world. Does all Western medicine actually
meet these criteria? Much of our sophisticated medicine is based
on plausible hypotheses, which at times lead to very dangerous

results. Furthermore, many of the modern medical prescriptions
are mere placebos! What do we call this, civilized magic? If this
is true of Western sophisticated medicine, there is little on which
to castigate a folk society whose traditions still maintain the
magico-religious ambience. Claude Levi-Strauss, who has studied
folk society in a scientific way, came to the defense of magic when
he observed that:

> One deprives oneself of all means of understanding magical
> thought if one tries to reduce it to a moment or a stage in
> technical and scientific evolution. . . . It forms a well-
> articulated system, and is in this respect independent of that
> other system which constitutes science. It is therefore better,
> instead of contrasting magic and science, to compare them
> as two parallel modes of knowledge.[18]

Levi-Strauss further observed that although science is more successful than magic, magic is also successful in producing results.
At the back of Levi-Strauss' mind was the old Frazerian idea that
magic is a pseudo-science which in the evolutionary scale of things
predated modern science. To Frazer, magic and science were two
separate things; on this point Levi-Strauss is totally opposed to
Frazer. To the African there is no such separation.

Having discussed the value of benevolent magic and the medicine men in African society, it is now necessary to discuss
malevolent magic, known as witchcraft, and its important func-
tionary in this context, the sorcerer. Unlike the traditional medicine man, whose talent is directed toward the health of the society,
the sorcerer and his witchcraft stand in opposition to the community. His work is destructive, not curative. Witchcraft in Africa
is feared as much as leprosy is feared in the West; consequently,
the ultimate fate of the sorcerer is social ostracism and/or death.
At the outset, let us make a distinction between the witch and the
sorcerer. A witch is one who, by his sheer will, can cause hurt to
another person. Witchcraft is a disposition to hurt which is
endemic. Sometimes a witch is not aware of his evil powers until
he is accused. In some African societies techniques are developed
to discover witches, but it is generally difficult to know who has an
"evil eye." It is believed that the witches diminish the force-vitale
of another person by devouring it. They are believed to be able
to change themselves into various forms in order to carry out their

dreadful nocturnal deeds. Little conclusive evidence can be brought against an accused witch; the contrary is true of a sorcerer. The sorcerer has much of the knowledge of the medicine man. His herbal and ritual techniques are so similar to those of the medicine man that they are generally indistinguishable by the uninitiated, but to the indigenous members of society the two are not confused. The sorcerer's speciality is the casting of spells, but his *coup de grace* is poisoning; in many instances his knowledge in this field makes his work almost undetectable. In a recent lecture given by a visiting African scholar who had himself been trained in folk medicine, the following examples of this technique were given. One method of poisoning is to add a small amount of a ground herb to a person's drink. This particular poison is activated long after it is administered; it is not effective until a certain amount of cold water has been consumed, subsequent to the poisoning. Another example is the mixing of juices from the barks of certain trees—three tablespoonsful to a gallon of water. One drink from this mixture will be fatal but death will not occur for approximately two to three months from the time of its consumption. The drink ultimately destroys the liver, and this generally goes undiscovered. Such is the work of sorcerers. As a footnote to this section of our analysis, it should be noted that both the medicine man and the sorcerer came to the New World on the slave ships—a blessing to the Africans and a curse to the plantation. It is our aim to show that the fear of African witchcraft became a potent weapon against the slave regime, and the means by which revolutions against oppression were fomented.

6. African wisdom—proverbs and folklore: A survey of Black heritage would not be complete without a short statement on the wisdom sayings and the lore of Africa, both of which have influenced New World Black culture and, in many cases, have become the dominant folk literature of the New World. We need only mention the "Uncle Remus" and "Br'er Rabbit" stories of the United States and Brazil, the "Ananse" stories of Jamaica and other English-speaking Caribbean Islands. Very little work has been done on the wisdom sayings of traditional Africa, but enough is available to give us a sampling despite the vast research yet to be done on this area.[19] All the research in African oral tradition suggests that the key to the African mind is hidden in the wisdom sayings, the proverbs and in the folklore.

a. The proverbs: The proverbs of Africa contain the true expression of the Black man's spirit. Those who have studied these sayings are impressed by their elegance, an elegance comparable to the high points of antique style. The proverbs of Africa are old. They are not attributed to any one sage; they simply exist as the wisdom of the nation. Bishop Vidal, quoted by Richard F. Burton in his book *The Proverbs: Wit and Wisdom from Africa,* and writing on the high quality of the proverbs of the Yoruba, observed that

> Were we to measure these people by the standard of their proverbial morality, we should come to the conclusion that they had attained no inconsiderable height in the development of social relations, having passed out of that savage barbarism, in which every man lives for himself alone, into a higher state of being, in which the mutual dependence of one member on another, is recognized, giving room for the exercise of social virtues as a sort of moral compact for the safeguard of society.[20]

Vidal concluded:

> Surely these [proverbs] are indications of no ordinary perception of moral truths, and are sufficient to warrant the inference that in closeness of observation, in depth of thought, and shrewd intelligence the Yoruba is *no ordinary man.*[21]

This view of Bishop Vidal has been confirmed for other African societies by men such as Captain Rattray, working among the Ashanti; Danquah, among the Fanti; Parrinder, in other parts of West Africa; and more recent writers such as John S. Mbiti and E. B. Idowu. All of these scholars are convinced that the proverbs are the philosophically garnered wisdom of Africa and that they continue to be very influential in the lives of contemporary Blacks.

Webster's New World Dictionary of the American Language defines a proverb as a short saying in common use that strikingly expresses some obvious truth or familiar experience or an enigmatic saying in which a profound truth is cloaked. The second of these definitions fits beautifully with the nature of African proverbs. African proverbs are by nature enigmatic; that is to say, they are puzzling; for the uninitiated. Deep reflection on the context in which they are spoken is required in order to perceive their

profound truths; the proverbs generally carry a moral reprimand
or are intended guides for future action.

African proverbs speak to various aspects of life. First and most
important are those which deal with man's relation to his God. The
second are those which deal with man's moral behavior, and the
third, those which deal with aspects of social virtues. Using the
Twi language of the Akan people of Ghana, let us illustrate these
three aspects of proverbs.

1) Proverbs dealing with man's relation to his God:

Obi nkyere abofra Onyame
God needs no pointing out to a child. [Omnipresence]

Akoko nom nsu a, ode kyere Onyankopon
When the fowl drinks water it shows it to God.
[Thankfulness]

Onyame nkrabea nni kwatibea
There is no by-pass to God's destiny. [Moral
obligation]

Onyame ne panyin
God is chief. [Omnipotence]

Wope aka asem akyere Onyankopon a, ka kyere mframa
If you want to tell God, tell the wind. [Omni-
presence]

Asase terew, ne Onyame ne panyin
The earth is wide but God is chief. [Omnipotence]

*Wuse wobesom nyankopon a, som no preko, na mfa
biribi mmata ho*
If you would serve God, be thorough, attaching
no condition. [Total commitment]

2) Proverbs dealing with human morality:

Obi nye yiye nnya bone
The pursuit of beneficence brings no evil.
[Goodness]

Obi se "bo wo bra yiye" a, onyaw wo e
If some one tells you to lead a good life,
that is no abuse. [Be open to instruction]

Biribiara nye yaw se aniwu
Nothing is more painful than disgrace. [Moral
rectitude]

Wobo bra-pa a, wote mu dew
If you live a good life, you enjoy its sweetness.
[Goodness pays]

3) Aspects of social virtues:

Abrofa kotow panyin nkyen
At the feet of the older, the young bends
its knee. [Respect]

Abufuw te se ohoho, ontra obiakofo fi
Anger is like a stranger, it does not stay in
one house. [Good social relationship brings
good harmony]

Wodo wo ni a, di wo ho ni
When people hold you in respect, hold yourself
in respect, too. [Dignity]

Oman rebebo a, efi afi mu
He treats you like a beast who does not recipro-
cate your goodness. [Kindness]

Enye tekerema na eboo nantwi nti na wanhu kasa
The cow never learnt to speak, and not because
she has no tongue. [Be careful of what you say]*

It may be observed from the sample of Akan proverbs above,
that there is a wide variety of simple and abstract proverbs. Proverbs are used for many occasions. They are used for correction,
warning, reprimand, praise, encouragement and most importantly
in traditional court proceedings. Many modern-day Africans, after
a few years' stay in foreign countries, informed this writer that they
are unable to follow the proceedings of community councils in
their society because they have forgotten the fine points of the
proverbs. It is for this reason that vast knowledge of the proverbs
is an essential tool in the legal tricks of traditional lawyers.

* For an extensive study of Akan proverbs, see J. B. Danquah: The Akan
Doctrine of God, London: Frank Cass and Co., 1968.

One of the most important characteristics of the proverb is its earthiness. Animals frequently are portrayed as the speakers of maxims. For example, the antelope says, or the fowl says, or the cow says, and so on. These animals have authority because the African sees in each species certain characteristics which he deems necessary to his own social survival, aggressiveness, shrewdness, doggedness, meekness or, perhaps, patience. Some of these qualities can be better observed as they emerge in folklore. The use of animals as the speakers in proverbs and folklore in general is a characteristic of Black culture to this day. One can still hear counseling and advice of this sort among Jamaicans.

b. The folktales: The folktales of Africa, like the proverbs, are just beginning to receive the attention of scholars both native and foreign. And much remains to be done, especially by African scholars who are well acquainted with their mother tongues. So vast is this oral literature that it will take several decades to catalogue even a small quantity of them; yet the work is urgent because the carriers of traditional culture are fast dying out.

The folktales of traditional Africa are the repository of traditional customs, beliefs and sayings, preserved unreflectively among the people. They are narratives which attempt to explain the origin of the universe, God, man, death and the afterlife. All students of African culture are aware of the importance of storytelling in these societies, for it serves educational as well as recreational functions. It is through this medium that moral concepts are taught, as well as history, theology and philosophy. Some scholars propose four different kinds of folk literature in African oral tradition.[22] The first type includes stories concerning the supreme being; the activities of the lesser deities; or the origin of the world, mankind, cultural artifacts and institutions as a result of the activity of sacred beings. The above are classified under the heading of "myths" because they are closely connected with religion as a whole. The second group consists of stories that seek to explain the environment and the nature of animals; these are concerned with the natural and the supernatural nature of these animals and are called "etiological" stories. The third group is made up of stories which deal with the founding fathers or ancestors, their activities and the people with whom they came in contact. These may be called tribal "histories" or "legends." Finally, there are tales which deal with characters who are neither ancestors nor deified beings, and they are repeated mainly in recreational situations. Our main interest here is in the second type, the so-called etiological tales.

Although many of the animals have been dramatized in folklore, there are a few which are given greater emphasis in West Africa. Two of these will be used in our example: The "Ananse" —the spider of the Akan people—and the tortoise, which is known all over West Africa. Knowledge of why these animal stories persisted in the memory of New World Africa is important. Ananse, the spider, the trickster god of the Akan people, compares well with Legba of the Fon people and Esu of the Yoruba. These divinities have one outstanding common characteristic and that is their ability to disrupt the plans of man. They delight in confusion and are not themselves unless they have some antics going. Ananse is the architect of confusion, he muddles everything he is engaged in, yet he always manages to come out on the better end of the deal. He is like the elf in European folktales, rather insignificant in size, but able to outsmart others one hundred times his size with his speed, shrewdness and dexterity.

Another important character of African folklore is the tortoise, which can be found in Yoruba stories and in the tribal literature of West and Central Africa. This creature is probably the slowest of all the forest creatures, yet figures prominently in the "sport pages" of African folklore as a consistent winner of all races. The tortoise is said to appeal to the African mind because it is uncanny and mysterious; and it is considered sovereign in the forest even though it is inoffensive and does not prey on even the smallest creature. Africans respect the tortoise because it subsists on a minimum of food and is practically immune to injury. There are only two enemies capable of hurting it: one is man; the other is the python. In most cases man carries away the tortoise for use in ritual ceremonies. The python, on the other hand, is said to be able to crush the young tortoise with its enormous power of constriction. Most of the other animals of the forest will not challenge a tortoise because of its ability to protect itself. Because of the above-mentioned characteristics and the additional ones of longevity, silent movement, and dogged determination in overcoming obstacles, one can easily understand why the tortoise figures so prominently in African folklore. It is a synonym for cunning, craft and exceptional intelligence. We shall meet Ananse and the tortoise in the New World and see how their stories became paradigms for human survival.

The proverbs and folktales of Africa found in the New World are examples of the selected aspects of traditional culture which the Africans in diaspora thought necessary for survival in their new environment. These stories in themselves are enough proof that the Africans did not enter the New World *tabula rasa,* but rather as culture bearers, who within a short period stamped the New World with their cultural inheritance. This general summary of African heritage is provided in order to throw light on those aspects of African survival which were carried over into the New World Black culture. Much has been written about these "strange" customs, but few scholars have adequately dealt with these findings in light of their origin.

Blinded by the cancerous prejudice created by slavery, early scholars wrote about Africa with a guarded pen and their observations were often highly questionable. Thus the literature on Africa is replete with discoveries of fetishism, animism, jujuism, magic, witchcraft and sorcery; and it is argued that this kind of religion has degraded the sons and daughters of Africa. It could be about these scholars that John Milton speaks when he says they were "well-versed in books but shallow in themselves." Their shallowness became the scholarly diet of their disciples but the true nature of Africa was distorted. Happily not all nineteenth-century scholars fell for this shallow analysis of African religion. Professor Max Mueller, in his Hibbert Lectures of 1878, exhibited the kind of scholarly maturity on the analysis of African culture that was not usual until the current writings of men such as Geoffrey Parrinder:

> I maintain, says Mueller, that fetishism was a corruption of religion, in Africa as elsewhere, that the Negro is capable of higher ideas than the worship of rocks and stones and that many tribes who believe in fetishes cherish at the same time very pure, very exalted, very true sentiments of Deity. Only we must have eyes to see, eyes that can see what is perfect without dwelling too much on what is imperfect. . . . Religion is everywhere an aspiration rather than a fulfillment; and I claim no more for the religion of the Negro than for our own, when I say that it should be judged not by what it appears to be, but by what it is—nay not only by what it is but by what it can be and by what it has been in its most gifted votaries.[23]

It is a pity that the missionaries who went to Africa in the very period in which Max Mueller wrote never paid heed to his guidelines. To them the religion of Africa was nothing but heathenism which was to be eradicated root and branch, and in its place the "undiluted brew" of European Christianity was to be established. However, even with all the Christian zeal and fanaticism for the eradication of African traditional religions, Western effort was a miserable failure. After years of seeking to plant the true word of God (whatever that may mean) in Africa, the Africans have not been diverted to any great extent from the traditional roots of their culture, because these roots are deep. Bishop James Johnston, of Western Equatorial Africa, although brought up in the creeds of European Christianity, expressed in a letter to Edward Wilmot Blyden in 1862, the failure of the Christian attempt to destroy the traditions of Africa.

> We have for a long time now been contending, and that rightly too, for a teaching and training that shall not destroy our Native African idiosyncrasies and that will not Europeanize us, but I fear we are practically giving over our contention now. We Africans in our pure and simple native state know not any distinction between what is secular and what is religious. With us, there is nothing secular. Religion enters into every department of life with us, and so it should be with beings who know that they are responsible to the great creator of their existence and all creation also for everything they do, and that they are expected to seek His glory in and through everything they do.[24]

The reaction of Africa to Europeanization through Christian missions was not felt by the bishop alone. This feeling was felt throughout Black Africa. However, as we shall show in the last chapter of this book, the soul of Africa could not long endure the frozen quality of European Christianity with its do's and don'ts. What the Africans did was to take the essence of the Christian religion and unite it with their traditional virtues and thus they transcended the trappings of European cultures and their irrelevant forms of worship and evolved a new religion of their own. Today, thousands of syncretistic religions are found throughout Africa, similar to those which the Africans in exile created out of the same mixture of Christian and traditional African elements. It is interesting to note that the African ethos, whether at home or in exile, produces similar reactions. In sum, the dehumanizing influence of Europe on the peoples of Africa has not been able to destroy their soul. If anything, it has given them new energies to kindle their force-vitale and to reinterpret their own destiny. Thus we hope to prove in the following chapters that the African came into the New World and brought with him his rich cultural heritage and that in his new environment he remained a variation or modification of his African self.

CHAPTER 3

SOUL IN CAPTIVITY:
Africa in the Americas

1. Slavery—English and Latin systems: This chapter attempts to give a broad picture of the nature of slavery in the New World by contrasting the two systems which dominated the area from the sixteenth to the nineteenth century. These are the English and the Latin systems; the first being dominated by the Protestant religion, the other by the Catholic Church. We will also look at the reaction of African slaves to slavery and the particular methods they used to overcome their oppression.

For over 350 years slaves were carried to the New World, and by the end of the slave-trading era, over eleven million Africans had been transported to the Caribbean and Latin America. This is the greatest mass migration of a forcible type that has ever taken place in the history of mankind. The suffering of slaves, the intrigues and rivalries which accompanied this forcible migration, are far too complicated to be recounted in this book. Let it suffice to say that the history of African slavery was one of the most greedy forms of man's inhumanity to man. It is even more revolting when one remembers that slavery was conceived within the context of, and blessed by, the Christian Church.[1]

For our purposes, we will deal with slavery as it appeared in North and South America and the Caribbean as if it were one large plantation under two different systems. First, we will survey the English colonies, those of North America, and those extending into the Caribbean Islands and the northern part of South Amer-

ica. Then attention will be turned to the Latin slave colonies which
spread over South America and parts of North America. These
include the Spanish, French and Portuguese colonies. Because of
their close similarity, the latter can justly be grouped under the
single heading, the Latin system.

a. The English slave system: The African slaves under the
English slave system were subjected to one of the most stringent
forms of domination known in the New World. The power of the
master was absolute. Slaves were nothing but chattel, liable to
seizure at any time by those to whom the master was indebted, or
to be sold to other slave colonies. Every inch of the slaves' lives
was regulated by a system in which they were forced to give un-
questioning obedience to the master at all times. The welfare of
the master was to be their total concern and any thought of themselves or their own welfare was strictly forbidden unless it contributed to the master's plan. This system of domination was
initiated and maintained by violence, or the threat of it, on the part
of the slave master under a system of strict law and order. It is
essential to understand that throughout most of the history of
slavery, the violence perpetrated against the majority (the slaves),
was indeed a *legal* violence, and that the main quantity and direction of violence came from the oppressive minority against the
oppressed majority, under the rubric of law and order.

Unlike the Latin countries, the English had no slave tradition;
consequently there was little or no protection for the slaves within
their legal system. Under the old English representative system
of government which prevailed in the colonies, constitutional
recognition was given only to the white minority, who in turn
legislated the power necessary for control of the slaves. Under the
English system the slave was without a legal personality. Thus he
was denied the right to personal security, property, marriage or
even parenthood. We shall examine these points more carefully
to see more clearly the difference between the English and the
Latin systems and the reaction of the slaves within each.

The concept of a legal personality suggests that a person has the
capacity to choose and, within limits, the ability to act on his
choices. It suggests that a person has the right to decide which of
his rights he will maintain as absolute and God-given and which
of them he will relinquish for the good of society. Under the English slave system, the slave was deprived of all rights: he became

the object of other people's rights and was the possessor of none of his own. He was chattel, a thing, a possession to be used, abused or destroyed without any questions asked of his master. An English jurist commented that slaves were "below the rank of human beings, not only practically, but physically, and morally."[2] Unlike the Latin slave system, the English system left authority totally in the hands of planters, whose power over their slaves was total. Every law concerning the control of slaves was made with a view to total suppression of every aspect of their free will. U. B. Phillips, America's apologist for slavery, puts it this way:

> The severity of the slave laws in the commonwealths of English origin . . . was largely due to the historic possession by their citizens of the power of self-government. A distant autocrat might calmly decree such regulations as his ministers deemed proper, undisturbed by the wishes and apprehensions of the colonial whites; but assemblymen locally elected and responsive to the fears as well as the hopes of their constituents necessarily, reflected more fully the desire of social control. . . . If this should involve severity of legislative repression for the blacks, that might be regrettable and yet be done without a moment's qualm.[3]

The British Government did have the power to review the early slave laws of the colonies. However, the surprising thing is that only in rare cases did the laws controlling the slaves ever receive a review by the English Government. There is some indication of review by the Crown but even this is disputed.[4]

Enslavement under the English meant not only the loss of human personality, but personal security itself. Under the Virginia law, the murder of a slave by his master was not considered a felony. Thus it was declared: "It cannot be presumed that prepensed malice (which alone makes murder a ffelony) should induce a man to destroy his own estate."[5] Since the slave was property, a part of the estate, and not a person, killing him brought no moral or legal judgment. Not only could he be murdered without the master incurring guilt, but what was even more serious was that the slave had no right to defend himself. The Virginia law of 1668, which was comparable to all the English slave codes, denied the slave every right to self-protection. It declared:

> If any slave resist his master (or other by his master's order correcting him) and by the extremity of the correction

should chance to die, that his death shall not be accompted a ffelony . . .[6]

furthermore,

> If any negroe or other slaves shall presume to lift up his hand in opposition against any Christian, shall for every offense . . . have and receive thirty lashes on his bare back well laid on . . .[7]

At the same time slaves were denied the privilege of a trial by jury.

Turning to another area of life, slave marriage was totally unrecognized by law. Under the English system, marriage between slaves was seen as depriving the master of his right of possession. And so the institution of parenthood was also without legal sanction. Here maternity was a fact; paternity was a fiction.

Manumission under the English was almost impossible, while in the Latin system this was so highly regarded that freeing slaves became a mark of piety on the part of the masters. In the Virginia law of 1691, no Negro or mulatto could be

> set free by any person whatsoever, unless such person or persons, their heirs executors, or administrators pay for the transportation of such negro or negroes out of the country within six months of setting him free.[8]

Throughout the period of slavery every obstacle was placed in the way of Black freedom. Because, in those days, it was believed that the only good Negro was either a slave or was dead. The designation "slave for life" was rigidly preserved and any deviation from this rule was resisted. However, despite such resistance, there were masters who, overwhelmed by a sense of duty or having experienced conversion, manumitted their slaves at great sacrifice to themselves and hardship to the slaves. It was a mark of their love of liberty at any cost that led the Blacks to accept freedom; and it was the freed slaves who, despite the degrading condition of life in their so-called free state, gave hope to their brethren in bondage. Unlike the Catholic Church in the Latin system, the church in the English slave colony was part and parcel of the oppressing class. The Church of England remained the staunch supporter of the slave/master relationship from the beginning of slavery until its very end. One reason for this was that the church

came to North America and later to Jamaica along with the slave
system. As such it was totally under the control of the slave masters, who had absolute power in making and breaking its clergymen. In England, the ministers of the church were under the
power of the bishops and, once invested with office, they were
accountable only to the ecclesiastical hierarchy. In the colonies,
however, the ministers were under the power of a vestry made up
of planters, who set up the church as an agent of their own inter-
ests. Whereas in England, at that time, the minister was appointed
to his parish for life, in the colonies he was hired and retained on
the basis of his good conduct in preserving the status quo.

Although directions dealing with the religious life of the slaves
were, from time to time, sent from the church in England to the
colonies, they were largely exercises in futility. A look at the
church's concern with the slaves provides a striking study in human ambivalence. The documents sent out from the Church of
England concerning slaves in the English-speaking world are
masterpieces of hypocritical piety. They are full of lofty instructions, and good intentions, but devoid of reality. The majority of
the preachers to whom these instructions were sent were themselves slave holders, often renegades from the English church and
upholders of the slave system with all its brutalities. Furthermore,
the majority of the planters were totally opposed to religion for
themselves, and so were naturally against it for their slaves.

As early as 1673, in his *Christian Directory,* Richard Baxter
included a chapter entitled "Directions to those masters in foreign
plantations who have Negroes and other slaves." The seventh
and last direction in this chapter reads in part: "Make it your
chief end in buying and using slaves to win them to Christ and save
their souls."[9] This was the general tenor of the church's directives
to planters in the English slave system. "Save their souls." And the
classic example of "saving the souls of the slaves" was undertaken
in 1701, by the prestigious organization The Society for the
Propagation of the Gospel in Foreign Parts, under the sponsorship
of King William III, and having as its president the Archbishop
of Canterbury, Thomas Lord.[10] It was preceded by a similar
society with a slightly longer name: The Propagation of the Gospel
amongst the Heathen Nations of New England and parts adjacent
in America, incorporated by Charles II, in 1661. The work of the
society consisted of "1) the care and instruction of our people

settled in the colonies; 2) the conversion of the Indians and
savages; 3) and the conversion of the Negroes." The society
operated from 1701 to 1783, yet despite the heroic attempt and
the dispatch of many missionaries to convert the Negro slaves, its
efforts were non-productive because the society's view of the
Negroes was inherently contradictory.[11]

In the now classic letter written by the Bishop of London to the
masters of slaves in America in 1727, in section II, the bishop set
in writing, in no uncertain terms, the doom of the hope of Blacks
ever to gain their freedom through the effort of the Church of
England. In this letter the bishop made it clear that baptism would
in no way change the slaves' status. He wrote:

> But it is further pleaded that the instruction of heathens in
> the Christian faith is in order to their baptism: and that not
> only the time to be allowed for instructing them, would be
> an abatement from the profits of their labour, but also, that
> baptizing them when instructed would destroy both the prop-
> erty which the master have in them as slaves bought with
> their money and the right of selling them again at pleasure,
> and that the making them Christians, only makes them less
> diligent and more ungovernable. . . . To which it may be
> very truly replied, that Christianity and the embracing of the
> Gospel *does not make the least alteration in civil property,*
> or in any of the duties which belong to civil relations; but in
> all these respects, *it continues person just in the same state
> as it found them.** The freedom which Christianity gives is
> a freedom from bondage of sin and Satan, and from the dom-
> ination of men's lusts and passions and inordinate desires;
> but as to their outward conditions, whatever that was before,
> whether bond or free, their being baptized and becoming
> Christians, makes no manner of change in it.[12]

The bishop then proceeded to shore up his edict with a reference
to the Holy Scriptures:

> As St. Paul has expressly told us, I Cor. 7:20, where *he is
> speaking directly to this point,* "Let every man wherein he is
> called therein abide with God."[13]

So in the mind of the venerable Bishop of London "baptism
and becoming Christians, makes no manner of change: in the

* [My italics]

slaves' external conditions or obligations." In the matter of their being ungovernable as a result of accepting the Christian religion, the bishop further instructed:

> It is certain that the Gospel everywhere enjoins not only diligence and fidelity, but also obedience for conscience sake: and does not deprive masters of any *proper* methods of enforcing obedience, where they appear to be necessary. . . . Christianity takes not out of the hands of *superiors* any degrees of strictness and *severity* that fairly appears to be necessary for the preserving *subjection* and government.[14]

In other words:

> You yourselves remain the judges as much after they receive baptism as before; so that you can be in no danger of suffering by the change; and as *to them the greatest hardship that the most severe master can inflict upon them is not to be compared to the cruelty of keeping them in a state of heathenism* and depriving them of the means of salvation as reached out to all mankind in the Gospel of Christ . . .[15]

The sentiments of the church as conveyed in this letter of the Bishop of London need no further elaboration. Henceforth, the church's main concern was to be the conversion of the slaves; but this was a devious piety, whose main intention was to make the Blacks more adaptable to all the brutality of slavery. Still, despite the attempt of the Society to convert the Africans, very few masters were willing to allow their slaves this luxury and very few slaves did not see through the hypocrisy. As late as the period of the Declaration of Independence, the Africans were almost wholly non-Christian.[16] There were some attempts made by the SPG's individual missionaries and a few pious planters to instruct the Africans in Christian doctrine, but the mass of them remained untouched. Many reasons were given for this failure to convert the slaves; some blamed it on the fact that there was not enough leisure time, others on the commotion generated by colonial wars. But it should also be remembered that the colonies were always at "loggerheads" with England and refused to carry out many of her directives. Still, perhaps the most important reason for the failure of a plan of religious instructions for the slaves was the general attitude of the population towards Blacks. Jones, in his book *Religious Instruction of the Negroes in the United States,* observed:

> Their degraded and miserable appearance and character,
> their stupidity, their *uncouth languages* and *gross superstitions,* and their constant occupation, operated as so many
> checks to benevolent efforts for their conversion to Christianity. And thus, those who advocated the slave-trade on
> the grounds that it introduced Negroes to the blessings of
> civilization and the gospel, saw their favorite argument losing its force in great measure from year to year.[17]

He further added:

> The Africans who were brought over and bought by us for
> servants, and who wore out their lives as such enriching
> thousands, from Massachusetts to Georgia and were members of our household, never received from the colonists
> themselves a solitary missionary exclusively devoted to their
> good; nor was there ever a single society established within
> the colonies, that we know of, with the express design of
> promoting religious instruction![18]

In the light of this it is not surprising that the preponderance
of Africans in the United States, from the time of their entrance
to the Revolutionary War, remained true to essentially African
beliefs and practices; and that, during this period, they laid the
foundation of a typically Afro-American life-style which was to
continue side by side with the white American ethos to the present
day.

In Jamaica, one of England's prime colonies, it was not until
the second decade of the nineteenth century that any real attention was given to the religious condition of the slaves by the
Church of England and even this was done under duress. It was
the nonconformist sects that finally made the church react. Thus
in 1815, the Jamaican House of Assembly voted unanimously to:

> consider the state of religion among the slaves, and carefully investigate the means of diffusing the light of genuine
> Christianity, divested of the dark and dangerous fanaticism
> of the Methodists which had been attempted to be propagated and which grafted on to the African superstitions
> . . . has proved, the most pernicious consequences to
> individuals, and is so pregnant with imminent danger to the
> community.[19]

We may conclude, then, that throughout the history of the English slavery system, the Church of England did little to alleviate the harshness and brutality meted out to the slaves. Here and there voices were raised, here and there some efforts were expended, but the moral responsibility of the church to point out the inhumanity of its leading members—the planter class—was largely neglected. It would not be until the coming of the Methodist and Baptist churches, with their radical reawakening of the dignity of the Christian man and their doctrine of liberty under God for the slaves, that many slaves were brought to the Christian religion. Yet even they failed to change radically the laws of "tooth and claw," that were the basis of slavery.

b. The Latin slave system: In general, an objective analysis of slavery in the New World will reveal that the system was riddled with inhumanity and brutality to our African forefathers and their descendants. In particular, the analysis will reveal that wherever the slaves were treated with any degree of respect and sympathy they responded with gratitude. Most scholars agree that the slaves under the Latin system were more humanely treated than those in the English system. However, even under the Latin system there was harshness and brutality. If one could set up a severity continuum within the Latin system, we would place the French at the harshest end, the Portuguese in the middle and the Spanish at the point indicating the most lenient.

We will have space for only a brief look at the institution of slavery under Spain in order to compare it with the English system previously discussed, and in this we will use Cuba as our case study.

The first and most important thing that distinguishes the Spanish slave institution from the English one is that the former was always under the effective control of the Spanish Crown and this control never was conceded to the colony at any time. Therefore it was decided that "because the Kingdom of Castile and the Indies are under one Crown, the laws and ordinances of government of the one and the other ought to be similar and consistent as possible."[20] It was further declared that the customs of these overseas kingdoms should be the same as

the customs and ordinances with which the Kingdoms of Castile and Leon are ruled and governed with regard of course for making room and allowing for the diversity and dissimilarity of these lands and nations.[21]

The nature of this declaration immediately places the situation in sharp contrast to that which evolved in the English system. Whereas in the Latin system the ancient laws of Spain were to apply equally in the Indies, new laws were constantly being made in the English system. Thus from the beginning of Spanish hegemony in the New World, there were established laws governing the treatment of slaves. This, as we shall see, was to have far-reaching results. The most important Spanish Law Code was developed in the thirteenth century and was known as *Las Siete Partidas del rey Alfonso el sabio*. It was compiled between 1263 and 1265, and contained seven divisions. An elaborate slave code was carefully spelled out here which became the Magna Carta of slavery in the New World.

The most far-reaching statement of *Las Siete Partidas* was that which says that slavery was *"contra razon de natura"* (slavery was against reason).

> Slavery is the most evil and the most despicable thing which can be found among men. Because man, who is the most noble, and free creature, among all creatures, that God made, is placed by it in the power of another . . .[22]

At the outset, the law made it clear that slavery is evil; man is a divine creation with a God-given humanity that ensures his personal freedom although this freedom is placed under the power of another. In contrast to the position of the slave under the English system, here his personal security was established by law, and we shall see that under the Spanish system every effort was made by the Crown to preserve the slave's personal liberty. In this respect, *Las Siete Partidas* clearly states:

> The father may punish his son moderately, and the master his slave . . . and the teacher his student. But because there are some of them who are so cruel and so excessive in doing this, that they do evil with stone, or with wood, or other hard things . . . and someone dies because of these wounds, although it was not done with the intention of killing him, the killer should be banished, to some island for five years. And if the one who punished with these wounds did it knowingly with the intention of killing him, he should have the punishment of homicide.[23]

We only need to compare the humanity of this law which governed slavery in Cuba with that developed in English Virginia during the same period to see how the two systems differed with respect to Christian enlightenment. In the Spanish institution both intentional and unintentional homicide were punishable by law. In the English system it was assumed that no master would kill his slave intentionally, therefore all killing of slaves by masters could be ruled unintentional. There was no area of personal security that was not protected under the Spanish law. The opposite prevailed under English law.

Also with respect to property, the slave under Spanish law was given many more rights than he was under the English system. Of course, even under Spanish law this did not amount to much.[24] One of the most important rights in this area was his right to inherit property.

The slave under Spanish law could buy his own freedom. In Cuba this system provided that the slave could employ the service of a third party (usually a priest) to buy his freedom with money provided by the slave himself.[25]

On the subject of the sanctity of marriage, the slaves under the Latin system were guaranteed this right both by the law and by the Church. No master could deprive the slave of the rights of marriage and parenthood.

In the Latin system manumission was not only possible but was a legal right, and in Cuba it was considered an honorable act on the part of the master. Once manumitted, the slave was free to participate in the society depending only on his ability. He was free to enter the professions if prepared to do so, and every effort was made to protect both slaves and freedmen in their status and this vigilance did not end with the laws of *Las Siete Partidas*. But before discussing the latter development of laws governing slaves, it will be helpful to look into the reason why the Latin institution of slavery differed so drastically from that of the English.

It will be observed that the governing of slaves in Spain existed long before Columbus; by the time of the discovery of the New World, the Spanish laws contained in *Las Siete Partidas* were over two hundred years old. Of course, the African slave trade in its most extreme form was not yet conceived. The provisions contained in *Las Siete Partidas* were designed to regulate the slaves who lived in Europe. Africans in Spain and Portugal were part

and parcel of daily life as a consequence of the Moorish invasions
of the Iberian Peninsula as early as the eighth century. It is fairly
well documented that African slaves were carried into Spain in a
large number from these early times; and as late as the fifteenth
century, West African slaves were still being imported to Spain by
Portuguese traders.[26]

It appears from the documents that Africans played a rather
important role in the history of Spain from this time until the slave
trade came to center on the New World colonies. Thus, in Seville,
for example, Antonio Dominquez Ortiz reported that the government of this city appointed a "Negro Count," or judge who ruled
over the Negro community.[27] He further stated that the same arch-
diocese had a population of 14,760 slaves.[28] A large number of
African slaves was also in Portugal, thus we hear that at Lisbon,
the center of Portuguese slave trade, as early as 1665, the slave
population numbered 9,950.[29]

Las Siete Partidas was written to protect slaves living in Europe.
When slavery was created in the New World colonies, new law
codes were necessary. When it became evident that the Indians
of the New World could not supply the needed labor for the
colonies and that Africans would have to be imported, it was de-
creed that only Spanish-speaking Blacks were to be taken. They
were called *ladinos*. It appears, however, that the ladinos were
both expensive and unruly as slaves, having been sold to planters
by the Crown after having become accustomed to the culture and
civilization of Spain. New sources of manpower and cheaper labor
were necessary. The only avenue open was the vast multitude of
"raw blacks from Africa." These were called *bozales*. As early as
1510, Spain agreed to the importation of Africans direct from the
continent, provided that no Mohammedans were included. For
this new departure, the Spanish Government granted licenses
known as *ascientos*. With these ascientos came complex laws to
govern the transportation and protection of the human cargo. New
laws were now added to *Las Siete Partidas* to cover this new type
of slave. These laws not only considered the master's protection
of his slave, but also dealt with the slave's relation to his master.
With the massive importation of new slaves to Cuba, new laws appeared; but in all cases these new laws were consistent with The
Law of the Seven Parts. Thus in 1693 in the *Real Cédula,* written

by the Captain-General of Cuba, it was provided that if at any time the master mistreats his slave, the captain-general:

> will apply the necessary remedy. For it is not just to consent to, or permit any excess in this matter, for their slavery is a sufficient sorrow without at the same time suffering the distempered rigor of their masters.[30]

Following the *Real Cédula,* an entire code dedicated to American Negro slavery came into being which was known as the code of 1789.[31] The Crown of Spain, referring to the multitude of new slaves in Cuba, said in the preamble to the code, "This class of human beings deserves from me their just attention."[32]

This code among other things provided for the instruction of the slaves in the Catholic religion and their admittance to the sacraments. It re-emphasized the sanctity of slave marriage and the provisions for their physical well-being—things such as food and clothing.

> These rules were then to be posted in all the local churches, on the doors of the *cabildo,* and in the parade grounds or shrines of the local *haciendas,* giving full notice to all masters "in order that none can allege ignorance" of them.[33]

The liberal code of 1789 was, as may be expected, greatly resisted by the masters. It was considered too restraining for the master and too lenient for the slave. This is an important point to note. What we hope to emphasize by the review of these codes is that in Cuba, the codes were more lenient with respect to the welfare of the slaves than, perhaps, in any other place in the New World.

The Catholic Church, unlike its Protestant counterpart, had a more Christian approach to its non-European inheritance. The first thrust of the Church was toward the Indians, but it later gave great energy to the evangelization of the slaves, and this energy greatly alleviated the sufferings that were the norm under the English system. This influence of the Church is copiously documented with regard to Cuba. With the extinction of the Indians, Cuba became populated by Africans from Nigeria, the Congo and other parts of West Africa. Because of its previous acquaintance with Blacks, the Church found no difficulties in attending to their religious needs. Thus we find that in Cuba the Church became the patron of the Blacks, a position which was to create for both the Africans and the Church a most amicable relationship.

Although the enslavement of Africans did not bring about the legal controversy in the Church as had the enslavement of Indians, many priests were opposed to slavery in any form. However, they were in the minority. But the Church did see to it that the provisions of the law were carried out. The power of the Church in this matter never was weakened. In various synodical pronouncements, the Church made it clear that not only were the laws to be carried out, but the periodic pronouncements proclaimed by the diocese were to be implemented, as well. Thus in 1680 the *Constituciónes* published by the Church synod in Cuba declared that: "No master [shall] prohibit his slaves against marriage, nor impede those who cohabit in it."[34]

The Church not only prohibited the master from preventing slave marriage, but also saw to it that no illegal marriage, adultery or concubinage was practiced among them. Thus it would seem that stable conjugal union prevailed among the slaves of Cuba, a condition which was unknown anywhere under the English system.

The clergy was most emphatic on the subject of manumission and, as the statistics show, the growth of the class of freedmen was phenomenal. Thus in the first census of 1774, 41 per cent of the colored population on the island was free. This amounted to 30,847.[35]

With regard to African religious institutions, Cuba to this day retains a large body of African tradition preserved for us in the native religion of *Santeria*. The well-known *cabildo* system created by the Spanish slave system was an African club that provided for each African nation present; it facilitated social interaction based on common language and customs. Thus in Cuba, the cabildo was the nucleus around which the strong African religious pattern now present in Santeria and *Nañiguismo* emerged. Santeria was basically religious, as we will see, while Nañiguismo was more a fraternal organization of a strongly benevolent nature. The combination of freedom that was given the Africans to preserve their own tradition and the encouragement they were given to participate in the Catholic yearly religious festivals led to the evolution of what is known today as the National Carnival. On festival days, the slaves from each nation in Africa would dress up in their traditional costume, and enriched the local festivities with their

special native dances. The extent of the African influence in the
National Carnival was described by an English visitor to Cuba in
1820, and although his prejudice is glaringly obvious his information is revealing.

> Each tribe or people has a *King* elected out of their number,
> whom, if they cannot enthrone in *Ashantee* glory, yet they
> rag out with much savage grandeur on the holidays on which
> they are permitted to meet. At these courtly festivals (usu-
> ally held every Sunday and feast days) numbers of free
> and enslaved negroes assemble to do homage with a sort of
> merriment that one would doubt whether it was done in ridi-
> cule or memory of their former condition. The gong-gong,
> cows-horn, and every kind of inharmonious instrument, are
> flourished on by a gasping band, assisted by clapping of
> hands, howling and the striking of every sounding material
> within reach, while the whole assemblage dance with maniac
> eagerness till their strength fails.[36]

The above quotation simply authenticates the fact that much
more benevolent attention was given to the slaves in the Latin
system than it was under the English. Consequently, not only their
personal security was guarded, but their spiritual and social welfare were cared for and their African customs preserved. One
Cuban bishop even proposed that his clergymen learn the various
African languages in Cuba so they would be better able to
Christianize the slaves.[37] We have no evidence as to whether his
directive was followed.

Despite the vigilance of the Catholics in Christianizing the
slaves, it is fair to point out that a real conversion of Afro-Cubans
to Christianity was never achieved. What took place was a syncretism of African religion with Christianity, where the Yoruba
pantheon gained supremacy over that of the Christians and
emerged as Santeria. The Babalawo of the Ifa oracle emerged as a
more respected religious official than the Catholic priest and, as
the Santero, or "saint maker," he was able to perform the re-
baptism of all the African gods, turning them into saints of the
Christian religion. However, having said this, we must give a final
nod to the Latin system as practiced in Cuba. Herbert S. Klein
wrote that the Church

> created the panoply of mores and attitudes that permitted
> the negro to be treated as a coequal human being and allowed

him to merge fully into Cuban society when the harsh regime of slavery was destroyed.[38]

Had this been the case in the English system, there would be no
use for this book. While the Latin system provided a climate of
leniency for the slaves' existence, the English system was bent on
destroying them as human beings. It is against this treatment that
the slaves revolted and became what Kenneth M. Stampp described
as "a troublesome property."

CHAPTER 4

SOUL IN CAPTIVITY:
The African Reaction to Slavery

It is a well-known fact of history that the forms of resistance are directly related to the forms of domination. The literature on Black revolt is rather full, and a study of it will prove that the intensity of resistance during slavery is in direct correlation to the intensity of domination exerted against it. Contrary to the myth that in servitude the Africans were the most satisfied, gentle and obedient of all enslaved peoples, it will be our aim to show in this section that the Black man was not long in asserting his human dignity in the New World. There have been few societies more rebellious and less law-abiding than the slave societies of the Caribbean, and those of North and South America. It was not long before the slaves understood that law under slavery was nothing but conspiratorial injustice subjugating the majority to the minority.

A careful look into the literature of slavery shows that despite the absolute power of the slave master, rebellion and the threat of rebellion were almost permanent features of the New World slave society.[1] Hardly a year passed between the seventeenth and nineteenth centuries when there was not some major slave upheaval. Even before the slaves landed on the shores of the New World we hear of revolt or mutiny on board the slave ships. So frequent had this mutiny become that slave masters were forced to insure their lives and their vessels against loss.

In order to examine the particular forms of resistance during slavery, we will consider the material under two headings: passive resistance and violent resistance. Passive resistance had various forms, from simply lagging on the job to outright running away from the plantation; another form was the pretense of being ill with an undiagnosable disease. But the most extreme form of passive resistance was that of suicide. This form was especially common among the Ibos of Nigeria, who preferred to take their lives rather than have the slave masters take them from them by degree.[2]

Violent resistance was carried out both on an individual and a collective level. Despite the fact that the legal penalty for even imagining the death of the master was a violent death to the slave, many of them did not only imagine the death of their master but actually brought it about. In this case the African sorcerer became prominent in administering deadly poison. The slaves who were trained in the herbal lore of Africa managed to use this technique rather successfully during the period of slavery, as the record will show.[3]

Historically, however, the most significant form of violence was collective violence. This was carried out by two different groups. First were the Maroons, or runaway slaves, who congregated in the mountain fastness of certain parts of the New World slave nations. An example of extensive maronage can be found in Jamaica where hundreds of Maroons fought the British in bloody warfare from the seventeenth to the eighteenth century.[4] In fact, it was not until Britain signed a peace treaty with them, giving them perpetual freedom, that peace was finally restored. Another example comes from Brazil, where the Republic of Palmares was created by runaway slaves and lasted for seventy years.[5] The presence of these Blacks in the forest caused no little harassment and bloodshed for the slave masters. A final example is the so-called Bush Negro of Surinam, who took to the forest in the seventeenth century and was not discovered until the first half of this century. However, the most bloody examples of collective violence come from the spontaneous uprising of plantation slaves in which the lives and properties of both masters and slaves were indiscriminately destroyed. This particular mode of resistance is important in three respects: first, its continuousness; second, its large-scale nature; and third, its effect on the final liberation of the slaves from bondage. As was already said, hardly a year passed from the time of the entrance of the slaves in the New World to the nineteenth century without a major slave insurrection. As for the large-scale nature of the rebellions, this varied from country to country; and in the United States of America we have the greatest exception to the rule. The ratio of whites to Blacks in the United States was always in favor of the whites. Consequently the largest rebellion in the United States, the Nat Turner Rebellion, which numbered less than one hundred slaves, was mild when compared to those of Jamaica, Cuba, Haiti and South America. To cite Jamaica as an example, the average number of slaves involved in revolts in the seventeenth and eighteenth centuries was approximately four hundred. The three most serious revolts on that island—the Maroon war of 1735–40, the 1760 Rebellion and the Sam Sharpe Rebellion of 1831—each involved over a thousand slaves.[6] And, when we turn to Haiti, we no longer see rebellion but, instead, war of a most savage sort.[7] This leads us to the third point, and that is the effect of these rebellions on the liberation of the slaves. When we speak of liberation, we must give the first nod to Haiti, where for the first time in history a slave population fought successfully against their enslavers. Here, under the leadership of the Africans Boukman, Toussaint L'Ouverture, Dessalines and Christophe, the Black slaves stopped the army of Napoleon and proved that they not only loved liberty, but that they could die for it.[8] Haiti became the second independent nation in the New World and has remained a Black republic to this day. And, turning to the English colonies, the massive revolts there were one of the major factors contributing to the downfall of the plantation system. For many years scholars have speculated that the collapse of the slave system was primarily the work of the humanitarian movement of Great Britain; however, scholars such as Eric Williams of Trinidad contend that one of the main reasons was that the system of production by slaves had become less profitable during the second half of the slave period. And to this may be added that it became less profitable because of the frequency and gravity of collective resistance on the part of the slaves. Slavery was fought not only physically but spiritually.

1. Invoking the African gods: Slavery was not a new institution to the Africans and although we have no record of when it actually began in Africa, we know that it was a part of the social structure of most African nations before the sixteenth century. Nevertheless, the brutal nature of European slavery made it as traumatic

for the Africans as the Exile was for the Jews or the unleashing
of the atomic bomb on Hiroshima was for the Japanese. Stanley
M. Elkins, in his book *Slavery: A Problem in American Institutional and Intellectual Life,* rightly observed,

> . . . that every African who became a slave underwent an
> experience whose crude psychic impact must have been
> staggering and whose consequences superseded anything that
> had ever previously happened to him.[9]

Elkins discusses these shocks under six headings, namely: "the
shock of capture"; "the march to the sea"; "the shock of sale"; "the
middle passage"; and "the shock of enslavement."[10] His conclusion is that these shocks were traumatic enough to obliterate every
vestige of African culture from the minds of the slaves. I disagree
with Elkins' conclusions and will argue, to the contrary, that it
was this very shock that drove the African to return to his traditional charter, to invoke the help of his traditional gods, as a means
of transcending the traumatic conditions of slavery. The literature
on "psychic shock" is just in its infancy, yet enough has been done
to show that it is in conditions of this type that an individual or a
people becomes more susceptible to dreams and visions of the
supernatural through which a renewed purpose for life is born.[11]
The Africans, like the Hebrews, found themselves in new and
frightening conditions, devoid of power, goods and worth, and,
like the Hebrews, they turned back to their native resources. In
this case, that means their supernatural beliefs, for these were their
only weapon against extinction. The Hebrews had their prophets,
who were able to advise them in new situations; the Africans were
not so fortunate. The Hebrews were dealing with an enemy with
a tradition which gave hope to exiles; the African had no hope of
a future amnesty. For him there was no way out of his calamity.
So out of the despair the Africans began to rebuild their belief
system, adapting it to the new conditions of slavery. We have
ample literature on the Caribbean and South America to prove
that the cultural institution that survived best in the New World
was the African traditional religion. However much it was modified, we now know that it was strong enough to outlast slavery.
African traditional religion has come down to our day in such
forms as Cumina in Jamaica, Shango in Trinidad, Santeria in Cuba,
Vodun in Haiti and Candomblé in Brazil.

2. Witchcraft–obeah: Before describing the nature of the African religions which became dominant in the New World we must first give attention to the question as to why, in every island where slavery was dominant, one specific mode of African religion dominated all others. For example, why, in Jamaica, did Cumina, the Ashanti form of ancestor worship, dominate over that of the Yoruba and other tribes; and why did the Arada form of ritual dominate in Haiti over that of the Congo? Similarly, why did Shango prevail in Trinidad and not others? The answer is conjectural because the early writers did not ask the Africans these questions–thus many of the answers we receive are only hypothetical.

Some writers believe that the tribe that was most active in fighting against slavery was the tribe whose rituals became routinized within the society, and that the rituals of other tribes were added on to this basic structure as they were felt to be necessary for the solidarity of the various peoples in their struggle. Other writers believe that because witchcraft became the most potent weapon in slavery, the tribe whose witchcraft proved the strongest, became the dominant religion of the society.[12] The present writer is inclined to believe that both theories are true and, as it will become evident, the second of these is more probable. But let us return to the description of the evolution of African religions in the New World using, first, examples from Jamaica.

One of the first reliable sources on the Africans in Jamaica is the Rev. William J. Gardner, a Congregational minister who worked on the island in the first half of the nineteenth century. His book *A History of Jamaica* was written in 1873. In the preface he tells us that in writing the book he availed himself of the labor of those who preceded him, but that the sources from which they derived their information had been carefully investigated. In addition, he used public records of the colony and a great mass of books and pamphlets, published from time to time. Referring to what he called "the social life of the slaves," Gardner said that, "little can be said with confidence as to the religious beliefs of these people. The influence of the *Koromantyns* seems to have modified if not obliterated whatever was introduced by other tribes."[13] The Koromantyns of which Gardner spoke are none other than the various tribes from the Gold Coast, whose place of departure from Africa was the famous Kormantine Castle of the Cape Coast, which now stands in ruin by the sea. We know from the slave period that the English were especially interested in these slaves because of their strength, even though they were also reputed to be ferocious and inclined toward mutiny and rebellion. It is now quite evident, from the slave records, that the Gold Coast Africans, that is, the Ashanti, Fanti, the Akim and some Adangwe, were most prominent in the early slave period, with the Ashanti and the Fanti peoples more numerous than the rest. This explains why the Ashanti influence became dominant. They were the first to arrive and it was they who determined the cultural mode that was to dominate all those who came after them. Edward Long, probably the first Jamaican historian, observed that:

> With the importation of slaves by the English, almost from the start, the irrepressible spirits among the Koromantyns fled to the mountains and found refuge with the Maroons in such numbers that they soon gained control of the entire body. Thus as early as 1693, we find a Cudjoe chosen as their general.[14]

The word "Cudjoe" is a rather interesting name which gives credence to the origin of the Koromantyns. The so-called day-names of the Akan remain the same to the present. Thus Cudjoe is a child born on Monday; Kwabena, Tuesday; Kwaku, Wednesday; Yao, Thursday; Kofi, Friday; Kwaame, Saturday; and Kwasi, Sunday. Each of these is a spirit name or the name of the deity who governs that day. No other people are so designated.[15]

R. C. Dallas in his book *The History of the Maroons* gives this interesting discovery that, "The Maroons continue to believe, like their forefathers that Accompong was God of the Heavens, the Creator of all things, and a deity of infinite goodness."[16] As we have discussed in the previous chapter, the earthly title of the Akan deity is Nyankopon, which means "the God who only is great." What seems to have happened here is that the word "Nyankopon" was changed to "Accompong" by the Europeans, who were unaccustomed to the African speech. This corruption has come down to the present in the name of the village where the St. Elizabeth Maroons now reside in Jamaica. But this has compounded the problem more. The name of the village probably should have been Akropong, which means the city of the chief, a name which

is commonly used in Ghana to designate a town in which a paramount chief resides.

But to resume our study, we may conclude that the name of
the Akan deity was the first to be known among the Africans in
Jamaica and that he was the one who was most ardently worshiped. Phillippo, a Baptist missionary writing on this point forty
years later than Dallas, said of the slaves as a whole, "Most of the
Negroes appeared to have possessed some notion of the Supreme
Being; though, like all uncivilized nations, their ideas of the deity
were confused and unbecoming."[17] He further observed:

> Superstition itself in its most disgusting form prevailed
> among them to a very great extent. Dark and magical rites,
> numberless incantations and barbarous customs, were con-
> tinuously practiced, the principles of these were *obeahism,*
> *myalism* and fetishism; and such was their influence upon the
> general mind . . . that they were accompanied by all the
> terrors that the dread of a malignant being and fear of
> the unknown evil could invest.[18]

The above quotation needs some analysis because it contains important insights into the nature of the slave system and into one of
the most important African survivals in the New World. These
are *obeahism* and *myalism*. Obeahism is the name for the type of
witchcraft practiced in Jamaica. This type of witchcraft was found
wherever the Ashanti and the Fanti tribes became dominant and
thus is mentioned in relation to many other English-speaking islands. Myalism is a type of possession which was the opposite of
obeahism and it was the state of spirit of possession in which obeah
was discovered.

As we have seen, the two professions, that of sorcerer and that
of legitimate priest, were transferred to the New World during the
slave trade and their functions were well known to the slaves in
the various societies. Herbert G. DeLisser, a native of Jamaica and
probably the first to clearly delimit the function of the legitimate
African priest and the work of the sorcerer within the Jamaican
slave system, wrote:

> Both witches and wizards, priests and priestesses, were
> brought to Jamaica in the days of the slave trade, and the
> slaves recognized the distinction between the former and the
> latter. Even the masters saw that the two classes were not

identical, and so they called the latter "myal-men and myal-women" . . . the people who cured those whom the obe-ahman had injured. . . . It is probable that many of the African priests became simple obeah-men after coming to Jamaica, for the very simple reason that they could not openly practice their legitimate profession.[19]

It is interesting to note that the word *obeah* can be traced back to Ashanti witchcraft and bears out our previous argument that the Ashanti influence became dominant at a very early date. In the Dictionary of Asante and Fante Language by J. G. Christaller, we have the Twi word *obayifo,* meaning a witch, hag, wizard and sorcerer. It is a combination of three words: *oba,* a child; *yi,* to take away; and *fo,* he who. The root meaning of the combined words yields: he who takes a child away. This simply supports the theory in witchcraft literature that the final test for one to enter into the fraternity of sorcerers is the sacrifice of a child, either his own or that of a relative. The opposite of the sorcerer is the *obirifo* or the *okomfo.* These names refer to the legitimate priests of the Ashanti people. According to DeLisser both of these func-tionaries were brought to the New World in the slave trade, but the two professions soon merged into one. This is an important point which needs more elaboration. A careful analysis of how witchcraft, the most dreadful profession in Africa, became the most important ritual force in the New World, has never really been attempted; however, recent observations have gotten closer to the root of the matter.[20] In Africa, although witchcraft exists and the sorcerer is one of the religious functionaries of the reli-gious system, his work is considered dangerous to the society. If he is discovered, he is generally killed or driven out of the community. There are built-in controls by which his polluting influence can be counteracted. In the social and religious system, the evil power of the sorcerer is always in conflict with the legitimate power of the traditional priest. Therefore, in African societies, at certain times there are witch-hunts or cleansing cults to clear out the pollution caused by the workings of the sorcerer. Whenever the society is in equilibrium, that is, when the society is under proper control, there is little use for witchcraft. On the contrary, whenever the society is in an unstructured state, whenever there is cultural con-fusion or social disorientation, witchcraft is likely to flourish. This being the case, it is easy to see why witchcraft became dominant in the slave societies. To the African slaves, the mass migration to the New World was explainable only as the sorcery of the white man. Outside the boundaries of his ancestral homeland, his kinship ties, his religious institutions, the Black was marginal, vulnerable and exposed to great danger. Although he recognized some priests and priestesses, they were devoid of the institutional accouterment to back up their performances. The priests themselves were at the mercy of the white man's magic, which had obviously proven stronger. Thus legitimate functionaries were powerless in an alien surrounding. However, this was not the case with the sorcerer. In this state of confusion, he was in his climate. The legitimate priest, finding himself in a powerless position and equally knowledgeable in the techniques of sorcery, joined forces with the sorcerer in the unleashing of psychic forces against the common enemy. But as sorcery is a two-edged instrument, it also was unleashed by Black against Black. Thus, the *obeahman* in Jamaica was feared not only by the masters who saw him as a threat to life and wealth, but also by the slaves. As DeLisser said, "the very name of them spread terror."[21] Every evil, every sickness and every disturbance, no matter how trivial, was attributed to the work of the obeahman. He became the source of authority among the slaves. He was the one who provided the talisman to protect the slaves' gardens against thieves and performed the ordeal to detect those who stole from each other; but most important, he was the one who administered the deadly oath during times of rebellion, sealing the mouth of each slave at the risk of death. He was also the one who mixed the potion which was believed to make one immune to the deadly weapon of the slave masters. The obeahman was the leader in the dancing and the drumming that preceded the slave rebellion.

From the earliest days of the slave system the masters recognized the growing danger of witchcraft and its potential for evil, especially as it related to the dancing and the drums. So, as early as 1696, the Jamaican legislature passed a law

> for the prevention of the meeting of slaves in great numbers on Sundays and Holidays, whereby they have taken liberty to contrive and bring to pass many of their bloody and inhuman transactions . . . no master, or mistress, or overseer, shall suffer any drumming or meeting of any slaves not belonging to their own plantations, to rendezvous, feast, revel, beat drum, or cause any disturbance.[22]

The law directed that if the owner of the plantation was unable to enforce order, he was to call for the militia. This law contains a very important insight into an extremely important slave custom, the meeting of the slaves on Sundays and holidays. Here was the possibility of preparation for resistance to the system; it was a custom that was designed to weld the slaves into a single unit, one which was ultimately to overthrow the entire "slaveocracy." Thus the important reason for the prohibition of the slave gatherings was not so much the jollification received from these gatherings, but the opportunity they provided to "contrive and bring to pass many of their bloody and inhuman transactions." These "bloody and inhuman transactions" were the works of the obeahman.

The Rebellion of 1760 was one of the most bloody revolts staged by the slaves of Jamaica. The leader was Tacky,[23] whose name has come down to us through the writing of the planter-historian Bryan Edwards, who referred to him as "a Koromantyn Negro . . . who had been a chief in Guiney." Recent research suggests that the name Tacky is an Ashanti word for a great warrior and not a chief.[24] Generally before a war, the Ashanti took an oath of victory or death. This oath was performed in the following way: To a quantity of rum, with which some gunpowder and grave-dirt had been mingled, blood, drawn from the arm of each individual, was added; then the mixture was drunk in turn by each warrior. Once this was done the covenant to fight to the death was sealed. This ritual might be the one referred to in the Law of 1696.

After the slave Rebellion of 1760, the fear of the obeahman was so strong that the white planters were forced to acknowledge his potency and introduce a law against him. This law was so drastic that it failed to receive royal consent. We quote the relevant part:

> And in order to prevent the main mischiefs that may hereafter arise from the wicked art of the Negroes going under the appelation of Obeahmen and women, pretending to have communication with the devil and other spirits, whereby the weak and superstitious are deluded into the belief of having full power to exempt whilst under the protection from any evil that might otherwise happen. Be it therefore enacted by the authority . . . that from the year One Thousand Seven Hundred and Sixty One, any negroes or other slaves who

shall pretend to any Supernatural power and be detected in
making use of blood, feathers, parrot's beak, dog's teeth,
alligator's teeth, broken bottles, egg shells or any materials
related to the practice of witchcraft . . . shall upon conviction thereof before two magistrates . . . suffer Death or
transportation.[25]

Here for the first time, *obeah* was enshrined in Jamaican law.
Some features of this law throw light on the nature of the craft
and the extent of its influence during slavery. First, obeah was
believed to be "communication with the devil and other spirits."
Second, it was thought to have full power to exempt one from any
evils that might otherwise happen. Although this law was rejected
by the King of England for its severity, it is interesting to note
that with a few modifications it remains the legal instrument
against witchcraft in Jamaica to the present day. The reason for
this is very clear. Jamaica, to this day, suffers from the ever-present
danger of obeah which was introduced in the days of slavery. So
powerful is the belief in obeah, that the words of the Reverend
J. Banbury, written in 1894, were not only true in his day but still
apply to all categories of Jamaicans to this day. Discussing obeah
and its pervasive influence, he said:

Whilst treating about obeahism and other superstitions of
Jamaica, we do not wish to leave the impression on the minds
of our readers that it is only the black people of the country
that have faith in them. The majority of the coloured people
also come under the category of the superstitious, and even
white people are not exempt. . . . there are but few among
the people whose minds are not imbued with a superstitious
dread of obeah influences, though they may not enter into
the practice of it.[26]

Here is the answer we sought: the psychic power contained in
African witchcraft was a powerful weapon not only against other
Africans, but against the masters, who lived in fear of the power
which made the Africans fearless of bullets. So strong was the
power of witchcraft against the masters that Herbert G. DeLisser,
in his classic novel *The White Witch of Rosehall,* informed us that
Miss Annie Palmer, the proprietress of her estate, indulged in
witchcraft herself, in order to control her slaves. Whether or not
this was an isolated instance we are not sure, but Banbury's and

DeLisser's observations throw light on the fact that witchcraft was used by many members of the society.

3. Cumina: The second of the dark magical rites mentioned by Phillippo was myalism. This word has caused much confusion in Jamaican study. Some writers believe the word to be of Dahomean origin, while others simply say that its origin is unknown. However, one thing that all writers agree on is that the work of the *myalman* is the discovery and the destruction of witchcraft. It is the myalman who rids the person of the spells of the obeahman. The work of the myalman is curative not destructive, and so the present writer is convinced that the word refers to that phenomenon in Africa known as "witchcraft cleansing." We have evidence from Africa of the periodic emergence of an anti-witchcraft cult whose purpose was to "clean" the society of the influence of witches. It can further be shown that the word "myal" is an Akan word taken from the Twi language, where *mia*, "to squeeze," or "to press" probably refers to the method for juicing the weeds used in curing illness. The word also appears in many combinations, such as *mia kuru*, "to treat or dress a wound or sore with water or medicine." Another combination is *omua noan*, meaning to exert or to strengthen one's self. With respect to the idea of healing, there is still a weed used by modern-day healers called myal weed. Myal is also the name for a vigorous dance in which a trance state is produced. We may conclude that the same thing happened to the word "mia" that happened to Nyankopon. The planters and the Creole Jamaicans unable to reproduce African speech, simply pronounced these words as they thought they heard them.

It is our intention here to show that myalism was the legitimate survival of the traditional religion of Africa and that myal and the Jamaican Cumina religion therefore are one and the same phenomenon. It will be remembered that both the sorcerer and the legitimate priest were brought to the New World in the days of slavery and that both of these functionaries aided in working witchcraft against the common enemy. It would appear, however, that the legitimate priest asserted himself as soon as it was necessary and emerged in a new role. According to John Joseph Williams, the *okomfo,* or legitimate priest of the Ashanti people, did not abdicate the role totally. Although he was unable fully to engage in his pro-

fession, he was able to instigate the one act which was common to
all African traditional religion, and this was the dance. Williams
observed:

> As a precaution against complete proscription the Ashanti
> Okomfo began to further disguise what was left of the old
> religious rites under cover of one of the dances that were
> permissible in the local amusements, until it was gradually
> appropriated to his own purpose. This dance in its adapted
> form became known to the whites, as the Myal-dance.[27]

Edward Long, the planter-class historian, also observed this dance
and referred to it as follows: "Not long since, some of these exe-
crable wretches in Jamaica introduced what they called the myal-
dance and established a kind of society, in which they invited all
they could."[28] Here we find the dance now enclosed in a society.
This society, as we are about to show, was none other than the
present-day Cumina cult found in St. Thomas and in St. Mary on
the island of Jamaica. Recent investigation of this cult suggests
that it is the oldest of the African cults to emerge in the New
World complex of cults and must be compared in age with Vodun
in Haiti, Shango in Trinidad, Santeria in Cuba and similar cults
of its kind in Brazil. These original cults which emerged early in
the slave societies of the Caribbean were basically ancestor cults
and have remained so to this day. The word "Cumina" is another
of those words which have been corrupted by the non-Africans
who first heard them, but we are now sure that the word is derived from two Twi words: *Akom,* "the state of being possessed,"
i.e., a temporary loss of one's personality or ecstacy, expressing
itself in dancing and gestures; and *Ana,* "relationship, or ancestor."
The two words combined give us the word *Akomana,* which means
to be possessed by an ancestor. The word "Cumina," then, is nothing but the Akan word for ancestor cult.[29]

A description of Cumina will make our point even more con-
vincing. Many writers believe that Cumina originated with the
Maroons and was introduced to the wider slave society during
slavery, and this does not seem unlikely when we remember that
the Maroons were predominantly Ashanti. Membership in Cumina
is a matter of birth. It is basically a dance used for all rites of passage. That means at birth, the introduction of an infant to society,
marriage and death. It is also performed at Christmastime as a

year-end festival. In Cumina, there are usually three drums used
to invoke the ancestral spirits. The drummers are of great importance to a successful Cumina festival; they must be very knowledgeable about the workings of the ancestral spirits and must be
able to detect which spirit is operating in the service and the kind
of drumbeat acceptable to that particular spirit. One of these
drummers said to the present writer that if the drumming is not
suitable, the spirits will stand far off and will not come into the
service. He also said that during his drumming he is able to see
the spirits as they approach the Cumina festival. A Cumina service
generally begins at about nine o'clock in the evening and continues late into the night or early morning. Much alcoholic bev-
erage is needed for a Cumina service. This is not only consumed
by the dancers, but is used for pouring libations to the dead.
On certain occasions, there is also a sacrifice in which a chicken
or a goat is offered to the ancestors. There are two types of Cumina, the first kind being simply a get-together for holidays and
special occasions such as marriage. The other is that which is called
because of sickness or death. One of my informants told me of
his uncle who was near death, having suffered a stroke by an evil
spirit. He called for a Cumina service and during this service he
was relieved of his stroke and was able to dance in the service
that very night.

When a Cumina is to be performed a hut is built by the people
of the community. Beginning on Saturday night at nine o'clock,
the service will continue until Sunday or may be danced nightly
for one week. The meeting begins when a sufficient number of
people are gathered; a slow shuffling movement commences with
the drum. The participants move counterclockwise to the beat of
the drum. As the service continues, there is a quickening of pace
until someone is possessed by an ancestral spirit. On a recent field
trip of the present writer, one of the dancers of Cumina recounted
the following experience:

> When I go to Cumina, the person for whom the dance is
> called may appear to me. When this happens, it is a sign that
> the person desires me to be his or her representative or me-
> dium. In this case I am controlled by the spirit of that person.
> I generally see the person in front of me. I am then con-
> trolled by that spirit from that moment. All my movements
> are directed by that spirit. If it puts its hand on its head, I

must do the same. If it holds its leg, I must do the same. If it whines, I whine; if the spirit calls for a song, I must sing that song. If it speaks, I must speak; although, the language is African. I may not know what I am saying but I must speak because the spirit has control of my mouth. If I am not assisted by those around me I would continue in that state as long as the spirit wishes. To release me, sugar and water or rum is poured on me or if they can get it into my mouth it generally breaks the spell and I return to myself. Generally I do not know what I am doing or what I did until someone tells me.[30]

The contemporary experience as told by a Cumina dancer throws light on the movement which began in slavery and continues to the present day. But the most important information gleaned from that particular interview was the meaning of the word "myal." In the course of the conversation the writer asked the Cumina dancer: "Do all persons dancing at Cumina receive possession?" Her answer was this: "Not all persons dancing in a Cumina meeting receive myal." I believe this was the first time I heard that word "myal" associated with Cumina; however, it is my opinion that the possession experience received at a Cumina service is generally called "myal." The Cumina woman continued to explain to me that during the state of "myal," she is able to detect evil and good spirits. She also indicated that under the experience of myal, she is able to discover the workings of obeah. Our conclusion then is that Cumina was the old Ashanti ancestor cult which was brought to the New World, and that within this context, ancestor possession was experienced along with other spirit possession which enabled the early Africans and their descendants to counteract witchcraft, divine and perform healings with herbs and other medicine.

Up to this point we have drawn heavily on Jamaican sources and that for good reason, as we shall presently see. Jamaica can be used as a paradigm for most of the English-speaking Caribbean, and although Trinidad came late to the English, it too falls in line. In fact, Akan slaves were brought to all the British islands early and in large numbers; consequently, their influence was the first to be established. But it must also be emphasized that both the Dutch and the Danes, who occupied the smaller Caribbean islands, had forts in the Gold Coast and brought Akan slaves to these islands. The records of slave revolts from the Virgin Islands to Surinam, from the seventeenth through the nineteenth century, show that the rebel slaves were typically the Akan- and Ga/adangwe-speaking peoples who originated in the area of modern Ghana. These are generally referred to as Koromantine, Coromantees, Delminas or Elminas. Their Akan day-names and their name for witchcraft—obeah—are the most important indicators of their origin.

In 1701 we find Governor Christopher Codrington of Barbados writing:

> My father who had studied the genius and temper of all kinds of negroes 45 years with a very nice observation, would say, no man deserved a Coromante that would not treat him like a friend rather than a slave, and all my Coromantes preserve that love and veneration for him that they constantly visit his grave and pour libation upon it. . . .[31]

If the above sentiment is true, this was one of the exceptional slave masters, but the important point here is that the Akan slaves were highly respected in Barbados, not only for their loyalty but for what they could do if aroused. In Guiana, it was a Kofi—Akan day-name for Friday—who led the great slave uprising in the eighteenth century and who has now become the folk hero in the independent Guiana.[32] Furthermore, a Mrs. Carmichael, who visited St. Vincent and Trinidad in the 1820's, found obeah to be widespread in those islands, again indicating the presence of the Akan people. She wrote:

> The Obeah of the Negro is nothing more or less than a belief in witchcraft; and operates upon them in such a degree, as not infrequently to produce death. There is not perhaps a single West Indian Estate upon which there is not one or more Obeah men or women; the Negroes know who they are, but it is very difficult for the white people to find them out.[33]

It is not surprising to learn that the man who sparked the Haitian rebellion, Boukman, came from Jamaica. In all probability he was an Akan.

4. The dance and the drums: Before closing the discussion of the period of slave reaction in the Caribbean and the establishment of African tradition in the New World, we must make a few statements on two important ritual forms within the African religious

tradition. These are the dance and the drums. The two are inseparable. They were the means by which Africans reinstated their
force-vitale in the New World. For the Africans in the New World,
the dance became the only language that every tribe could understand. It, like the drum, was the instrument of non-verbal communication. In Africa, the dance occupied and expressed every
significant emotion. There was a dance for every occasion—even
death. Dance was not a separate art, but a part of the whole complex of religious and secular life. The dance was strong magic,
vivifying the spirit. Through the dance the whole being entered
into the rhythm of nature and the supernatural. The body, through
the dance, turns to liquid steel. It is through the dance that the
emotions are conveyed symbolically. And it was during the dance
that, while the masters looked on with great amusement, the message of rebellion was disseminated. The Reverend Phillippo, one
of the early missionaries to Jamaica, witnessed the African dance
and left us this vivid description:

> The dance was performed to a monotonous music which was
> manufactured in Africa. . . . The people were arranged in a
> circle, with a leader in the center. Male and female danced to
> the music of the drums. A female led a chant followed by
> choral response from the rest. This was accompanied with
> the stamping of the feet, with strange contortions of the body;
> the head of the dancers sometimes erect; sometimes inclined
> forward; the hands united in the front; the elbows fixed point-
> ing sideward, the lower extremities being kept firm; the whole
> body was made to move from the ground without moving
> the feet off the ground.[34]

Anyone who has visited Ghana during a festival season can
well appreciate the accuracy of Phillippo's description of this
dance. The movements and the positions of the hands and feet
are quite accurate. Examples of the dance from Haiti would involve a quite different description, in that the movement of the
Akan peoples and those of Dahomey are not the same.[35] The
African dance was always interpreted by the slave masters as a
sign of the contentment of the slaves. Little did they know that
the Africans expressed their entire culture in the dance. Speaking
on the role of the dance and the dancer in African life, A.
Mawere-Opoku of the University of Ghana had this to say:

> To us, life, with its rhythms and cycles is Dance. The Dance
> is life expressed in dramatic terms . . .

We, the people accept the dancer's special role as the centre of our life—in his subtle flexions of hands and fingers, our prayers; in his thrusting arms—our thanksgiving; in his stamp and pause—our indignation; in his leap and turns, our frivolity—our foolishness; in his tensed frame—our defiance; in his bow—our allegiance; his halting steps—our reverence. Thus he dances, not alone but with us and we with him. We are not spectators, but co-creators and participants in the drama of the African way of life.[36]

However, if the dance was misunderstood, it also took a long time before the masters became aware of the secret of the drum in African tribal life. The drum to the Ashanti, especially, was a very important instrument. Not only was it used for religious and recreational purposes, it was an instrument of speech. To this day, the talking drum is still used among the Akans. Speaking about the use of the drums among the slaves in Jamaica, John Joseph Williams observed:

The early Ashanti slaves in Jamaica must have numbered among them some really expert drummers who would naturally exchange messages throughout the island while their fellow Ashanti could perfectly understand the conversation. And even when the use of the drums were prohibited, native ingenuity made use of barrels, gourds, boards or any other medium of producing notes that would correspond with those of the male and female drums.[37]

As early as the year 1717, the legislature of Jamaica became wise to the powers of the drum in the lives of the slaves. In that year, the following law prohibited the use of all instruments of sound:

. . . and for as much as Negroes can, by beating on drums, and blowing horns, or other such like instruments of noise, give signals to each other at a considerable distance of their evil and wretched intentions: Be it further enacted, that in one month's time after the passing of this Act, no proprietor, attorney, or Overseer . . . shall . . . suffer any beating of drums, barrels, gourds, boards, or other such like instruments of noise on the plantations and settlements. . . .[38]

Judging from the numerous laws against the Africans in the slave societies, we may infer that the white slave masters and lawmakers had no easy time. The strange ways and customs of the

Africans kept the planters on constant alert. So persistent and cunning were these Africans in their pursuit of freedom and so insistent were the masters on retaining their superiority, that the English Caribbean became an armed camp. Phillippo summed up the situation as he saw it in the nineteenth century as follows:

> These colonies' whole past history . . . presents only a succession of wars, usurpation, crimes, misery and vice . . . . All is one revolting scene of infamy, bloodshed, and unmitigated woe, of insecure peace and open disturbance, of abuse of power, and of the reaction of misery against oppression.[39]

5. The Africanization of the New World: There is no accurate record of the exact number of Africans who came to the New World. Some writers estimated it to be as high as one hundred million, others contend that the number is much lower.[40] We probably will never be able to arrive at the exact figure at this late date, but one thing is clear—the best of African manhood entered the New World and so thoroughly marked it with African customs that in a short while, the sound of the New World was the sound of Africa. There is no place in which the African influence has not made an inroad. This influence on the language, folklore, medicine, magic and religion, music, dress, dancing and domestic life of the New World, can be called Africanization or indigenization. How did this come about? The first answer to the question must be sought in the numerical imbalance of the slave population over the whites. The slaves outnumbered the whites, especially in the Caribbean and Brazil, in such a large proportion that the influence of the whites was totally ineffective in shaping the mass of the slave population. It is true that those slaves who were close to the masters were affected by European culture in many ways, but in the broader context, there was little contact between the few whites of the plantations, who garrisoned themselves in the "great houses," and the large body of field slaves. In the British Caribbean, the slaves were supervised by their own countrymen, who reported to the masters and received instructions from them. In either case, little or no contact was made by the whites with the slaves, who had their own quarters, and their own piece of ground on which they raised their own food crops. The Blacks had their own markets where they sold their excess provisions and their particular days for religious and secular dancing. These

were the basic institutions around which the slaves recreated
Africa in the New World. We will look at these institutions more
closely.

First, the plot of ground: The piece of ground given to the slaves
on their arrival in the Caribbean was more than a provision
ground. John Taylor, writing about Jamaica in 1685, said:

> When a planter hath purchased some 20, 30 or more slaves,
> he first gives to each man a wife without which they will not
> be content or work. Then he gives to each man and his wife
> a half acre of land for them to plant for themselves . . .
> maize, potatoes, yam etc.; which land they cleared (in their
> leisure hours) and build them a wigwam on it, and then
> plant it as fast as they can . . .[41]

This description of the early life-style of the slaves in the West
Indies shows the beginning of the indigenization process in the
New World. What the master intended by this gesture was totally
an economic affair. The slave was to be self-supporting, while he,
the master, got all the benefits of the slave's labor and a handsome
profit as quickly as possible. What he failed to consider was the
unintended benefit of this gift to the slave. Land to the Africans
meant more than provision ground. The African felt himself
rooted in the earth. To the Akan the earth was next to God. Via
this little piece of land the African was able to transfer his peasant
relationship from Africa to the New World. In the early slave
period, the African viewed the New World as alien soil; he had
no ancestors buried in the earth; he viewed the new surroundings
as a land of exile. Writing in 1740, Sir Charles Leslie gave us an
example of this alienation in the funeral custom of the slaves in
exile. He observed:

> When a Negro is near about to expire, his Fellow-Slaves kiss
> him, wish him a good journey, and send their hearty Recom-
> mendations to their Relatives in Guiney. They make Lamen-
> tation, but with a great deal of Joy intere his body firmly
> believing he is gone home and is happy.[42]

Gardner also witnessed this custom and left us this description:

> In the early part of the century they [funerals] were frequent.
> The scene presented on these occasions was wild in the ex-
> treme, though rarely witnessed by white people, and only
> then by stealth. One or more Negroes played upon the

goomba, and another, at intervals, blew a horn made of conch shell; another took the solo part of a recitative of a wild funeral wail, usually having reference to the return of the departed to Africa.[43]

Then he concluded: "In later years it became common to use more expedition at the grave, and when the funeral was over, and a few dirges sung, to return to the house and spend the night in feasting, often accompanied with dancing."[44]

Here we have an example of what happened before indigenization and what happened after. The early slaves took pains to send their dead back to Africa at death, because they had no relationship to the new land. Death was one way of returning to the homeland. But as the years grew and indigenization took place, this solemn custom turned to celebration. The funeral rites were shortened and "the slaves returned to their homes for feasting, often accompanied with dancing." No more wailing for the departed, because the departed were now with them. A new African society was being developed. And that little piece of land had a lot to do with it; it brought about a new ecological relationship.

A second process of indigenization was created by the development of the African market pattern in the New World. Any one traveling in the Caribbean and South America will not fail to see that the New World markets are duplicates of those of West Africa. The markets of Africa are not just places where things are bought and sold, they are the vehicles of social and tribal interaction. They are places for recreation, information gathering and interaction. African markets have the flavor of a festival, and they soon became one of the dominant slave institutions in the West Indies and have remained so to the present. Here, African customs were re-developed in the New World. The markets, above every other institution, became the new African forum for the spreading of news among neighboring estates and a means whereby new associations were formed and rebellions plotted. Although the tribes came from different parts of West Africa, as the years passed, the barriers of language also passed. The custom of scattering tribes on the plantations also facilitated the breaking down of tribal custom, thus fusing the tribes, their customs and folklore. If our theory holds that the Ashanti set the cultural pattern at an early time in Jamaica, then we can assume that in each

new slave society, within a generation, the indigenizing process
had taken place with a specific dominant tribal flavor in each. So
we find that in Haiti, the Dahomean-Arada custom became the
integrating influence; and in Cuba and Brazil the Yoruba prevailed. Once this indigenization took place there was no real
problem in the African slaves uniting behind their common African identity, because, as Simon and Phoebe Ottenberg observed:

> Underlying the great regional or tribal differences . . . there is
> a widespread substratum of basic ideas that persists in the
> rituals, myths, and folklore of West African peoples.[45]

We may conclude, then, that despite the strangeness that existed in early years among the different tribes in slave societies,
they eventually recognized that they were one people and co-
sufferers. This alone was enough to unite them in their endeavor
to survive.

If one reads the slave literature carefully, one gets the idea that
the problem of identity which has plagued Blacks in the New
World in the modern period was almost non-existent in the time
of slavery. It is obvious that slaves of all tribes rallied around a
leader who pitted himself against oppression, regardless of the
tribe to which he belonged. So we found a Cudjoe of the Ashanti
in Jamaica, a Kofi in Guiana and a Boukman in Haiti and various
others who became would-be deliverers of their people, amassing
great numbers in time of rebellion.

The plot of land and the marketplace were successful instruments of indigenization; however, the institution which figured as
the greatest single indigenizing force was the traditional religion
of Africa. What are known in our day as Cumina, Shango, Vodun
and Santeria and Candomblé are nothing but the fusing of the
beliefs and practices of various tribes in one mold. It did not take
the Africans long to people the New World with their supreme
beings, their lesser deities, spirits and powers and, above all, their
notions of witchcraft. They soon discovered that the river gods
of Africa could be found in the rivers of the New World, and that
there were African spirits in the great cotton trees of Jamaica as
well as the Mapu trees of Haiti. The herbs of the New World came
to possess the same effective medicine as those in Africa. The
drummers began to make their drums, on which they beat the
same rhythms that called up the gods, and the gods came as in

Africa. With the drum, the dance also came and with this phenomenon Africa was recreated in the Americas. The rhythm of
Africa, the vital force which is the soul of Black people had now
taken possession of the New World and cast its magical spell on
all things. From now on, Europe would rule the New World but
Africa would govern.

6. Religious retentions, a comparative analysis: The African religious institutions which emerged in the New World are unique
in the history of religion. Very few references have been made
to this aspect of the African religious genius in New World literature. A glance at the tribal units taken to the New World would
suggest that as many as fifty tribes were represented in the slave
trade. Each of these tribes had a religious system of its own. Each
had its own pantheon, belief and practice. But the African genius
for amalgamation and inclusion prevailed in the New World and
emerged in unique institutions; this was their religion. As already
suggested, the numerically dominant tribes established the cultural mold to which all the other tribes contributed their religious
practices and beliefs as needed. Thus we find Vodun (a Dahomean word for spirit) as the base or mold in which the spirits
known as *loa* (a Congo word) operate. In the Vodun temple there
are altars to a Nago divinity, an Ibo divinity, a Dahomey or Arada
divinity and a Congo divinity. In a Vodun ceremony, one may
distinguish a Nago, Congo and a Dahomey drumbeat all in one
polyrhythm. In the Trinidadian Shango ceremony we have the
"drum of the nations," which means a drum on which all the
tribal rhythms are played. Thus the Africans in diaspora forged
a pattern of ecumenicity long before the word became popular
in the West. They developed a religious pattern unique in history
and proved beyond a doubt that as Africans they were conscious
of their situation and had the organizing genius demanded of them
for survival in a harsh New World situation.

It would be a formidable task for one to provide a detailed study
of the various African traditional religions which have come down
to the present day. But it cannot be denied that these religious
systems, which are usually called cults in our day, were so well
established that, despite the onslaught of the European ruling class
with their numerous laws aimed at eradicating them, and despite
the onslaught of the Christian missionaries who spent their lives
and their financial resources in an attempt to convert the slaves

to Christianity, these New World African religions have remained
to this day as the psychic monitors of the vast majority of New
World Blacks. And, although their confessed devotees may be
few, in some areas of the Caribbean and Brazil, these cults still
dominate the consciousness of the majority of the inhabitants,
both peasant and elite. More important, the folk tradition which
forms such a large part of the culture of former slave-holding
countries, has its roots in the African religious cults of the slave
days. Religion is the mother of the dance, and the dance of the
New World had its roots in the religion of the slaves.

We shall now attempt to give a broad comparative outline of
the nature of the slave religions of the New World, using certain
general topics common to all as our guide. The Africans had in
common the following: religious ancestor cults, songs, dances,
drums, spirit possession and curing by herbs.

We have already seen how the Africans indigenized their new
surroundings in order to be able to function as a united people
in the New World context by establishing a relationship with the
land—Mother Earth—and by invoking the African gods, spirits and
powers. This process of indigenizing the New World was accom-
plished in different ways by different peoples. The Africans in
the New World fell into two separate groups. The first were those
with a highly developed pantheon, in which the deities played a
dominant role. In this category are the Fon people of Dahomey
and the Yoruba, generally called Nago, of Nigeria. Wherever these
people were represented in large numbers, their religion with their
pantheon of numerous deities predominated. Examples of this
are found in Haiti, Brazil, Cuba, Trinidad and New Orleans. The
second group of Africans emphasized a religion with a strong ancestor cult, but a weak pantheon of gods. This group seems to
have blended their form of ritual with the dominant Fon- and
Nago-speaking peoples. Thus we hear little of the Akan and Bantu
gods, but much of Shango, Ogun, Damballah and Vodun.

The New World setting also contributed much to the nature
of the African religious elements which were transported and it
needs to be emphasized that there is a big difference between
the nature and form of the African religion which developed
within the Latin system and that which developed in the British
system. In the Latin system, much emphasis was laid on the religious participation of the slaves in the Catholic Church. Days

were set aside for religious observation. Consequently religion became and always was a part of the slave experience. The Catholic ritual, festivals and the adoration of saints were in nature and content not very different from the religious ritual practices in Africa; and therefore the slaves found the Catholic pattern of worship rather suited to their religious upbringing. It was relatively easy to reinterpret the Catholic ritual and theology in the light of Africa. What happened then was an Africanization of Catholicism. The Catholic gods became African gods and the Catholic saints became African voduns in the Dahomean pantheon and orishas in the Yoruban pantheon. The problem of integration into Christianity was therefore easily solved by the Africans, who outwardly manifested no tension as they shared in the religion of the masters but who inwardly were simply worshiping the gods of Africa in Christian dress. Furthermore, New World Catholicism was colored with gaiety and festivity, unlike its austere counterpart, the puritan Protestantism. The former better fitted the natural African love of life.

In the British system religion was for the masters, not for the slaves. All religious practices on the part of the slaves were suspect and the practice of African religious custom was vigilantly suppressed. In the Latin system, very little attention was paid to the African religious practices, if they did not interfere with work and the observance of the Catholic ritual. In some of the British islands, religion of any kind was prohibited for Blacks for well over a hundred years. Consequently, African religion in the British system was limited to cults, whose rituals could be performed in secret. The suppression of the African religious rituals of the legitimate kind gave way to the development of witchcraft in the British system; consequently, the elaborate African religious rituals manifested in Vodun in Haiti, Santeria in Cuba, Shango in Trinidad and Candomblé in Brazil have no counterpart in Jamaica and the United States, where Protestant religion dominated. This is not to say, however, that the African religious dynamics were completely destroyed. From time to time Africa reasserted itself in periodic witchcraft-cleansing cults such as myalism. An outbreak of this cultic phenomenon occurred soon after emancipation in Jamaica in 1832–34, and finally crested in 1860–61, ultimately forming the base for the Afro-Christian cults now existing in that island. All evidence points to the transportation of this from Africa, for the establishment and development of this institution is evident in the early part of the once slave countries.

In summary, we shall review these distinguishing marks of the elements of African religions in the New World. The first element of the African religion transplanted in the New World is the *dance,* which was the soul of the religious life of Africa. Students of New World African culture are convinced that the first appearance of African religious life in the New World was in the dance. The dance is the medium through which the deepest emotions are expressed by Africans, be they joy or sorrow. Each dance has its own symbolic language and each emotion, its symbolic expression in a dance. The Africans, like the Asians, have a complex cosmic metaphysic which could not be expressed in verbal symbols. The dance, then, was the medium of expression. Through the dance the African is able to break the structure of physical boundaries and through rhythm be united with the cosmos. In the dance, the African becomes one with the spirit world, thus uniting himself through vibrations with his ancestors and the lesser deities. In the dance he is immortal. It has been said by one authority that African religion is not thought out but danced out. This observation, although greatly misunderstood, contains some profound insight. In the dance, one becomes one with reality. Almost every writer on slavery has made some reference to the dance, the most prominent element in the behavior of African slaves. Most of these early writers spoke ignorantly of the lewdness and obscenity of these dances. Many of the dances referred to concerned fertility rites, which were part of the African religious heritage. These dances naturally emphasize pelvic movements; rarely does any African dancing include the close-hugging couples that characterize European dances. In the light of the early reaction to these dances, it is interesting to note that almost all the religious dances of the Africans in modified form were soon to become court dances in Europe. Some scholars have advanced the idea that there are very few dances in the New World after the eighteenth century which cannot be traced to an African origin and, at that, a religious one.[46]

The dance for Africans was the means by which the force-vitale was reinforced. Before every war in Africa, there was a dance, and we have evidence that most large-scale rebellions in the Caribbean were carried out after a religious dance. Vodun in

Haiti is known primarily for its dance, so is Cumina in Jamaica. African religion danced its way into the New World culture and became the basis for the rhythmic pattern of our present culture.

A second characteristic of the African religion in the New World is its utilization of the drums. The drum is Africa. It is the key to the rhythm which initiated the dance. Rhythm is the universal life-force, the essence of the African universe; it is the fluid that runs through all beings from God to man and from man to inanimate things. Without the rhythm of the drum, the dance would be impossible. In Akan philosophy it is said that in the beginning God created the drummer. The drum in Africa was the medium by which the voice of the king was heard among the people and the voice of the king was in many cases the voice of God. It is through the drums that the spirits come to possess the dancers. The drum controls the dance. It dictates the movements of the body in the dance. The drummer has the power to control even the spirits, since, by the beat, he can inhibit their entrance or invite them in great numbers. The Vodun drummer knows the beat suitable to each loa, whether he be a Yoruba, Arada or a Congo deity. One Cumina drummer told the author that he is able to see the spirits as they appear and is obligated to play the rhythm suitable to each spirit or else the spirit will leave the meeting or create a disturbance among the devotees. So important was the influence of the drum upon the slaves that numerous laws prohibiting its use were soon enacted. Wherever the drum was suppressed, the Africans' soul severely suffered. This was what happened in the puritan United States. It is important to note that it was in the Latin slave system of North America that the soul of Africa was preserved. Here, jazz had its origin, in New Orleans and not in Boston or Philadelphia, solely because the Africans had access to the drum.

There were drums of all kinds in Africa. There were the male drums and there were female drums. Drums that were played while resting under the arm; drums that were played by drummers who sat in a straddling position; drums that were played from a position seated in front of them; and large drums which demanded the player to stand at full height; and, finally, the sacred drum, which was played only on the most stately or solemn occasions. All these were transported to the New World. The drum

is Africa and the drumbeats of Africa were the prime method of
Africanizing the New World.

A third characteristic of the African religion in the New World
is that phenomenon known as spirit possession. Spirit possession
is the central religious experience of African traditional religion.
In this experience the person becomes the tabernacle of the god
or spirit who possesses him. His ego is displaced for the period
of possession, whether it be for a few minutes or a few days. The
possessed person is totally unconscious of his behavior and is, for
the period, himself the god or the ancestor. The behavior of the
possessed may be passive, active or erratic, depending on the nature of the spirit. The person possessed becomes a medium
through which the spirit may warn, encourage, prophesy, reveal
hidden mysteries or make known some wishes which the god or
ancestor has for the living to perform on his behalf. Possession
can take place on various occasions. It can happen in a dream or
with the sound of a drum, or at a family ritual or at a festival. The
author has witnessed possession on various occasions both in
Africa and the New World. The most dramatic was that of the
priestess in the *Homoa* festival of the Ga people in Accra,
Ghana, where the ancestors are fed at the beginning of the plant-
ing season. After all the traditional dignitaries had assembled,
the priestess became possessed—a sign that the ancestors had accepted the offerings. The possession in this case was unexpected;
the priestess was dressed in elaborate ritual paraphernalia. At the
signal of the first sign of possession, her attendants quickly removed the many skeins of expensive beads which she wore because of the vigorous movement which was to follow. Not only
did they remove her beads, but her robe and her blouse, leaving
her naked to the waist. This unexpected possession enlivened the
festival for some time, until the drums brought her out of possession and her garments and beads were replaced.

Possession generally begins from the head of the devotee. Eyes
closed, there is a twitching movement of the shoulder, then the
back and legs become rigid. The devotee may break out in a leap-
ing dance, falling from side to side; or he may remain rigid as a
stump in one place or fall abruptly to the ground. The possessed
generally becomes the center of attention and his comrades who
are not possessed take every care to see that no harm comes to
him under possession. Possession common to Africa is found in

all Afro-religious cults in the New World. It varies in intensity
from the Afro-pentecostal religions to a more truly African
tradition.

Much has been written on the psychological aspects of possession. Some believe that it is a means of releasing aggression,
others see it as hysteria, but these are mere descriptions of the
outward appearance of the phenomenon. The fact that those who
undergo possession have rarely written anything about the experience makes the problem even greater. But despite the apparent
traumatic shock which seems to accompany the experience, most
devotees of African cults see possession as the great assurance
that they are in close touch with the gods. The capacity for repeated possession sets apart certain individuals within the cults.
They are the religious elite and are highly esteemed by those who
appear incapable of the experience.

Possession seems to be valuable on two levels: first, at the
spiritual level, where the individual becomes a medium of the
gods. On this level the individual sometimes receives clairvoyant
and clairaudient powers. Capacity for possession is generally considered to be the first step toward religious leadership. On the second level, possession has a physical benefit for the possessed. It
releases tension, it has therapeutic values and heightens one's prestige in the cult.

All religions seem to have a high point of spiritual attainment.
In Buddhism it is called illumination, in Christianity it is called
"being filled with the spirit," in African religion it is known as
possession. We shall see later that when Evangelical Christianity
and African religion met in the New World, there was a unique
marriage that took place, a marriage which helped produce what
we now call pentecostalism, with its shouting, dancing, speaking
in tongues and receiving of the spirit. We will later show that in
these meetings Christianity rarely overcame the African element
but rather the reverse was usually the case: Christianity generally
became Africanized.

A fourth and final characteristic of African religion is its emphasis on the power of curing through the herbal art. As we have
seen, the African is a man who is totally concerned with his force-
vitale. Anything that diminishes this is unnatural. Sickness is therefore viewed as an unnatural force working against man's
equilibrium. At the first sign of illness the African seeks a cure

for it. If the illness is of the common variety, most Africans will prescribe a remedy out of the vast knowledge handed down through generations of experimentation with the herbs which grow in abundance all over the land. Most African homes contain a small patch of medicinal weeds which are used to cure common illness. If, however, the illness is of a serious nature, the medicine man is called in for a diagnosis. If the sickness is sufficiently serious, it could require divination, in which the spirit world is explored for the cause of the illness. The cure may call for a ritual procedure involving sacrifices and offerings. However, it may only call for a special herbal treatment or it may call for both. In either case, the medicine man is highly capable. Generally, both ritual and herbal remedies are required in instances of major illness. In that all sickness is considered an intrusion by an outside spiritual force, or the result of a spell cast by a spiritual practitioner, the medicine man is the mediator, standing at the point of intersection of the spirit world and the natural world.

African medical art is not utilized only in emergencies but is also used preventively. Preventative medicine involves charms, amulets, talismans, commonly known in the West as fetishes, to protect the weak against diseases or free-floating spells. These are worn for such things as:

1. to obtain a child of the desired sex.
2. to win or restore love, or to insure success in courtship and marriage.
3. to prevent failure in business undertakings.
4. to give one power in quarrels, fights or lawsuits.
5. to operate against adultery.
6. to increase fertility or to insure fertility of the soil.
7. to prevent misfortune of all types.

All these medical items must be ritually prepared by the medicine man, who energizes them through incantation. The energized article then becomes a center of force which must be carefully protected by special taboos. Periodic rituals may be required to reinforce its powers until the work which it was originally designated to perform is no longer required. It is then buried or may simply be discarded.

Ritual and herbal art was brought to the New World with the slaves and has continued to influence New World Blacks to the present day. There are at the present time many herbalists in the

Caribbean and South America, and the evidence of their influence is found in the United States wherever there is a heavy concentration of Afro-Americans. Every island of the Caribbean is a veritable pharmacological garden in which there can be found every type of herb and root sufficient for the healing of the nation. One only needs to spend a day with an old woman to be impressed by the assortment of weeds necessary for each ailment liable to occur. Further, numerous "balmyards" are still in operation in most Caribbean islands, where one may take a bath with the mixture of seventy-seven different weeds. So influential are these African healers that many doctors have complained to government officials about the constant competition that exists between European-trained doctors and the traditional African specialists. The availability of these specialists and the faith vested in them by the common folk make them an essential part of the health service of most Caribbean and South American communities. In fact, their service is sought by the majority of the peasants and few of them will seek a European-trained doctor except for the gravest of illness and then only when the African specialist recommends it. The Vodun *houngan* and *bocor,* the Shango and Candomblé priests and the Jamaican *papi* and *mammi* are generally more highly respected than the Oxford-trained surgeon. So important has been the role of healing in African traditional religion in the New World that medical students in the Caribbean have recently begun to observe the techniques. A short history of a healing center in Jamaica will show how closely the healing art of the New World is related to Africa. The founder of one of the Jamaican centers was known by the familiar name Mammy Forbes. Her mother is reported to have been an "African" who knew all kinds of herbs and seemed to have been a healer. In 1871, an angel appeared to Mammy Forbes and commanded her to "rise up and heal the people." She immediately experienced a strong spirit possession under which she was taken by the spirit to a nearby forest, where she spent seven days without eating or drinking. When discovered by her husband, she was in a cave surrounded by various kinds of herbs, the knowledge of which was revealed to her in the spirit. Returning from this desert experience with an extensive repertoire of herbs and their specific use, she was also told by the spirit to build a tabernacle, and the dimensions and the symbolic colors for decorating it were also revealed to her. She was told the

kind of ritual dresses to wear on all occasions and one of the
specific commands was that she should go without shoes. Seventy-
seven herbal medicines were revealed to her. These were boiled
in water to 50 per cent consistency and were used both internally
and externally. The power of immediate diagnosis was revealed
to her. In other words, she used clairvoyant means to arrive at
one's illness. The patient may appear in person or simply send a
piece of clothing and she is able to tell what kind of illness the
patient suffers from simply by holding the garment. The price for
diagnosis in her lifetime was three cents. Under the present leadership of her daughter it is now seventy-five cents. Mammy Forbes
worked at the center that she founded for fifty-nine years. She
died in 1930. Before her death, the gift of healing was handed
down to her daughter, Rita, who is the present priestess of the
center. Rita is now seventy-eight years old and has been working
in her mother's place for the last forty-one years. A total of one
hundred years of healing has continued unbroken from August
1871 to August 1971.[47]

The present priestess follows her mother's methods of diagnosis
and the author was privileged to tape some of her diagnostic sessions. Below are some of her prescriptions transcribed verbatim
from slips of paper during my research.
1) *Name A*—Severe pain in the head and general weakness:
   Buttonweed, sweet-cup weed, half a leaf of leaf-of-life, Aloes
   and Juba bush; boil in 10 pints of water to 5 pints, mix it with
   Gilby's wine, take 2 tablespoonsful three times a day.
2) *Name B*—Gastric ulcers:
   One bottle of gas tonic [name not specified], poor-man's-friend
   weed, 10 sprigs of balsom leaves, sucumber bush, dead-and-
   wake weed, Qwakuo bush, garden bitters, black jointer; boil
   in 10 pints of water to 5 pints, mix with Gilby's wine.
3) *Name C*—Nervous conditions:
   Sassaparilla, horse bath, dead-and-wake, ½ leaf of Aloes,
   sea thyme, camphor weed, chana roots, buttonweed; boil in
   9 pints of water to 4½ pints, mix with Gilby's wine.
4) *Name D*—Pain in the back, feet and itching in womb:
   One set of womb tables, sucumber bush, buttonweed, sweet
   cup, womb weed, three leaves of leaf-of-life, some wild grapes
   and water grapes, bitch weed; boil in 9 pints of water to 4½
   pints, mix with Gilby's wine.

5) *Name E*—A child suffering with recurring fever:
Semen-contra weed, two leaves of horse bath, two sprigs of sucumber bush, two sprigs of buttonweed, two sprigs of blue-fever-grass; mix with a bottle of Virol Compound and Brandy.

6) *Name F*—A child suffering discomfort in the womb:
Womb weed, garden bitters, bladder weed, horse bath, buttonweed, strong back, leaf-of-life; boil in 3 pints of water to 2½ pints, mix with Gilby's wine. Take Indian Root Pills as prescribed.

7) *Name G*—A businessman in trouble:
One bottle of High-John-the-Conqueror oil. Anoint the hands with oil and make the sign of the cross; concentrate on your desires. Sprinkle a few drops around the room and place of business; read the 23rd Psalms while sprinkling.

These are only a sample of the varied practices and prescriptions given out daily by one of the health centers of Jamaica. The herbal prescription predominates, but the last prescription is rather important because in this we are introduced to a more sophisticated syncretistic formula which is rather different from the purely African herbal treatment. In this prescription we are dealing more with the modern trend of healing in Jamaica, a trend that incorporates the esoteric formulae of the East Indian guru with the occult art of Europe and America. To this occult art Christian rituals are added, especially the sign of the cross and the reading of the Bible.

The "balmyard" might be considered the center for the herbal art in the Caribbean, and it has its counterpart in Africa today. The author has had the privilege of observing the balmyard both in Africa, at the traditional healing center at Larteh, Ghana, and in St. Elizabeth, Jamaica, West Indies. A comparative study of both these centers yields invaluable insight into the process of African retention in the New World. However, only a brief survey can be undertaken here. The Larteh Healing Center, unlike the Jamaican center, is elaborate and efficiently run. It is as efficient as a small hospital in a country town. Here people suffering from every kind of illness, from insanity to barrenness, are given ritual and herbal treatment. Yet it is also a center for the training of priestesses. In Jamaica the balmyard does not have the facilities for long-term sufferers and it has no provision for training priestesses. It is interesting that both centers are run by women, and both practice balming in herbal waters. The balm may be either water of boiled herbs of various varieties or may be the water of fresh green herbs crushed and juiced. Both centers dispense boiled medicine and also give various species of herbs to the patient with the prescription for preparing them. Both centers conduct daily rituals. In Africa this is done in the traditional way to African gods. In Jamaica, the Christian God prevails, along with the biblical angels, who figure prominently in revelation and divination. The Jamaican healing center uses a total of seventy-seven different herbs in preparing the herbal bath; whereas ninety-nine are used in Africa. The methods employed at the healing center at Larteh, Ghana, are the duplicate of those used in Jamaica, although the healers of Jamaica have no direct knowledge of the contemporary practices in Africa.

There seems little doubt that orthodox practitioners of medicine have, to some extent, contributed to the popularity of such healers by their failure to recognize the psychological aspects of illness and to meet the emotional needs of their patients as well as the physical needs. *It would be a mistake to underestimate the importance and influence of these religio-magic practitioners.* Even among the middle-class there is often a tendency for the patients to consult the obeah-expert or "science man" surreptitiously. Even obviously physical ailments still occasionally reach the obeahman. In a culture in transition from religio-magic thinking to scientific-pragmatic thinking, it is most important that not only the psychiatrist but every doctor be taught the social/anthropological background of the patients with whom he deals and how these patients perceive him; for the doctor from the middle classes is usually surprisingly unaware of his patients' beliefs and value system.

This medical practice of roots and herbs is deep and still dominates the Caribbean; thus it only emphasizes the heritage of our African forefathers. It is interesting to note that the Caribbean slaves found almost all the herbal medicine that their forefathers had known in Africa. Speaking on the herbal practices of the people of Haiti, Sir Spencer St. John, the nineteenth-century British ambassador, had this to say:

> And if it be doubted, that the individuals without even common sense, can understand so thoroughly the properties of herbs and their combinations . . . I can say that tradition is

a great book, and that they receive these instructions as a sacred deposit from one generation to another, with the further advantage that in the hills and mountains of this island grow in abundance similar herbs to those which in Africa they employ in their incantation.[48]

But the Caribbean did not have a monopoly in the knowledge of African folk medicine. The slaves in America were equally well versed in the art. Herbert M. Morais, in *The History of the Negro in Medicine,* points out that the "old wife" carried out all of her old country duties on the slave plantation and was often in charge of all obstetrics on the plantation. And it is believed that these midwives brought with them medical knowledge concerning birth by cesarean section.[49] Some American slaves attained not only fame, but their freedom, on account of the medical skill. One of the most significant transplantations of African folk medicine was revealed by the Reverend Cotton Mather, 1663–1728, who is said to be the man responsible for the adoption of inoculation against smallpox in America. He later confessed that this method, which was to save countless lives, was disclosed to him by one of his slaves, who told him that this particular method had long been in use in Africa.[50] Recent study has shown that smallpox was one of the ravagers of Africa from time immemorial and that elaborate folk medicine was developed against it long before it was probably known in the West. In the Yoruba language the name of the god of smallpox was Sopona, and Shakpata in Ewe. A regular cult is maintained to the god to this very day and his priests are some of the most respected leaders in Africa.[51]

Space will not allow us to review the various incidents of cure revealed by slaves in North America but two more incidents are worth recording. In 1729, Lieutenant Governor Gooch of Virginia reported that he had:

met with a negro, a very old man who has performed many wonderful cures of diseases. For the sake of his freedom, he has revealed the medicine, a concoction of roots and barks. . . . There is no room to doubt of its being a certain remedy here, and of singular use [in the cure of syphilis] among the negroes; then he concluded, "it is well worth the price (£60.0.0) of the negro's freedom since it is known how to cure slaves without mercury."[52]

There is much in Governor Gooch's statement that could be commented on, but it need not delay us here. It is only sufficient to note that the old African was also able to cure a New World disease.

One more incident of African medical lore is the famous case of the slave Caesar. In 1751, it was reported that Caesar was freed by the General Assembly of South Carolina for disclosing his famous cure for poison and rattlesnake bite. He was also allotted an annual stipend of one hundred pounds sterling. Here is the formula:

> Take the root of plantane and wild hoarhound, fresh or dried, three ounces, boil them together in two quarts of water to one quart, and strain it of its decoction. Let the patient take one third part, three mornings fasting successively, from which, if he finds any relief, it must be continued until he is perfectly recovered. On the contrary, if he finds no alteration after the third dose, it is a sign that the patient has not been poisoned at all. . . . During the cure the patient must live on spare diet, and abstain from eating mutton, pork, butter, or any other fat or oily foods. . . . The plantane or hoarhound will either of them cure alone, but they are most efficacious together.[53]

He then went on to describe the symptoms of poison as follows:

> The symptoms attending such as are poisoned are as follows: a pain of the breast, difficulty of breathing, a load at the pit of the stomach, an irregular pulse, burning and violent pains of the viscera above and below the navel, very restless nights, sometimes wandering pains over the whole body, a retching inclination to vomit, profuse sweats (which prove always serviceable) . . . those who have been long poisoned are generally very feeble and weak in their limbs, sometimes spit a great deal, the whole skin peals, and lastly the hair falls off.[54]

Caesar's cure for rattlesnake bites:

> Take two roots of plantane or hoarhound (in summer roots and branches together), a sufficient quantity, bruise them in mortar, and squeeze out the juices, of which, give as soon as possible, one large spoonful. This generally will cure; but if he finds no relief in an hour after, you may give another

spoonful which never hath failed. If the roots are dried, they must be moistened with a little water. To the wound may be applied a leaf of good tobacco, moistened with rum.[55]

We need no further elaboration on the medical skill of the African in slavery. The above is proof enough of the existence of a class of men and women who, though uprooted from their land and brought to the New World under conditions of abject inhumanity, nevertheless adapted their skill to save their brothers from the dangers of the plantation life. In a period when modern medicine was still in its primitive state in the West, there were African slaves with expert knowledge in the cure of smallpox, syphilis and various kinds of poisoning. Although some persons with keen insight threw away their prejudice and recorded some of this knowledge, most of the medical knowledge existed outside the view of men who could write. It is only in our day that the interest in folk medicine is growing, but many feel this is too late. The miracle of the Africans' survival in the New World must in some measure be attributed to the technical skills of the medicine men.

CHAPTER 5

SOUL UNDER STRESS:
Redemption Cults — Caribbean

Our aims in this chapter are to explore the confrontation of African and European culture; to trace the reactions of Africans in the New World; and to understand their struggle through the missionizing attempts of Christianity and the rise of millenarian cults. The reaction of the slaves in captivity was naturally one of sustained hostility. This hostility, which continued throughout the slave period, was aggression of a collective type. In their struggle against oppression they invoked their African gods, especially the war gods, Ogun and Shango and others. They resorted to their own culturally approved techniques of resistance by practicing deception, and by reinterpreting their native folklore, especially the "trickster lore," which delights in lengthy description of the technique of escape by disguise and trickery. Such folk knowledge served well when used against the masters. They also resorted to forces of a psychic nature, employing the sorcerer against the powers of oppression.

As the original Africans died out and their descendants took over, a new type of African emerged in the New World. The descendants of the slaves had acquired new languages; they were exposed to new ways of life and had imbibed a culture with new assumptions of power. The Europeans with their controlling technological skill and their efficient way of amassing wealth appealed to the Africans in new and different ways. A new sense of awareness broke upon their consciousness. They saw themselves as spiritually and socially deprived and as a people of little or no worth. Unable to recall their past, and seeing no future remedy for their existing condition, they sought redemption.

Black redemption cults are the product of a long process of incubation and result from the mixture of Christian ideas and African traditional beliefs. Christian ideas were grafted on to traditional African roots. The Christian God became an African God, who, if not considered more powerful than the traditional gods, was perceived to be at least as great as those in the traditional African pantheons. And the angels of Christianity were identified with the lesser deities of Africa. In this way, the Christian religion opened new avenues of thought to the slaves.

The message of Christianity based on the Bible was, for the slaves, above all, the message of salvation and deliverance. If there were only one message that Africans welcomed, it was this message of salvation from present oppression and a future in heaven where God would wipe away all tears. Both the Old and New Testaments are full of accounts of the activity of the Judaeo-Christian God on behalf of the downtrodden. The God of the Old Testament manifested himself to the Jews as a God who stood firmly against oppression; as one who would stop at nothing to bring down the oppressors and set the oppressed free. The New Testament introduced the Africans to Jesus of Nazareth, the Messiah, the one who was sent to earth in human form to liberate the oppressed. It was this message of redemption that the Africans understood most clearly and that they soon grafted on to their traditional beliefs, giving the millenarian flavor to the Afro-Christian movements in the New World.

In the Latin system, where Christianity was introduced to the Africans at the start of their New World experience, this syncretism merely enriched the traditional African religion and became a routinized part of African ritual. In the English system of slavery, however, the acceptance of Christianity was a dramatic and powerful precipitator for the rise of millenarian and messianic movements. As a matter of fact, the confrontation of traditional African religion and Christianity is still spawning cults in the New World.

Redemption cults have been observed all the way from New Zealand to Melanesia, to Africa, to North America and the Caribbean.[1] They vary on a continuum from low to high assimilation of Christian doctrine. That is, redemption movements are found which have taken only a few ideas from Christian teaching, while others have allowed only a few of the traditional elements to remain within a highly developed Christian ideology and ritual.

The majority of these cults emerged in the nineteenth century as a reaction to the shock of culture contact between primary societies and their colonial masters. Of special importance in this was the fact that, in every case, colonial domination was accompanied by European missionary outreach. So almost all of these redemption cults arose as delayed reactions to the cultural confusion brought about by the heightened expectation that had been created by the Gospel message of the missionaries on the one hand, and the corresponding stress and frustration of colonial domination on the other. The message of abundant life, equality, justice and love taught by the missionaries became a haunting mirage to the people in these primal societies as they came to realize that their lands were gradually being appropriated, their prestige destroyed, their ancestral religion proscribed, and that a new economic system was being introduced which left them in what they felt was a deprived condition in their own ancestral homeland. As the cultural mazeways of these societies became more restrictive and the stress on the society heightened, the desire to break out of this bind became urgent and pressing. A process of serious reflection set in, in which the Africans compared the present with the past, the present with the future, and the relative status of the Europeans over against that of those who were by right the legitimate owners of the land. From this followed a period of acceptance-repulsion behavior toward all that represented the intrusive culture. This produced what is known as cultural distortion, and as a result the Africans urgently sought new ways to restore equilibrium. A rearrangement of society was necessary. However, few leaders of the old mold could provide a satisfactory solution to the problem of unifying society; a "new man" was needed. This man had to be a mixture of the new and the old. He had to be a true representative of traditional values; he had to understand viscerally the stress felt by his society, yet he had to be equally knowledgeable in the ways of the new intrusive culture that had brought about the unsettled conditions. At the points in history where such a man appeared we speak of a prophet or a charismatic leader.

Redemption cults appear in many forms. They can take the form of nativism, in which the society seeks to meet the crisis of the present by a return to certain aspects of its traditional religion that proved satisfying in the past. Revivalism is another form of redemption cult which also returns to remembered cultural values, although in this case, certain valuable aspects of the intrusive culture are retained. But whatever the various outward forms of these movements may be, reliance on the supernatural or the magico-religious dimension is characteristic of all of them.

The role of the leader is of less definitional importance. Redemption movements can emerge without a leader; however, such movements are generally not prone to aggressive social action. The emergence of a singular charismatic figure appears to be necessary for sustained social action.

With or without a single leader, these movements are essentially "collective." The society experiences a shared stress, for the relief of which, common action is taken. Such a movement may have begun in response to unacceptable socio-economic conditions that precipitated mass reaction, or it may have been the immediate result of a prophet's ability to perceive the direction of new trends within his society, this perception literally forcing him to recruit a collective. In both cases, however, redemption cults generally must have leaders in order to inspire and/or consolidate the dynamics of change.

The descriptions and analyses of redemption movements the world over, have, in the last quarter of a century, grown to many volumes, most of which are easily available to the student of Third World religious movements. And any attempt to repeat those findings here would take us far afield, since our particular interest is in Black movements in the New World and very little has been written on these movements. Our desire is to point out the dynamics of African religion that persist in the various religious and social movements in the New World and give these movements their particular flavor. This will enable us to understand the many different ways in which the African force-vitale manifests itself in Black survival.

A. Cults of Redemption—The Caribbean: Haiti and Jamaica

During and after slavery, cults of redemption emerged in great numbers in the English slave colonies, but rather infrequently in the colonies of the Latin system. This may be attributable to the greater religious restraint imposed on Blacks within the English system. Classic examples of these cults are found in Haiti and in Jamaica; and, as a matter of fact, these cult dynamics are formative within the culture of these two islands to the present day. Using Haiti and Jamaica as examples of all types of revivalism in the Caribbean, we shall see the background causes for the emergence of redemption cults, the forms of emergence and their influence on the peasant society.

1. Vodun in Haiti:

> *Papa Legba, ouvri barrière pour moin: ago-e*
> *Papa Legba, ouvri chemin pour li: ago-e*
>
> (Creole)
>
> Papa Legba, open the barrier for me: pay heed
> Papa Legba, open the road for him: pay heed

No discussion on African religions in the Caribbean would be complete without the recognition of Vodun in Haiti. For, despite its caricature in various books and television melodramas, Vodun represents the most potent ingredients of the African soul in the West Indies. No student on Vodun has been able to trace the exact date when the Africans came together and fused their various beliefs around the Dahomean concept—Vodun—but be that as it may, one thing is clear: the priest and priestess who came under French brutality soon perceived that they were in danger and that their survival depended upon the protection of the gods of Guinea.

The invocation to Legba, written above, represents the faith of the Haitians in their African gods, and anyone who is familiar with Haitian history will doubtless agree that their gods heard their prayers. If Moreau de Saint-Méry is correct, Haiti had one of the most impressive mixtures of African peoples of all the islands. According to his research, from Senegal came the Yolop, Bambarras, Foulas, Poulords, Kiambaras, Mandingos; from West Central Africa, the Aradas, Makis, Honassas, Ibos, Yorubas, Binis, Takwas, Fanti, Agonas, Sobos, Limbas and Adjas; from Angola and the Congo Basin, the Solongos, Mayombes, Mosombes, Bumbas and Kangas.[2]

Several of the above peoples are readily identifiable, others are not, but if this list is correct, it bears out the thesis of this book, which is that, although many tribes were present in the New World, only those with the strongest religious traditions were able to wield cultural influence and so leave their impression on the New World. In Haiti, although there was a variety of African peoples assembled, the Dahomean Vodun religion was not only the most powerful, but flexible enough to incorporate all religious beliefs within its ritual manifestations.

The word "vodun," or "voodoo," which never fails to conjure up visions of heathenish revelries in the mind of non-Haitians, is a Dahomean word which means God, protective spirit, or the company of gods. The last term, "the company of the gods," is rather fitting for an understanding of the religion of Haiti, for, as we shall see, Vodun is a conglomeration of various African divinities with the further addition of the Christian Trinity, plus the roster of saints of Catholicism, all thrown together. Vodun, then, is a religion which leaves no powers outside its orbit. It is a prime example of the African genius for assimilating other religious forms; further examples of this are Macumba in Brazil, Santeria in Cuba and Shango in Trinidad.

Space will not allow us to analyze all the intricacies of Haitian Vodun. Our main emphasis will be to point out some aspects of the development of Vodun as a religion and the place of Vodun in Haitian liberation.

James G. Leyburn suggested four stages of development in the history of Vodun.[3] The first he called the period of its gestation, a period which began in 1730 and ended in 1790. During this period, we see from the records that the new Africans underwent a traumatic period of forced indoctrination into the rituals of Catholicism. Baptism was the magic word which for Western Christendom covered a multitude of sins. So as early as 1685 the decree was given in *Le Code Noir,* that "all slaves will be baptized and instructed in the Catholic religion."[4] It commanded that those who are engaged in buying new slaves should notify within eight days all the governors and leaders of the said island and, "that under serious penalty of a fine, that necessary orders are that slaves should be instructed and baptized as soon as possible."[5]

The vagueness of the wording of this decree points up the half-heartedness of the governance of slavery in Haiti. With few exceptions, most planters paid little attention to these decrees. However, those who were under the watchful eyes of the Church did submit their slaves to baptism. An example of how it was done is recorded for us by Ralph Korngold's research from records of slavery. He writes:

> A hundred or so Negroes freshly arrived from Africa would be herded into a church. Whips cracked and they were ordered to kneel. A priest and his acolytes appeared before the altar and mass was said. Then the Priest followed by the acolytes carrying a basin of holy water, walked slowly down the aisle and with vigorous swings of the Aspergillum scattered the water over the heads of the crowd, chanting in Latin. The whips cracked again, the slaves rose from their knees and emerged into the sunlight, converts to Christianity.[6]

What took place here was not a conversion to Christianity but a legitimization of Vodun. Among those Africans herded into the church were several priests and priestesses who we may believe watched carefully every movement of the Catholic priest and who later incorporated every movement in his or her rituals, which were not too different from those they had learned in Africa. Between 1730 and 1790, the African rituals and those of Catholicism merged in what may be called a religious symbiosis in which Vodun copied just enough of the Catholic ritual forms to disguise the real religion of Africa. This was necessary because from the earliest contact of the Africans with French Catholicism there was a fanatic reaction on the part of the Church against what they described as "heathen practices." The battle between Africa and Rome in Haiti has never known a "cease-fire"—from slavery to the present time.

The second period, according to Leyburn, should be dated from 1790 to 1800.[7] This is called the period of expansion and self-assertion. In this period, Vodun grew and managed to fuse the numerous tribes under its banner and became the life-force of the Haitian revolution. The power of Vodun in the Haitian revolution is now a matter of record. The Oath of Bois-Caiman, which signaled the Black revolt, is known by all Haitian schoolchildren; this will be discussed later.

The third period in the development of Vodun came between 1800 and 1815, after the smoke of the battle finally had blown away, and was a period of systematic suppression of Vodun undertaken by the Black rulers, especially Dessalines and Christophe.

Their attitude toward Vodun was not that of those who saw it as a useless superstition; they knew and feared its power. In the fourth period, from 1815 to 1850, Vodun, despite being suppressed, quietly diffused itself through the masses.

Since 1850 Vodun has had its ups and downs. But the dynamics of Vodun within the Haitian subculture have never lost their force. Religiously it is still the spiritual source for all peasants. Politically, it retains the potential power to guarantee elections and is quite capable of maintaining the political tenure of any President who is bold enough to identify with the masses. The example here is, of course, the late François Duvalier, who, as an ethnographer, was sympathetic to the people's ethos. He boldly extolled the value of Vodun, claiming himself to be the African messiah, the reincarnation of those dead heroes who fought for Haitian liberation. His mystical demeanor and his love for the peasants made him a political *houngan,* or priest, to his people. The period of Duvalier's reign may be called the fifth period of Vodun. It is too early to say what influence Vodun will have in the new regime, but Vodun had been able to meet and overcome all previous challenges.

a. Vodun as a religion: Like the children of Israel in exile, the multitude of Africans in Haiti cried to the Lord in their troubles and their Lord saved them from destruction. Thus Vodun became, for the Haitians, a religion of survival, a remedy for their ills. Jean Price-Mars, the legitimate father of Négritude, had no inhibitions about defending Vodun's status as a religion. "Vodun is a religion," writes Price-Mars, "because its initiates believe in the existence of spiritual beings who live partly in the universe, partly in close contact with men, whose activities they control."[8] According to Price-Mars, these invisible beings in Vodun form an Olympus of gods, the highest of whom bears the title of Papa or Great Mother and claims special veneration. But the gods of Vodun are many and the ones referred to most often are the lesser deities, who are known by the generic name loa—a Congo word which signifies power. The most popular loa is Damballah-Wéda —the name, a contraction of Dangbé and Allada, countries of West Africa—who is symbolized by one or two snakes.

Wéda or Ayida is another West African province closely connected to Dangbé and Allada in the minds of worshipers. Damballah is the god of fertility, the bringer of rains. According to

Maya Deren, Damballah and Wéda represent the "sexual totality, encompass the cosmos as a serpent coiled about the world." "The egg, the world egg is the special symbol for them."[9]

Although Damballah-Wéda seems to hold the most prominent position in Haitian Vodun, the loa most frequently called upon is Legba. He is omniscient and omnipresent, the mediator between the world of man and the spirit world. He is the one who opens the door for other loa, he is the god who breaks all barriers. All Vodun ceremonies invoke his presence as the first order of ritual. Maya Deren said of Legba:

> As principle of life, as the initial procreative whole, Legba was both man and woman. . . . As navel of the world, or as its womb, Legba is addressed in prayers at childbirth with the phrase which signals him: "Open the road for me . . . do not let any evil spirits bar my path."[10]

He is god of the marketplace, the common square and, above all, the crossroads, where his blessings of fertility fall on all who pass by. His representation is a cross.

Another important loa of Vodun is Agwé, the god in charge of water, sea, boats and fishermen. He is represented by a small boat with sails aloft. Another goddess is Erzulie-Freda, the goddess of femininity and fertility. She is the African counterpart of the Catholic Virgin Mary. She represents love, beauty and luxury.

One final loa in this series is Nana-bouclou (in Africa, Nana-buluku), the guarder of racial origin, priesthood, healing powers and parental discipline. It is interesting to note that the name of this god is known in Dahomey as that of the original creator of the world. His twin descendants Mawu and Lisa, the sun and the moon, came to usurp his authority as he retreated from man's affairs. All the loa discussed above are those of Dahomean origin and are part of that variety of Vodun practiced under the Arada rites. Along with these are gods of the Yoruba and Ibo pantheon such as Obatala, Ogun, Shango and others. The Arada divinities of Vodun are said to be traditional, initiatory and benevolent.

Alongside the Arada rite is that of Petro and, by contrast, this type of Vodun is considered magical, malevolent and demonic. The same divinities mentioned above appear in Petro rites but with hyphenated names indicating their different manifestations. Erzulie-Lemba, Legba-congo, Damballa-ossange. The most powerful loa in the Petro series is Guede, or Ghede, the god of death. The difference between Arada and Petro rites is not always clear, but it is generally believed that the spirit of Haitian revolution was precipitated in the Petro rites. It is also believed that in the Petro rites blood sacrifice is performed, while in Arada rites it is rare. It is this writer's opinion that all this is academic. Because for the *serviteur,* the follower of Vodun, such fine definitions are pointless. The attempt to divide Vodun into good and bad categories is probably the work of scholars who would like to discredit the revolutionary spirit of Vodun that played such a major role in Haitian liberation. Maya Deren sees the Petro rites as a local creation, one that emerged to meet the oppressive situation brought about by slavery and the Catholic Church. In a footnote she wrote:

> It is still true, and extremely significant, that wherever Voudun has been especially suppressed (at the insistence of the Catholic Church) it is the Petro rite that becomes dominant.[11]

And she added:

> Suppression always destroys first what is gentle and benevolent; it inspires rage and reaction; encourages malevolence and magic, and so creates the very thing which, theoretically, it would destroy.[12]

b. Priesthood and organization: Price-Mars said of Vodun that:

> Its cult developed for its gods demands a hierarchical body of priests, a community of believers, temples, altars, ceremonies and finally an oral tradition. . . .[13]

At the center of Vodun is the *houngan,* or *papoloi,* who is both feared and respected. His female counterpart is called a *mambo,* or *mamaloi,* and is equally feared and respected. These Vodun votaries are people with a high degree of folk knowledge. They are not only priests and priestesses, but seers, healers, fortune-tellers, the guardians of African tradition and public entertainers as well. They are trained in the tradition handed down to them by their forefathers, a training which included herbal medicine, psychoanalysis, music and ritual instruction. They know the tastes of the loa and the various ceremonies appropriate to each of them. No one visiting a Vodun ceremony leaves with the impression that the work of these votaries is an easy one. The authority of the priest or mambo is symbolized in the *asson,* a gourd filled with pebbles that is used to summon the gods. Only a trained priest may lawfully use the asson.

Below the priest and priestess is the *hounsi.* The houngan is the master of ceremonies and controls the gods; the hounsi is one who is under his training and assists the houngan. Below the hounsi is the *houngenikon,* the one who is in charge of the chorus of *vodunsis:* the *bossale* and the *canzo.* The Bossales are those who are in the initial stages of training; while the canzos are those who are trained in the mysteries of Vodun. A priest or priestess with an hounsi, or houngenikon and a company of vodunsi form what is known at present as a *société.*

A société conducts ceremonies in a *humfo,* or *humfort,* commonly known as a temple. Humforts vary from area to area. In the countryside they may be nothing but improvised thatched constructions, while in the city of Port-au-Prince one can find quite elaborate structures that are usually attached to the rear of a compound or a dwelling house. One of these, with which the author is most familiar, is on the outskirts of Port-au-Prince. There are several ritual areas to a humfort. The large rectangular area known as the peristyle is the place where ceremonies and dancing take place and at the center of it is the great post called the *Poteau-mitan.* This post is the focal point of ritual activities. Theoretically it is rooted in Africa and extends upward into the spirit world. It is not clear whether the loa come up the post from Africa to possess the devotees or down from the spirit world; however, it is the Poteau-mitan around which the houngan operates. Adjoining the peristyle are altars dedicated to the loa. In the humfort under discussion there are four altars, each in a separate room. Each contains a table on which can be found various objects peculiar to the deity to whom the altar is dedicated. Here one may observe bottles of alcoholic spirits of various kinds and strength, beads, combs, mirrors, various pictures of Catholic saints, candles, incense, stones, cups, basins and various other objects. There are also rooms for flags, the coat-of-arms of the société, and various robes in a variety of colors suitable to the various loa.

It would take us too far afield to discuss the various types of ceremonies which take place in a Vodun temple; suffice it to say that it is here in the humfort that one may witness all the emotion,

the possession and the various expressions in song and dance that
constitute Vodun ceremonies. But as Harold Courlander rightly
said:

> Vodun means more to the Haitian than temple ritual. It is an
> integrated system of concepts concerning human activities,
> the relationship and ties between the living and the dead. It
> has its own cause and effect system to explain otherwise
> unexplainable events. It provides guidelines for social behav-
> ior and demands that the gods be responsive. In short, it is a
> true religion which attempts to know the unknown and es-
> tablish order where there might otherwise be chaos.[14]

c. The *vevers* and the drums: For some the dance is the most
intriguing thing about Vodun; for others it is the magic; but to
the author the art forms of Vodun are most exciting. The vevers
represent the most intricate religious art form in Haitian Vodun.
Vevers are Vodun symbols drawn on the floor of the peristyle during a ceremony just before the loa enter the service to possess
the devotees. They are what Metraux calls the material repre-
sentations of divinity. Each of the vevers represents a god or a loa
drawn in intricate geometrical patterns. In each service or ceremony the vever of the loa to whom the service is dedicated is
traced on the ground. It is generally done by the hounsi, who in
most cases is a woman. There is a strict formula involved, as each
vever is accompanied by a ritual incantation and by drumming. The
hounsi takes flour, ashes or cornmeal in hand, dances toward the
drums and begins the intricate patterning of the loa. After this is
done, candles are placed at appropriate places on the vevers.
Metraux said of them:

> These emblematic drawings have a magical nature. Merely
> by tracing them out a priest puts pressure on the loa and com-
> pels them to appear. Their function is to summon loa.[15]

The author has witnessed several such ceremonies and can agree
with Metraux that real spirit possessions rarely takes place before
the tracing of the vevers. As we have already indicated, some of
these symbols are simple, others complex. It appears that several
vevers can be combined according to the nature of the ceremony.
There are few scholars who really understand the true meaning of
this aspect of Vodun, but these cabalistic signs have now begun to

enter into the world of Haitian painting and sculpture and they are even to be seen in architecture.

The drums are an indispensable part of Vodun. Just as in various nations in Africa, in Haiti, there is a drum which is a symbol of the nation's spirit. This is the *assotor* drum. According to Michelson Paul Hyppolite: "it [the assotor] has been exalted to the rank of a deity by the people and is the object of a special cult. A living symbol of our African origin, it is submitted to a ceremony of consecration before being used in a Temple."[16] The assotor is so sacred in Haiti that a statue is dedicated to it in the heart of the city and it also appears in the coat-of-arms of the Republic.[17]

The typical Vodun ceremony of the Arada rite calls for three drums. The largest of these, the *manman,* varies in size but it generally is not less than thirty-six inches long. The next in size is the *ségond* and the smallest, the *bula*. These drums are played in a variety of ways. The manman is generally played with a stick with cricks at the end, while the others are played with the heels of the hands and the fingers, and the palm is shaped to create the desired sounds. Some beats demand that the drummer run his thumb across the surface of the drums to effect a mourning sound.

Different national rhythms are preserved in Vodun. Thus one may hear an Ibo, a Shango, a Congo, or a Damballah rhythm all intertwining in a given ceremony. The drummers may not be devotees of Vodun, but they must know the beats necessary to satisfy the loa or must be able to "beat" a vodunsi out of possession if this is needed. Drumming in Vodun, as in other African religions, is not an improvised mélange of sounds. Drumming is a tradition which must be learned. No houngan would gamble with a novice on the drums in a ceremony that demanded intricate changes of rhythm at intervals, for without the proper rhythm, confusion would reign.

Even from this rapid survey of Vodun, it is not too difficult to perceive that the religion of the Haitian people is the real life of the nation. It was Price-Mars who, after years of training in the very seat of French culture and imbibing the best that France could offer, came to the conclusion that the source of soul for the Haitians is not in French culture but in Mother Africa. It was this initial insight that ignited others of the same French tradition, thinkers such as Aimé Césaire and Léopold Sédar Senghor. Other

voices have from time to time echoed the same call for a return to
the African roots; in his book *Les Daimons du culte vodu,* Dr.
Arthur C. Holly of Port-au-Prince said in praise of his native religion:

> We are Latin-Africans. But our Latin civilization is on
> the surface; the old African heritage prolongs itself in us and
> dominates us to such an extent that in many circumstances we
> feel ourselves moved by mysterious forces. Thus, our sensibility
> and our will undergo strange emotions when the unequal
> rhythms of the sacred dances of voodoo, now melancholy,
> now passionate, always full of magic effects, are heard in the
> silent night.[18]

Reflecting on the elite whom he observed, and who try overly hard
to simulate a bastard French culture, denying with every breath
the roots of his origin, Holly said:

> By a sort of dilletantism, the cultured Haitian possesses the
> elegant art of deceiving himself. By constantly counterfeiting
> his ideas and sentiments, and feigning to adapt himself, with
> facility to a borrowed estheticism, the Haitian has lost his
> personality as a human type. Unconsciously he joins his
> voice to the doctrinal error erected against the traditions of
> his race; he humiliates himself and discredits himself by be-
> coming a witness in the serious accusation formulated by the
> white against the moral spirit and the manifestation of mysti-
> cal ideas of his Negro ancestors whose group constituted in
> times gone by a luminous landmark and the most living and
> fecund center of religious humanity.[19]

Holly is here voicing a sentiment that is badly needed in the
Caribbean and throughout the Black world. It should be remembered, these words were spoken long before the call of Black
Power and the "Black is beautiful" revival. But we must hear him
to the end. Voicing his deepest conviction about the Vodun religion, he said:

> Our salvation will not be secure until the day when, ridding
> ourselves of vain scruples and putting aside all fears of criti-
> cism, we shall resolve to perpetuate the purified cult of voo-
> doo and shall raise to Legba and the powerful Damballa
> hymns of prayer coming from the bottom of our hearts.[20]

These were truly the sentiments of liberated Haitians. Many of the elite have followed in the sentiments of Dr. Holly but there is still a large residue of "borrowed estheticism" yet to be discarded before all Haitians raise their hymns to Legba and Damballah.

d. Vodun and Haitian Liberation: Maya Deren, in her book *Divine Horsemen: The Voodoo Gods of Haiti,* said: "Even today, the songs of revolt of 'vive la liberté' occur in Petro ritual as a dominant theme."[21] The author witnessed a Ghede ceremony in Haiti in the summer of 1971, in which a unique military parade occurs as a part of the ritual. The mambo and her followers changed to military uniforms of eighteenth-century soldiers and performed a mock battle. When he asked what this signified, the author was told that it was a re-enactment of the War of Independence and that this has become an important segment of the Ghede rites.

In the public square south of the presidential palace in Port-au-Prince stands the statue of a muscular Maroon, kneeling on one knee, blowing the conch shell, known in Haiti as *lambé.* This statue commemorates a special breed of Haitian Black who, like the Jamaican Maroon, fled to the mountains and from there harassed the French even before the Haitian revolution began. It was in these mountains, sometime before August 1791, that a Jamaican-born African joined the Haitian Maroons. For all we know of him, which is very little, he could have been one of the Jamaican Maroons captured by the British in the wars with the Ashanti runaways and sold to Haiti. Whatever the circumstances surrounding his appearance in Haiti, all the records agree that he was born in Jamaica, and when we meet him in Haiti he was in the mountains as *"un N'gan* [houngan]"[22] or *"Prete du Voudou* [a Vodun priest]." Some writers referred to him as a "bocor," a medicine man.[23] It was this houngan or Vodun priest of the so-called Petro rite who ignited the flame of liberation in Haiti. The story runs like this: On August 14, 1790, several of these Maroons assembled at Bois-Caiman near Morne Rouge (Red Mountain). To most, this must have seemed like just another assembly to plan another local raid on a nearby plantation, but that night was a signal for greater things ahead. The climax of this meeting was dramatic.

In the middle of this impressive scene, motionless, petrified in sacred awe, the assembled slaves behold an old Negress rise up, her body shaking from head to foot. She sings, she

pirouettes and over her head she brandishes a huge cutlass.
. . . At this moment a black pig is produced. The din of the
storm drowns his grunts. With one vivid thrust the inspired
priestess plunges her cutlass into the animal's throat. The
blood spurts—and is gathered smoking to be distributed in
turn, to the slaves: all drink, all swear to obey Boukman.[24]

This incident is remarkable for its intensity. The austerity of the
natural setting, the authentication of their plan by spirit possession, the sealing of their oath by blood, all reminds one of Africa.
The sealing of an oath by blood is reminiscent of the Maroons in
Jamaica, and the Mau Mau of Kenya. According to popular tradition, just after the incident, Boukman spoke the following words:

The god who created the sun which gives us light, who rouses
the waves and rules the storm, though hidden in the clouds,
he watches us. He sees all what the white man does. The god
of the white man inspires him with crime, but our god calls
upon us to do good works. Our god who is good to us orders
us to revenge our wrongs. He will direct our arms and aid us.
Throw away the symbol of the god of the whites who has so
often caused us to weep, and listen to the voice of liberty,
which speaks in the hearts of us all.[25]

It is clear that Boukman was not referring to the Christian God.
He was praying to the God who created the sun. The one who,
though hidden in the clouds, rules the storm. Many in his audience
were new arrivals from Africa who knew whom he meant, but
some were undoubtedly Christians of a sort who might even have
worn the crucifix as a talisman; to them he said: "Throw away the
symbol of the god of the whites." Our conclusion, then, is that the
Haitians invoked their African gods in their liberation and they
did not fail them. Steeled with the Oath of Bois-Caiman, the slaves
stormed down the mountain and for one month swept the slave
masters before them. It is needless to go into the details of this
initial skirmish, but it is tremendously important to emphasize
the significance of the Oath of Bois-Caiman. One month after Bois-
Caiman, Toussaint L'Ouverture joined the battle and the rest is
history.

There is no need to amass elaborate proof to convince the
skeptic of the centrality of Vodun in the Haitian struggle for independence. It is much more appropriate to allow the Haitians to

speak for themselves. In this chapter we have heard their words, and their assessment of their struggle. Let us conclude by giving them the floor once more. In an address to the Alliance Française of Kingston, Jamaica, on the occasion of the one hundred and fiftieth anniversary of the Republic of Haiti in 1954, Monsieur Reynold St.-Cyr, Consul General of Haiti, reflected on the battle for Haitian independence in the following words:

> Now, what were the forces that were responsible for that national epic? What were the forces that caused the rallying of 1804? The Haitian Creeds, we would answer with pride. Yes, these only could give this transcending dynamic to accomplish those wonders of heroism before the indomitable soldiers of Arcole and Rivoli; they alone, could electrify the immortal vagabonds of St. Dominque, so that they could carry out with integrity the sacred order of the Emperor [Dessalines]: "Cut off the heads and burn the houses!;" they alone could give to Capois that sullen contempt of death at Vertiere, as he called to his men; "Forward! Forward! Cannon balls are dust!," when a bullet had just killed his fearless and impetuous horse under him. Such passion, such ardor could find their crystallization nowhere but in Vodoo, for, opposing the precepts taught by the Catholic Religion, Vodoo rather advocates protests, impetuosity and violence, as expressed in that song: *"Si yo ba ou, ba ya tou, pinga poté knot' ban moin"* (If they hit you, hit them back, do not come and complain).[26]

Haiti, though economically depressed and sometimes politically unsure of itself, is a reminder to all the world that Blacks not only crave liberty but, if needs be, will die for it. The drum and the conch-shell statues which stand in the city of Port-au-Prince will always remind the Haitians and the tourists of those Africans who, though ragged, ill armed and hungry, were inspired by the ethos of Vodun, to march against the French armies fully confident that if they were victorious they would be free of their chains; but, even if they died, their souls would go to Africa.

2. Revivalism in Jamaica: There probably was no other English slave colony in which there was such total resistance on the part of the landowners to the dissemination of Christianity among the slaves as there was on the island of Jamaica. As early as 1696, through the insistence of the Church of England, an act was passed

by the legislature mildly suggesting that all slave owners should see to it that the slaves be instructed in the teachings of the church and receive the sacrament of baptism "when fit for it." One hundred years after this act, it was reported that no effort was made to implement it. Few, if any, of the clergymen were willing to take this responsibility, and few, if any, of the masters were so disposed.

The first missionary enterprise to Jamaica was undertaken by the Moravians, who arrived in the parish of St. Elizabeth in 1734. Their efforts were so frustrated by the planters that very little progress was made toward a wide-scale evangelization of the slaves. And the Methodists, who arrived after the Moravians, met even more bitter opposition. So it was not until 1815, as we have documented in chapter 3, that the House of Assembly finally voted unanimously to:

> consider the state of religion among the slaves, and carefully investigate the means of diffusing the light of genuine Christianity . . .[27]

This quotation gives us an important insight into the planters' attitude toward preaching the Gospel to the slaves. They thought that the doctrine of the Methodists when combined with African superstition was "pregnant with imminent danger to the community." From the planters' resistance we can justly infer that the introduction of Christianity was at that time bringing about a new sense of self-awareness in the minds of the Africans. And this is further support for the contention that such revival movements emerged as a result of the meeting of Christianity and traditional African religion, within the contexts of slavery and colonialism. At any rate, in Jamaica, it was not until 1820 that any real missionary outreach was undertaken and the records will reveal that even this effort was soon to be frustrated.

In any discussion of the Christianizing of the Blacks in Jamaica, the most important event has got to be the founding of the Baptist Church there. The special significance of the Baptist mission lies in the fact that it was founded by a slave from the United States and that it was this slave religion which became the foundation of the Afro-Christian cult of Jamaica.

The Jamaican Baptist Church was founded by George Liele, in 1784.[28] He is also known by the name of George Sharp; Sharp being the name of his owner, a Loyalist in the American Revolution. At the death of his master, Liele received his freedom, but was soon thrown into prison. Through the help of a Colonel Kirkland he was released, and at the evacuation of Savannah, Georgia, Colonel Kirkland sought refuge in Jamaica, taking George Liele with him. According to the record, Liele was ordained as a Black Baptist minister before leaving Savannah and also did some preaching in the United States before his departure. He arrived in Jamaica about 1783, and here we quote his own words:

> I began, about September 1784, to preach in Kingston, in a small private house to a good smart congregation, and I formed the church with four brethren from America besides myself and the preaching took very good effect with the poorer sort, especially the slaves . . .[29]

We cannot overstress the importance of the work of George Liele. First, his slave origin gave him an important entry into the slave community in Jamaica. Second, his method of preaching to the slaves made him somewhat acceptable to the planters. The record shows that unlike the Methodists, he first received written consent from the planters before accepting anyone into his church; as a result, slave masters began to seek out his service on their plantations in and around the vicinity of Kingston, Spanish Town and St. Andrews. The record also shows that his colleague Amos Baker (one of the "four brethren" mentioned above) and probably others received calls to the parish of Westmoreland, and, starting churches on several estates in that region, succeeded in converting hundreds of slaves to the Baptist denomination.

Looking ahead to our discussion on the Rastafarians, a recent militant cult formed in Jamaica, which believes their heavenly home is "Ethiopia," it is rather interesting to note that George Liele named his denomination the Ethiopian Baptist Church.[30] This also gives us an insight into the African orientation of the Black Baptist Church existing in America in the eighteenth century. So successful was the Ethiopian Baptist Church among the slaves in Jamaica, that six years after its founding date, George Liele numbered five hundred members under his supervision, not counting those in the areas under the leadership of Amos Baker and other of his American brethren. The Ethiopian Baptists made the first important missionary outreach in the slave population of Jamaica, and they were successful, as was said, because of their slave origin and African orientation. But perhaps equal credit for the success should go to the organizational structure of the Baptist movement, which was a loose one, using newly converted lay leaders to supervise the African converts. Such flexibility allowed for the inclusion of elements of traditional religion; the drums, handclapping, dancing and traditional healing common to myalism today were part of the original slave tradition.

To support this point we now turn to other missionary efforts of the orthodox type which began in earnest from 1820 to 1860. The Church of England continued to hedge on the instruction of slaves for membership in the Christian church. Their most vigorous endeavor was their persistent opposition to the nonconformist churches, the most important of which was the Methodist. The Moravians, of which there is little mention in the records, made little real progress in Christianizing the slaves, although their work grew slowly in the last half of the eighteenth century. The Black Baptist Church continued to outdistance all other denominations and became the most favored religion of the slaves.

The teaching of the Christian message through missionary effort which was begun in 1734 by the Moravians, Methodists and Baptists, crested in the years 1860–61, when the whole island was swept by an unprecedented religious revival, known as the "Great Revival." This phenomenon was like an earthquake, tremors of which are still felt in the island to the present day. An eyewitness to this revival wrote the following:

> During the first week we were in the church night and day, and could only snatch short intervals of repose. The whole family including children slept at the church. During the last week the intense excitement which existed at first had in great part subsided, and our morning and evening services were conducted with perfect quietness and decorum.[31]

The writer, in describing the behavior patterns of the members, referred to the "stirring prayers," "prostration on the floor" and those "struck down." All this leads us to believe that what was happening in Jamaica during the "Great Revival," was similar to that which took place in the Great Awakening of the United States, which has been acknowledged as having been greatly influenced by Black religious behavior. Another writer a half of a century later, reflecting on the result of the Great Revival, was even more descriptive: W. J. Gardner, a Congregational minister, wrote:

> In 1861 there had been a very remarkable religious movement known as "the revival" . . . Like a mountain stream, clear and transparent as it springs from the rock, but which becomes foul and repulsive as impurities are mingled with it in its onward course, so with this most extraordinary movement. In many of the central districts of the island the hearts of thoughtful and good men were gladdened by what they witnessed in changed lives and characters of people for whom they long seemed to have laboured in vain; but in too many districts there was much of wild extravagance and almost blasphemous fanaticism. This was especially the case where the native Baptists had any considerable influence. Among these, the manifestations occasioned by the influence of the myal-men . . . were very common. *To the present* time, what are called revival meetings are common among these people.[32]

How can this Great Revival be interpreted? Was it really a revival of Christianity? The answer is no. There was no Christianity to revive among the slaves. What actually happened was a result of the confused state in which the Blacks found themselves after the Emancipation of 1838. Their expectation that Emancipation would result in freedom and self-betterment was disappointed and instead they found themselves disenfranchised, landless, homeless and without the means to support themselves. The missionaries, who played a great role in the liberation movement, had built up their expectations of a better life in a free Jamaica, but this proved to be nothing more than empty talk. The Great Revival is thus better understood as a rejection of Christianity and a revival of the African force-vitale. According to a recent writer, the Great Revival of 1860–61, brought the final surge of missionary hope and the final depth of missionary despair. What really took place was a forcible amalgamation of Christianity with the African ethos, a liaison made possible by George Liele and the Ethiopian Baptist Church. Gardner, speaking just fifty years after the Revival, supports this thesis when he associates "the wild extravagance and almost blasphemous fanaticism" not with the Moravians, to whom he mistakenly attributed the beginning of the Revival, but with the Baptists. Referring to this "wild extravagance," he said, "this was especially the case where the native Baptists had any considerable influence. Among these, the manifestations occasioned by the influence of the myal-men . . . were very common." The behavior patterns of seizure, or spirit possession, stirring prayers and dancing were thus nothing more nor less than the surfacing of traditional African religion which had been suppressed for almost a century.

a. Pukumina and revivalism: Following the Great Revival several new religious developments occurred in Jamaica. The effects of the missionary message on African consciousness brought about the emergence of Afro-Christian cults with a strong millennial emphasis. First, there was Pukumina and other revival cults which grew out of the myal cult of the slave period; and, second, the native Baptist Church, basically Christian in ritual but with a strong millennial focus. An analysis of these cults will provide us with a glimpse into the nature of the Caribbean millennialism and set the stage for our study of similar movements in the United States.

Having discussed the salient African features of the beliefs and practices commonly found in Black cults in the Caribbean at this point, we need only give a description of Pukumina and the revival movement existing in Jamaica.

The word Pukumina is without doubt a corruption of the name of the old ancestor cult Kumina, or Cumina, a cult which can still be found in the parishes of St. Thomas and St. Mary. And Pukumina, in turn, has been further corrupted in Jamaica to Pocomania—"a little madness." The peculiar behavior of the cultists, their dancing, possession and speaking in unknown languages may appear to the outsider as a "slight case of madness"; yet it seems incontestable that the name of the cult, Pukumina, originated not in parody, but in the memory of Cumina, or ancestor possession.

Pukumina as we know it today has passed through many phases. At first it was the pure African ancestor cult which was practiced by the majority of Akan peoples who came to Jamaica during the period of slavery and went by the name Kumina. About the year 1760, when the African religion was proscribed by law, it went underground, but was revived about 1834, under the name of myalism, disguised as a witch-hunting cult. By this time, witchcraft had become so entrenched in the society that even the planters were in sympathy with any attempt to rid the society of it.

Myalism, as described by contemporary observers, appears to have been still quite African in all features. The Moravian missionary J. H. Buchner, writing from his own personal observations, gave the following description:

> As soon as darkness of evening set in, they assembled in crowds in open pastures, most frequently under *large cotton trees, which they worshipped, and counted holy;** after sacrificing some fowls, the leader began an extempore song, in a wild strain, which was answered in chorus; the dance followed, grew wilder and wilder, until they were in a state of excitement *bordering on madness.** Some would perform incredible revolutions while in this state, until, nearly exhausted, they fell senseless to the ground, when every word they uttered was received as a divine revelation. At other times, *Obeah** was discovered, or a "shadow" was caught; a little coffin being prepared in which it was to be enclosed and buried.[33]

The above quotation is by far the most helpful description of myalism to be found in print. It is therefore worth a few comments. The reference here to the "cotton tree" is important. In many parts of West Africa great religious significance is attached to certain trees. In Nigeria, the Baobab tree is still of great religious significance, and, in Ghana, it is the *"Nyame dua,"* the tree of God. Similar trees are to be found in the West Indies, and the African slaves appear to have attached their traditional religious beliefs to these. In Jamaica it is the silk-cotton tree, which grows to a tremendous size. For many Jamaicans, it remains a supernatural tree to this day. The writer was pleasantly surprised on a recent trip to Haiti to learn of the religious significance which the Haitians attach to the Mapu tree. When, on my request, this tree was pointed out, it turned out to be the same "silk-cotton tree" found in Jamaica. In Haiti, as in Jamaica, the peasant folk have an abnormal fear of this tree since it is believed to shelter the spirits of the dead. Very few Jamaicans or Haitians will ever take shelter under the silk-cotton tree.

The second important element in the above quotation is the reference to "sacrificing some fowls," for this points to another of the African elements in myalism. The sacrifice of fowl in a re-

* My italics.

ligious ceremony is essentially an African custom, but it can still be found in Cumina in Jamaica, Vodun in Haiti, Macumba in Brazil and others.

Third, the reference to singing is rather revealing: "the leader began an extempore song, in a wild strain, which was answered in chorus." Here we have the statement/response singing common to West Africa, a mode of singing still found in Jamaican Cumina songs, and Vodun ceremonies in Haiti. In fact, the statement/response pattern is the basic one for the Negro spirituals in the United States.

And the fourth point worthy of note in that quote from Buchner has to do with the "dance," which, as the most important element in myalism, led up to the moment of possession, when revelation occurred and/or the *obeah* was detected. Here we notice that Buchner himself refers to the myalism ritual as "a state of excitement *bordering on madness*"! This same attitude is surely what led later observers to think Pukumina was "Pocomania" or "a little madness."

A significant change occurred in Jamaican native religion soon after Buchner's observation, and this was the Great Revival mentioned above. The entire island experienced a spiritual awakening and the persisting African religion, being flexible, underwent a transformation as a result of it. It is during this period that the Christian elements now common in Pukumina and Revivalism were grafted on to African roots. The Christian God, angels, prophets and evangelists took precedence over the gods of Africa. The Bible became the magic book, and new types of Afro-Christian movements came into being. Myalism and Christianity when merged produced a variety of cult groups which can be described on a continuum from those basically African to those mostly Christian.

At present, there are two or three of these cults existent in Jamaica. The Pukumina group, which is basically African and so has a somewhat "shady" reputation among the upper classes; and the Revivalist group, which claims to be Christian, hence "good." Actually there is very little difference in their forms of organization, as the following summary will show.

1) In both Pukumina and the Revivalist groups, there are divisions known as "bands." A band is a collective of believers, men and women, who are under the leadership of a papi or a

mammi. Sometimes these cult officials are referred to as "shepherd" or "shepherdess." The leader has dictatorial powers over the band and is recognized as the one with the highest spiritual attainment. He acts as preacher, healer, judge, diviner and the one through whom important revelation is transmitted. Although his followers are "spirit-filled," their revelations are not thought to be genuine unless they are authenticated by the leader. The "band" contains many functionaries who assist the leader in ritual ceremonies. These assistants carry such titles as "captain," "lieutenant," and "armor-bearer," while the ordinary member is usually referred to as a soldier. Some bands bestow offices such as that of the "wheeling shepherd," who supervises the ritual dance during a service; or the "warrior," whose duty is to protect the band from intervention by evil spirits, or by persons who might disturb the smooth performance of a ceremony. There may also be a "water shepherd," whose duty it is to see that water is available at all times, for without the ritual role of water the spirits would have no pathway into the ceremony. The water shepherd is also prominent in the baptismal ceremony and heads the ritual processions to the sea or the river. In practice, there is no one hierarchy; each band has its own division of functionaries, which depends on its size and its overall organizational pattern.

2) A band is generally housed in a permanent compound, called a "yard." This area of ground is rather important to both Pukumina and Revival. It is a kind of "holy ground" to the cult. Every square inch of this compound is ritually sacred. It contains the tabernacle and, although the majority are small and poorly constructed shelters of wattle and mud, they can at times be elaborate church-type buildings with a seating capacity varying from twenty to two hundred. In the compound is also found the house of the shepherd and/or shepherdess or in some cases shelters for important functionaries. In addition there is usually a house for ritual baths in every compound. Yet far more important than any of these features are the ceremonial grounds which contain the "seal." The seal is the religious power-center and in the middle of it a pole is placed on which a flag or insignia of the band is hoisted. It is around this pole that dances take place. The location of the seal can be identified by ritual markings on the ground, which bear some similarity to the "vever" of Haitian Vodun, and can only be understood by those who are spiritually initiated. The

yard may contain other esoteric signs and subordinate seals for other kinds of rituals, but the great seal is clearly the most important. Among the various pieces of ritual equipment that can be found in a yard are white bottles, filled with water, and usually placed on raised wooden stands. It is through these that the sky spirits descend. There are also stones in assorted shapes and banners of red, white and blue in evidence. Among the other ceremonial objects are fowls and medicinal weeds. The fowls used in sacrifices are usually red, white and black but the most important fowl of a "yard" is the one known in Jamaica as "sénsé" and in Africa as "asense." This fowl is easily identified by the peculiar growth of its feathers, which curl toward its head, giving a fuzzy appearance. In Jamaica, as in Africa, it is used to detect witchcraft. This fowl is considered so sacred few people in Jamaica will eat the flesh or eggs. The medicinal weeds found about the yard are used for external purposes (ritual baths) as well as for internal consumption.

3) Common to both Pukumina and Revival is the ritual dance around the pole of the seal ground. This dance has varied purposes. It is, first of all, a process by which devotees strengthen their contact with the spirit world. But it is also the means by which problems are worked out, and the process by which spirit possession is induced. It is called by various names: "trumping," "laboring," or "travailing." The members form themselves in a circle and, with the rhythm of the drum, move in perfect time, counterclockwise around the pole. The dance is accompanied with a song. Any song will do, and the rhythm is accommodated to the song. The hands swing back and forth, the head bending always toward the center pole. As the rhythm increases in speed, the singing gives way to guttural sounds as air passes in and out of the lungs and throat. The mixture of these guttural expressions is harmonious to the ear, as it takes on a pure musical form with various tones. This exercise may continue for hours, as different musical airs are introduced to the same rhythm. Then, possession occurs. The devotees become unconscious; some may fall to the ground abruptly, while others fall into the hands of their comrades, and some simply run with closed eyes out into the yard. One or two may receive revelations of imminent deaths, earthquakes or hurricanes, and these are proclaimed on the spot. Some receive

a new song and sing it then and there; some receive answers to their deepest personal questions and experience tremendous relief and joy. Only to the outsider does the service appear to be a "slight case of madness."

4) Both Pukumina and Revival can be identified by their peculiar ritual dress. The colors red, white and blue are symbolic for these cults. Black is also used, but sparingly. Various meanings are given to these colors; for example, white is for purity and is probably the most popular color among the cultists. It is used for fasting ceremonies and especially for services which are conducted in the daytime. Red is said to stand for the blood of Christ, and is used in ceremonies connected with sorrow and problems. Blue is for perseverance, the spirit of the firmament, and is commonly used by the band on preaching missions. Black is death, evil and trouble and is used in divination and conjuring. The headdress of the cultists generally matches the dress, the size of the turban indicates the rank of the wearer. The turbans of the shepherd and the shepherdess are naturally the most elaborate. They can be done in a single color—red, white or blue—or in a combination of all three. The author has never seen a black turban or any combination of black with other colors used in a turban. As might be expected, the ritual garments of the cults are influenced by the vestments of the orthodox church prominent in the community. For example, in the areas where the Episcopal Church is dominant, both the dress and ritual of the cults will have a noticeable Episcopal flavor. One of the most progressive Jamaican cult groups observed by this writer is found in the hills of St. Andrew. The leader was originally a Catholic layman, and his church, vestments and rituals all have the appearance of the Catholic Church. The most common cult bands, however, follow the unstructured Baptist form of worship.

5) Both Pukumina and Revival bands have adapted the Christian Bible to their worship. The Old Testament prophets are given prominence in their preaching and of these, Isaiah, Jeremiah, Ezekiel, Jonah and Joel are the most favored. The Psalms also serve as important devotional readings in special worship situations, and in the New Testament, the Evangelists are frequently read. However, by far the most important New Testament Scripture is the Revelation of John, in which the angels play such a

prominent part. Angels are the message bearers in both cults, and
their names, especially Gabriel, Michael and Rutibel,* are to be
heard in all ceremonies. The cult services are always directed by
one or another of the angels. The Christian Bible is also used for
confirmation of dreams and visions. If a dream or vision is not
supported by Scripture (and a specific text is usually mentioned
in the vision itself), it is not considered true, but if a Scripture is
given, it is considered "sealed and signed." That is to say, the
message has divine approval.

6) Both cults practice Christian rituals such as baptism and the
Lord's Supper. Of the two, baptism is of the greatest importance
and preparation for this ritual is elaborate. The procession to the
sea or the river is planned with great care in order to draw the
attention of the community. In some areas of Jamaica it even
takes on a festive air. The Lord's Supper is also elaborate, the
altar of the tabernacle containing not only bread and wine, but
fruits of every kind, basins of water, flowers, sugarcane and candles of various colors.

7) Pukumina and Revivalism both practice the healing art. Both
use medicinal herbs, roots, water, powders and patent medicines
sold at drugstores. Both operate "balmyards," where the sick
receive herbal baths. It is often reported that in Pukumina the art
of witchcraft is practiced, while among the Revival bands it is not;
however, I am inclined to believe that both groups are adept at the
practice of obeah, even though it may be true that the practice is
more prevalent among the Pukuminas.

Contrary to the often repeated report that Pukumina and Revival
cults are dying out in Jamaica, as a result of a recent research
trip to the Caribbean, this writer is convinced that such reports
are incorrect. There are still many active branches of both cults
in the interior of the island; there are various healers and folk
doctors to be found in every country town. It is true that a part of
the native membership of the cults has transferred allegiance to
the various American pentecostal sects which now flourish in Jamaica, but still their influence remains strong. Pukumina and Revival remain the source of folk medicine and folk dance, which
of late has been given prominence in the Jamaican folk festivals.

* Rutibel is the messenger of evil. His origin is obscure. Other references
to him—see G. E. Simpson, "Jamaican Revivalist Cults," *Social and Economic Studies,* 5, no. 4 (Kingston: December 1956), p. 344.

Their dance movements have been choreographed by the brilliant Jamaican scholar and director of the National Dance Theatre Company, Rex Nettleford, through whose influence the Pukumina dance has now been introduced to a wide audience both in Jamaica and America.

Like Vodun in Haiti, Pukumina and Revival bands are becoming a tourist attraction. This I am afraid will affect the cult in urban areas, giving way to commercial performance—the process has already begun. Pukumina and Revival cults have never manifested revolutionary tendencies. They may more accurately be categorized as thaumaturgical-utopian cults, yet with an implicit militancy which was to manifest itself later in more radical groups such as the Rastafarians. The term "thaumaturgical" suggests that the cults' main emphasis has been magico-religious; they have turned to the powers of the supernatural to accomplish their ends, and are primarily concerned with the cure of illness, the placation of the spirits and the comforting of the aggrieved. They take great pride in protecting the individual from the hatred of other men by rooting out witchcraft, providing charms against evil spirits and relieving tensions said to be caused by the fear of obeah. They are adept at communication with the spirits of the dead and with angels, good and evil. These cults thus fill a special place in a society where deprivation and insecurity abound and their popularity increases with the degree of faith the community places in their ability to relieve these tensions. Faith in the movement increases with each demonstration of their ability to heal and to bring good luck to their followers.

The second term used in describing these cults—"utopian"—suggests a strong hope for a perfect society, at some future date, in which every institution is under the direct leadership of the supernatural. In short, utopian movements look forward to a reversal of the present situation, where the first shall be last and the last, first. It is generally thought that this will come about after the cataclysmic destruction of the wicked, which, in this case, means the rich, the oppressive rulers of the poor. Keeping within the utopian spirit, the Pukuminas and the Revivalists withdraw into small communities which are, among other things, prototypes of life in that ideal future time. They preach the imminent destruction of the world, and the coming of the "new world," the New Jerusalem. The classical example of such utopian fervor in Jamaica is to be found in the emergence of the Native Baptist Church, a group better known as the Bedwardites. Its importance demands a short analysis.

b. The Native Baptists: The Native Baptist Church is relevant to the theory of redemptive movements because it is the most dramatic movement of this kind to have emerged in Jamaica. Actually, very few Jamaicans are aware of the name Native Baptist, but that is only because the movement is better known as the Bedwardites, after the charismatic leader who played the starring role in this millenarian drama. Bedward was born of slave ancestry in the year 1859, and lived most of his life on the Mona Estate, the site of the present prestigious University of the West Indies, where buildings of the former estate can still be seen.

Bedward seemed to have been greatly influenced by the Great Revival and he probably was taken to some of the meetings by his parents. When the estate broke up, he traveled to Colón in Panama, where he received an urgent vision to return to Jamaica to save the souls of his countrymen. He was ordered by the spirit to fast three times weekly and during this period the gift of healing was given to him. Once in Jamaica again, he returned to his native village of August Town, adjacent to the Mona Estate, and in 1891 began his ministry. His fame as a speaker was unique and, had it not been for the peculiar African flavor of his church, he might have become one of the greatest preachers in the annals of Jamaican church history. Instead, he has come down to us only in folk history. Yet this is certainly not to say that his influence has diminished because of it. Unique to his ministry were the instances of healing using the water of the Mona River, which runs near his home. After achieving seven miraculous cures from the use of this water, his fame spread throughout the island. Thousands flocked to hear him, and to receive healing; some carried the water away to their homes in bottles and other contrived containers. But at this period in Jamaican history, such a charismatic figure was a threat to the government and they soon began to put pressure on Bedward.

Bedwardism rose to meet the challenge in a magico-religious way. The leading members began to dress in military fashion with white uniforms and bush hats, similar to those worn by white officials. They engaged in military processions with a peculiar strut and swinging of the hips which recalled the warlike stride of African warriors. But the high point of Bedwardite millenarianism came when Bedward declared himself the incarnate Christ on earth, and declared that he, with his followers, would ascend to heaven for a while, during which time Jamaica and the world would be renovated. Only then would he and his disciples return to rule in the new kingdom.

Martha Beckwith, the American anthropologist who was in Jamaica a few days before the projected flight to heaven, gave us the following report:

> It was on the morning of December 26, 1920, that I visited Bedward at August Town. This was a critical time for the Bedwardists because their leader had predicted his own ascension into heaven on the last day of December of that very year, the destruction of the whites, and the reign of Bedwardism on the earth. The faithful were, I think, expected to accompany their leader into heaven, for they were all selling or giving away their property and gathering in response to his call to August Town. In Kingston the wildest rumors were afloat. Even the intelligent whites believed that something out of the ordinary was about to happen; they, too, were hypnotized by the man's enormous conviction. . . . some feared a Negro uprising. Even the educated colored were not without interest; one spoke of another Christmas day and of another prophet who was to the wise foolishness but whom the common people had heard gladly. . . .[34]

The charisma of Bedward was not only felt in Kingston, but over the entire island and even across the sea. The Jamaican *Daily Gleaner,* on the last days of December 1920, carried many articles reflecting the general pitch of excitement created by Bedward. We quote only one of them.

> Yesterday there was great excitement at the railway. Every train brought in a large number of people, men, women, and children all bound for August Town. But they came from Colón [Panama] as well, on a steamer travelling across the sea to see their "Lord of August Town" ascend. In King Street all tram-cars travelling to Hope Gardens were besieged by men, women, and children, some infants in arms, others hardly able to help themselves, but they were all bundling in with their clothes, baskets and fowls. All have sold out to come up and see their Lord and master do the disappearing trick. There are more to come. . . .[35]

Surprisingly, Beckwith is the only person to leave us a physical description of Bedward.

He was a large fine looking Negro with a rapt brightness on his face of a visionary clouded by the peevishness of accustomed tyranny. I looked into his face in vain for any trace of an imposter. All was gentle, even reasonably spoken except for that moment of pettishness about his identity with the Lord.[36]

What finally happened in this drama appears to be the common fate of the leaders of this kind of movement the world over. *The Gleaner* of December 31, 1920, gives the following report.

Bedward sat in this chair in a white robe and turban. He postponed his flight from 10 in the morning until 12, and from 12 until 3, and from 3 until 10. Finally he told the five thousand white-dressed followers who were with him that he had received word from the Almighty that he should postpone the Ascension until the end of the [next] year. . . . Then he ordered the people to return to their homes. He was arrested on a lunacy charge, convicted, and sent to the Asylum.[37]

Bedward died in 1930, nine years after he was committed to the asylum. His movement, although greatly diminished in numbers and influence, continues to the present day; his name and his activities linger on in Jamaican folklore.

The Bedwardite movement gives us many insights into the nature of the Afro-Christian cults in the Caribbean and the New World. Here we may point out a few of them by way of summary. First, there is a strong belief in dreams and visions and spirit communications. Second, there is the powerful role of the charismatic leader, who, whether man or a woman, seldom has his spiritual guidance questioned. Third, there is a firm belief in healing, either by water or herbal medicine. Fourth, there is the notion of the cataclysmic breaking up of the old world order, which, if it does not bring total destruction, will, by a kind of table-turning, make slaves out of the masters and vice versa. In other words, the meek shall inherit the earth, and those who are first shall be last. A fifth characteristic of the Afro-Christian cult, especially as seen in Bedwardism, is the latent militancy. It is this which comes to the fore in the revolutionary cults which will be taken up in the closing chapters.

Of course Caribbean, or specifically Jamaican, cultism is only one aspect of that redemption dynamic which characterized the African spirit in diaspora. This never-ending drive to rid themselves of New World bondage found expression in various ways from collective violence to the dependence on psychic forces, to millenarian dreams, to the open militancy of our present-day Black Power movements. To the wider society, these quests for freedom have been viewed from various points of view. From the point of view of the slave master, the redemption dynamic was simply a continuous manifestation of the savage nature of the Africans and of their intention to destroy the civilizing influence of a superior race. To present-day society, such feelings on the part of the Black man are often viewed as the corrupting influence of the communist world, in one more attempt to destroy Christianity and capitalism. To the Africans and their descendants, however, it is nothing but the righteous cause of a people to rid themselves of imposed bondage.

SOUL AWAKENING:
The Garvey Movement

A. The Man:

As children of captivity we look forward to a new, yet ever old, land of our fathers, the land of God's crowning glory. We shall gather together our children, our treasures and our loved ones, and, as the children of Israel, by the command of God, face the promised land, so in time we shall also stretch forth our hands and bless our country.[1]

Thus spoke Garvey, the founder of the Back-to-Africa movement and one of the greatest leaders of Black Americans. A man who envisioned a mass repatriation of the Black man to his homeland, Africa. This vision was his driving mission until his death in 1946. His tremendous energy was all channeled into this movement and, between 1920 and 1924, it became the dynamic Black movement not only in the United States but also in South and Central America, and the islands of the Caribbean—its influence even spread to Africa.

Garvey was born in Jamaica on August 17, 1887, in the garden parish of St. Ann. His father was a Maroon, and traced his lineage to those early freedom fighters in Jamaican history who had stood up against the British Army for nearly a century and then finally won their independence in 1739. Marcus Garvey in his youth must have heard the stories of great Maroon heroes such as Quaco, Cudjoe and Champong Nannie, as well as those of the rebels

Three-Finger Jack, Paul Bogle and William Gordon, all of them
the honored heroes of the Black man's struggle against white enslavement. He grew up knowing that his father bore the proud
Ashanti blood in his veins. His mother, as Garvey portrayed her,
was the direct opposite of his father, "a sober conscientious Christian, too soft and good for the time in which she lived."

In Jamaica, young Garvey spent his youth like most Jamaicans,
playing with other boys and girls in his neighborhood, paying no
attention to color. The whites in St. Ann's Bay were mainly children
of missionaries and landed gentry, but he never seemed to note
the difference until he was about fourteen years old. The incident
that brought this new awareness was the departure for England of
the white minister's daughter with whom he had a boyhood relationship. She was told not to keep in touch with Garvey because
he was a "nigger." Garvey never forgot this incident. He began to
observe Jamaican society and was disturbed at the privilege shown
to boys of white or near-white parentage. They were given preparation for government posts, being sent either to the few prestigious schools in Jamaica or to England to study. In contrast, the
blacker boys were given menial trades as laborers on the large
plantations, or in a few cases, when they were especially bright,
they became teachers in government and private schools.

As a boy, Marcus Garvey was strong-willed. He hated defeat
and as he later said in his autobiography: "It annoys me to be
defeated; hence to me, to be once defeated is to find cause for an
everlasting struggle to reach the top."[2] Thus when, at an early
age, he decided on the printing trade, he naturally went on to become one of the best in that business. When Garvey left St. Ann's
for Kingston and became a foreman in one of the large printing
companies, he soon became interested in public life, and engaged
in barbershop politics, which was about the extent of political
consciousness in Jamaica during his day. Observing the plight of
Black Jamaicans, he became thoroughly dissatisfied with their conditions and soon was even more involved in civic affairs. He developed an urge to perfect his speaking ability and so visited the
churches in Kingston, observing the most effective pulpit orators
of his day. At home he practiced various gestures in front of the
mirror while reading from schoolbooks, and became so advanced
in oratory that he organized the first classes in elocution in

Kingston. This training was to be invaluable for his success as a
Black leader.

By 1910, Garvey felt the need for further self-expression and
started a periodical known as Garvey's *Watchman*. Although this
seems to have had no lasting success, he later helped to set up one
of the first political organizations in Jamaica, The National Club,
and assisted in the editing of a periodical called *Our Own*. But his
eyes and heart were on more dramatic adventures, and so in 1912,
when Garvey found himself in a position to travel, he decided to
observe the conditions of the Black man in other parts of the
West Indies and in South America. He later visited England as well.
In these countries he found that the same conditions of deprivation
and disenfranchisement prevailed among the Blacks. In England,
he learned about Africa and its people, its ancient history and its
economic potential, and here he also heard about the exploitation
of Africa by the Europeans. He met West Indian soldiers returning from the Ashanti War, and learned of the atrocities the British
perpetrated on the land of his forefathers. Garvey pondered these
things and wondered how long this deception could continue.
The call suddenly seized him and in his own words he recorded
his experience as follows:

> I went travelling in South America and other parts of the West
> Indies to find out if it was so elsewhere, and found the same
> situation. I set sail for Europe to find out if it were different
> there, and again I found the stumbling block—"You are
> black." I read the conditions in America. I read *Up From
> Slavery* by Booker T. Washington . . . I asked: "Where
> is the Black man's king and kingdom?" "Where is his Presi-
> dent, his country, his ambassador, his army, his navy, his men
> of big affairs?" I could not find them and I declared, *I will
> help to make them.*[3]

He continues:

> My young and ambitious mind led me into flights of great
> imaginations. I saw before me then, as I do now, a new world
> of Black men, not peons, serfs, dogs and slaves, but a nation
> of sturdy men making their impress upon civilization and
> causing a new light to dawn upon the human race . . . My
> brain was afire. There was a world of thought to conquer. I
> had to start ere it became too late and the work be not
> done.[4]

Here then, in London, in 1912, a Black charismatic leader emerged, and he was only twenty-seven years of age. Marcus Garvey wasted no time, he immediately took ship for Jamaica and arrived in Kingston on July 15, 1914. Five days after his arrival he organized the Universal Negro Improvement Association and African Communities (Imperial) League.[5] The aim of the movement as he conceived it then was to *unite* "all the Negro peoples of the world into one great body to establish a country and government absolutely their own." The name of the movement had been revealed in a vision. He relates:

> At midnight, lying flat on my back, the vision and thought came to me that I should name the organization the Universal Negro Improvement Association and African Communities (Imperial) League. Such a name I thought would embrace the purpose of all black humanity. Thus to the world a name was born, a movement created, a man became known.[6]

Because of the social division in Jamaica, the Universal Negro Improvement Association appealed only to the common man. The Jamaican elite rejected it with hostility. The word "Negro" as a part of the movement's name was an insult to all the middle-class Jamaicans, who would never refer to themselves by such a term. This word was reserved for the poor masses of society and was extremely distasteful to the Black-English gentlemen of that period. In those days, the average Jamaican with the slightest shade of pink considered himself to be white. To them, blackness was degradation and so naturally Black leadership was looked upon with disdain. So it is no surprise to learn that the Garvey movement drew little support from the middle and upper classes of Jamaicans, but rather garnered its numbers from the masses, the lower working class, who, then as now, formed the overwhelming majority. It is paradoxical that the greatest encouragement to Garvey in his fight to lift up his people came, not from the Black elite, but from a small group of the white ruling class, including the governor and the colonial secretary of that period and some of the former members of the planter class.[7]

Despite this initial rebuff by the Black elite, Garvey and his association established a hold on the masses, and in a short while, Garvey had established himself as a leader of, and an inspiration for, a Black consciousness unheard of in the island before his time.

It is reported that thousands went to hear him at Edelweis Park, and hundreds of these became his followers. These Jamaican followers, some of whom were later to precede Garvey to the United States and become the early nucleus of his American group, saw in him the great hope of immediate redemption from colonial oppression.

With the nucleus of the Jamaican movement established, Garvey, the man of action, began to look about for ways and means to extend his vision and broaden his organization. His thoughts turned to America, to the man whose work he greatly admired, Booker T. Washington, who was then at Tuskegee Institute in Alabama. It was Washington's book *Up From Slavery* that precipitated the moment of decision to become a race leader. Marcus Garvey felt that such a man could not only aid his project in Jamaica, but could also give him an introduction to a wider Black community. In a letter addressed to Booker T. Washington, he explained his plan and was invited to the United States. No one can envision what the future of the Garvey movement might have been had he actually met Booker T. Washington, for the philosophies of the two men on racial matters were miles apart. Washington died in the fall of 1915, and Marcus Garvey did not arrive in the United States until March 23, 1916.[8] Garvey's arrival in New York City at that point was auspicious: the death of Washington, the great compromiser, left the mass of American Negroes without a leader. And the few intellectual Negroes had become more and more disenchanted with the "Tuskegee machine" anyway and had vigorously denounced the leadership of Washington. The most prominent among Washington's critics was the brilliant scholar W. E. B. Du Bois, then head of the NAACP, whose main interest lay in putting the Negro case before the American white conscience by means of his gifted pen. Still, there was no Negro intellectual from the United States really capable of controlling and using the great tide of social change about to sweep the American scene.

Thousands of Blacks were in uniform fighting for democracy abroad; and thousands were on the march from the Southland, their traditional home, to fill the empty benches on the industrial front in the northeastern cities. Yet the racial situation in the United States was as wretched as ever. Between 1910 and 1916, there was an average of seventy lynchings a year. When the Negroes moved

in any significant numbers into the cities of the North, they met
with hostility which led, in many cases, to open race riots. Despite
the Negro's attempt at being a part of the United States, contributing his due share to the country's growth, he suffered from
every kind of discrimination.[9]

Returning to Garvey: his first duty on arriving in the United
States was to visit Black leaders and observe their programs for the
improvement of the Black's situation. He was shocked to find that
none of them had a true picture of the suffering of the masses of
their people. It also surprised him to see that most of the Negro
leaders were mere opportunists, dependent on white support, and
accomplishing little more than preserving the status quo. None
of them really looked for the future independence of the Black
community. After an extensive trip through thirty-eight different
states, Garvey decided that a program such as he had developed in
the UNIA was necessary in the United States. Returning to New
York, he organized a branch of the UNIA in 1916, and had fully
decided to return to Jamaica to carry on his work as head of
the movement from there.[10] But this was not to be. The new
branch established in Harlem enlisted about a thousand members,
but no sooner had the movement been established than a power
struggle broke out.[11] The Harlem politicians wanted to use it as
a political club to promote their own careers, but Garvey objected,
and finally the movement was reduced to only about fifty members.
He was able to rejuvenate the UNIA within a two-month period,
but, not being an American citizen, he was blocked from actually
assuming its leadership. He did finally become the president of
the organization but only after great difficulty. However, by June
1919, he was claiming a membership of over a million both in
and outside the United States.[12] It will be of interest at this point
to observe some of the highlights of Garvey's movement.

B. The Movement:

When viewed in the context of social movements, the UNIA was
highly practical in some aspects and highly utopian in others.
Working under Garvey's motto "One God! One aim! One destiny!"
the objectives of the association were: (1) to establish a universal
confraternity among the members of the Black race; (2) to assist
in civilizing the backward tribes of Africa; (3) to develop independent Negro nations and communities and a central nation for
the race; (4) to establish Negro representation in the principal

countries and cities of the world; (5) to promote conscientious spiritual worship among the tribes of Africa; (6) to establish educational institutions for the racial education of the Black people; and (7) to work for better conditions of Negroes everywhere.[13]

Obviously the aims of this movement were far-reaching. Let us look at them more closely. First all, they were universal in scope; not just the Negroes of the United States, but all Black men everywhere were the objects of their efforts. Further, they aimed at reestablishing Africa for Africans, and this was practically an obsession with Garvey. "Africa must be free" was an ever-recurring statement in his speeches. He saw the independence of Africa as a prerequisite for the dignity of Black men all over the world and it was his belief that American Negroes and Negroes of the West should help in bringing this into being. Yet, even though the movement was separatist in orientation, it was to be devoid of bigotry in that it held to the doctrine of the brotherhood of man and the fatherhood of God. The rights of all men were to be respected, but this, of course, included the right of the Black man to claim his homeland, Africa. Not only political, the UNIA was also a spiritual movement. Its motto confesses "One God," the nature of whom was never actually made clear by Garvey, but all signs point to a Black God—the God of Ethiopia. On several occasions members pressed Garvey to be more precise about this God, but he remained noncommittal. At least in one place in his writings a Black God is referred to, and once, in discussing religion at the International Convention in Jamaica, he seemed to imply that the Son of God came from Africa and not Palestine. The motto confesses "One aim," and this is clearer. It can only mean the improvement of the life of the Negro race. This is made explicit in the title page of his newspaper *The Negro World,* which reads: "A newspaper devoted solely to the interest of the Negro Race." Finally, the motto aims at "One destiny," which could only mean the ultimate repatriation of the Black man to his African homeland. If the aims and objectives of the Garvey movement were innovative, the social philosophy on which they were based was equally surprising. The constitution of the UNIA states:

> The Universal Negro Improvement Association advocates the uniting and blending of all Negroes into one strong healthy race. It is against miscegenation and race suicide. It believes

that the Negro race is as good as any other, and therefore
should be as proud of itself as others are. It believes in the
purity of the Negro race and the purity of the white race. It is
against rich blacks marrying poor whites. It is against rich
and poor whites taking advantage of Negro women. . . . It
believes in the social and political, physical separation of all
peoples to the extent that they promote their own ideals and
civilization, with the privilege of trading and doing business
with each other. It believes in the promotion of a strong and
powerful Negro Nation in Africa. It believes in the rights of all
men.[14]

Marcus Garvey was not only a realist as the above quotation
shows, but a man with an acute prophetic vision. He foresaw the
gradual diminution of the Negro blood and its absorption into the
lifestream of the white race. He therefore detested miscegenation
and advocated racial purity. Garvey wanted Black separatism, not
in the sense of a nation within a nation as the Black Muslims are
now advocating, but a total geographical separation of Negroes
from this continent. Garvey wanted the Blacks to return to Africa,
where they could develop a culture of their own with a political
and economic base strong enough to compete with other nations
if they cared to do so. It was only on this basis that Garvey believed
the Black man could become a dignified person.

In the light of the above discussion it is instructive to compare
Garvey with Theodor Herzl, the Zionist visionary of the late nineteenth century, since there is some question of Garvey having been
influenced by him. Herzl found the Jews in a situation similar to
that of the Negro; they were peoples in diaspora. It was the vision
of Herzl that the Jewish problem could never be solved until the
Jews regained their homeland and revived their ancient culture.
His famous book *The Jewish State* became the blueprint of the
New Israel. He states: "We are a people—one people."

We have honestly endeavored everywhere to merge ourselves
in the social life of the surrounding communities and to preserve the faith of our fathers. We are not permitted to do so.
In vain are we loyal patriots, our loyalties in some places
running to the extremes; in vain do we strive to increase the
fame of our native land in science and art, or by wealth in
trade and commerce. In countries where we have lived for
centuries, we are still cried down as strangers, and often by

those whose ancestors were not yet domiciled in the land where Jews had already had experience of suffering.

No one can deny the gravity of the situation of the Jews. Wherever they live in perceptible numbers, they are more or less persecuted. Their equality before the law granted by statute, has become a deadletter. . . . They are debarred from filling even moderately high positions, either in the army or in public or private capacity.[15]

Herzl goes on to enumerate further indignities suffered by Jews: attacks in parliaments, in assemblies, in the press, in the pulpit, in the streets and on journeys, expulsion from certain hotels and places of recreation.

Is it not true that in countries where we live in perceptible numbers, the position of Jewish lawyers, doctors, technicians, teachers and employees of all descriptions becomes daily more intolerable? Is it not true that the Jewish middle class are seriously threatened? Is it not true, that the passions of the mob are incited against our wealthy? Is it not true, that our poor endure greater sufferings than any other proletariat? I think that this external pressure makes itself felt everywhere. In our economically upperclasses it causes discomfort, in our middle classes continual and grave anxieties, in our lower classes absolute despair.[16]

He concludes: "Everything tends in fact to one and the same conclusion, which is clearly enunciated in that classic Berlin phrase: 'Juden Raus! [Out with the Jews].' "[17] His question was picked up by the persecuted people of his race all over the world. "Are we to 'get out' now and where to? or, are we yet to remain? and how long?"[18]

Let us compare Garvey's assessment of the Black situation with that of Herzl. In the constitution of the UNIA we read:

We complain that nowhere in the world, with few exceptions, are black men accorded equal treatment with white men, although in the same situation and circumstances, but, on the contrary are discriminated against and denied the common rights due to human beings for no other reason than their race and color. We are not willingly accepted as guests in public hotels and inns of the world for no other reason than our race and color. . . . The physicians of our race are denied the right to attend their patients while in the public

hospitals of the cities and states where they reside in certain
parts of the United States . . . We are discriminated against
and denied an equal chance to earn wages for the support of
our families, and in many instances are refused admissions
into labor unions, and nearly everywhere are paid smaller
wages than white men. . . . In Civil Service and departmen-
tal offices we are everywhere discriminated against and made
to feel that to be a black man in Europe, America and the
West Indies is equivalent to being an outcast and a leper
among the races of men, no matter what the character and
attainments of the black man may be. . . . Against all such
inhuman, unchristian, and uncivilized treatment we here and
now emphatically protest, and invoke the condemnation of
all mankind.[19]

The Garvey movement has often been referred to as Black Zion-
ism because the Negro problem was so similar to that of the Jews.
The scene from which Herzl viewed the Jewish problems was
Europe; the scene for Garvey was America. The places were different but the conditions suffered by the people were the same.
In Herzl's case his vision bore fruit; in Garvey's case it was aborted
by the American system. Thousands of people caught the vision
of Herzl and rallied behind his cause; and, with the help of sympathetic nations, though not without heartaches and disappointment,
that vision became a reality. On the other hand, while thousands
of people also rallied to the banner of Garvey, the nations decried
his effort as impractical, fantastic and the idle dream of a Negro
fanatic. Garvey and Herzl were men of rare insight. A. Jacques
Garvey (Garvey's second wife) speaking to this point said of charismatic leaders:

Heredity and environment seem to influence them, and use
them to carry out a spiritual urge in a given line—an experi-
ment, a mission or a task—they seem to have a supreme
purpose in life, and once started, even against personal interest they will not give up. They are, as it were, impelled to
go on even to death.[20]

An analysis of Garveyism reveals that the present-day protest
has not advanced in any appreciable way beyond his demands.
The call for racial autonomy, vocalized in the demands of the Black
Power movement today, was characteristic of Garvey. And his
call to ignore laws that are "especially directed towards the Ne-

groes" was one of the mainstays of Martin Luther King's philosophy. Garvey's demand for the teaching of Black history is being re-echoed by Blacks all over the United States. Garvey probably was the first to demand that the word "Negro" be capitalized, and his insistence on respect for Negro women has had a new flowering in the Black Muslim movement, whose present leader was, himself, a Garveyite. Garvey's emphasis on African repatriation is still supported by many Negro leaders at the present time and the Black Muslim demand for separate Black states is but a variation on the most basic theme of the Garvey movement.

The appeal of Garvey was to the common man and especially to the darker Negroes. He exalted everything Black. To him Blackness stood for strength and beauty, an idea which, in Garvey's day, was new in Harlem and the Black community in general. At that time prestige was attached to the "light and the near white." Thus, in Harlem, where he expounded this theme, thousands of Black men and women listened with attention and thousands joined the Jamaican prophet. So powerful was this message that the Blacks from Canada to Florida joined ranks to form the greatest Black mass movement ever seen in American history.

However, the Negro intellectuals and preachers were soon to draw swords with Garvey. They would have nothing to do with the movement and only an occasional figure among them spoke on its behalf. However, the Black sociologist E. Franklin Frazier did see the importance of the movement and wrote an acute analysis of the reasons for its success. Under the caption: "Marcus Garvey: Mass Leader," he wrote the following in the *New York Nation,* August 26, 1926.

> The Garvey movement is a crowd movement essentially different from any other social phenomenon among Negroes. For the most part American Negroes have sought self-magnification in fraternal orders and churches. But these organizations have failed to give support to the Negro ego-consciousness which the white masses find in membership in a political community, or on a smaller scale in Kiwanis clubs and the KKK. In a certain sense Garvey's followers form the black klan of America.
>
> The reason for Garvey's success in welding the Negroes into a crowd movement becomes apparent, when we compare his methods and aims with those of other leaders. Take for

example the leadership of Booker T. Washington. Washington could not be considered a leader of the masses of Negroes, for his program commended itself chiefly to white people and those Negroes who prided themselves on their opportunism. There was nothing popularly heroic or inspiring in his program, to captivate the imagination of the average Negro. In fact the Negro was admonished to play an inglorious role. Certain other outstanding efforts among Negroes have failed to attract the masses because they have lacked the characteristics which have distinguished the Garvey movement. It is only necessary to mention such an organization as the national Urban League and its leadership to realize that so reasoned a program of social adjustment, is lacking in everything that appealed to the crowd.

The leadership of Dr. Du Bois has been too intellectual to satisfy the mob. Even his glorification of the Negro has been in terms which escaped the black masses. The Pan-African Congress which he has promoted, while supporting to some extent the boasted aims of Garvey, has failed to stir any considerable number of American Negroes.

The National Association for the Advancement of Colored People which has fought uncompromisingly for equality for the Negro, has never secured, except locally and occasionally, the support of the masses. It has lacked the dramatic element . . . Garvey came to America at a time when all groups were asserting themselves. (Many American Negroes have belittled his influence on the grounds that he is a West Indian. The truth is that Garvey aroused the Negroes of Georgia as much as those of New York, except when the black preacher discouraged anything that threatened his income or where white domination smothered every earthly hope. Moreover, this prejudice against the West Indian Negro loses sight of the contribution of the West Indian to the American Negro. The West Indian who has been ruled by a small minority instead of being oppressed by a majority is more worldly in outlook. He has been successful in business.) By his example he has given the American Negro an earthly goal. Garvey went even further. He not only promised the despised Negro a paradise on earth, but made the Negro an important person in his immediate environment. He invented honors and social distinctions and converted every social invention to his use in his effort to make his followers feel important. While every one was not a "knight" or "sir" all his followers were fellow-

men of the "Negro race." Even more concrete distinction
was open to all. The women were organized in Black Cross
Nurses—and the men became uniformed members of the vanguard of the Great African Army. (A uniformed member of a
Negro lodge paled in significance beside a soldier of the army
of Africa.) A Negro might be a porter during the day, taking
his orders from white men, but he was an officer of the Black
Army when it assembled at Liberty Hall. Many a Negro went
about singing in his heart that he was a member of the great
army marching to the "heights of achievements". . . . A
closer examination of ideals and symbols which Garvey always
held up before his followers shows his mastery of the technique of creating and holding crowds. The Negro group becomes idealized. Therefore he declares he is as strongly
against race-mixture as a KuKluxer. He believes in a pure
black race just as all self-respecting whites believe in a pure
white race.

Garvey gave the crowd that followed him victims to vent
their spleen upon, just as the evangelical turns the hatred
of his followers upon the devil—Every rabble must have someone to blame for its woes. . . . Therefore Garvey was always
attributing the misfortunes of the Negro group to traitors and
enemies. Although the identity of those *traitors* and *enemies*
was often obscure, as a rule they turned out to be Negro
intellectuals.

The magic hold of Garvey on the people came, as we have seen
from the above quotation, from his movement's ideals, symbols,
slogans, ceremonials and the promise of a new life. These are
important characteristics of a true mass movement, and their ma-
nipulations—the key to the success of charismatic leadership.

The movement reached its zenith in 1920, when the first international convention was held in New York City at Liberty Hall,
then the Garvey headquarters in Harlem. Garvey announced that
this would be the greatest gathering of Black people in the history
of the race. Delegates from all over were to attend and to report
on the worldwide conditions of the Negro people. "As the date
approached," according to one reliable source, "the colored world
was aroused to a fever pitch of excitement."[21]

It was in this convention that the Declaration of Rights was to
be drawn up and sent to all the governments of the world. But the
convention was also intended for another purpose: to make a

public show of the strength of the movement. Cronon observes that it was such a magnificent affair that even Harlem, a place long accustomed to the spectacular, found it an extravaganza not soon to be forgotten, and for the first time white America began to take notice of Marcus Garvey.

> Harlem streets rang with stirring martial airs, and the measured tramp of smartly uniformed marching bands. . . . The magic of Garvey's spell and the power of his organizational ability were never better demonstrated than at this first great international convention. Throughout the Black world people were stirred to a sense of their power and destiny by a fierce nationalism that pervaded every activity of the gathering.[22]

This convention was enough proof of Garvey's charisma and it placed him in the forefront of Black leadership.

Yet the convention was more than parades and spectacles; it also had deeply religious overtones. This aspect of the Garvey movement is rarely emphasized, and that is hard to understand because actually the religious dimension was the most important part. The UNIA was a mixture of high-church, Baptist and African festivals. The meeting was opened with a regular high-church ritual with litanies, Scriptures and prayers. One can only imagine the spiritual fervor that was established by the first hymn:

> God of the right our battles fight,
> Be with us as of yore,
> Break down the barriers of might
> we reverently implore.
>
> Stand with us in our struggles for
> The triumph of the right
> And spread confusion ever o'er
> The advocates of might.
>
> And let them know that righteousness
> Is mightier than sin,
> That might is only selfishness
> And cannot, ought not, win.
>
> Endow us Lord, with faith and grace
> And courage to endure
> The wrongs we suffer here apace
> And bless us ever more.[23]

The convention ended with the song that became an inseparable part of every UNIA meeting:

> God bless our president
> Father of all creation
> Allah Omnipotent
> Supreme o'er every nation
> God bless our President.[24]

The president, of course, referred to Garvey. During the convention, various groups within the UNIA appeared publicly in Harlem for the first time. The African Legion, the Black Cross Nurses and the Juveniles marched down Lenox Avenue and brought business activities to a standstill. In the evening, Garvey addressed his delegates in Madison Square Garden and that is said to have been one of the largest gatherings in the history of the hall—25,000 strong.[25]

In his presidential address, Garvey timed his words not only to suit the occasion but to set the tone for all subsequent speeches delivered as leader. He knew that if he failed to establish himself then and there as the great Messiah, it would be disastrous for him as a leader. Every word was chosen to instill that hope which is the lifeblood of messianic movements.

> We shall now organize the 400,000,000 Negroes of the world into a vast organization to plant the banner of freedom on the great continent of Africa. . . . We shall ask, demand, expect of the world a free Africa. . . . We say it, we mean it. . . . The other races have countries of their own and it is time for the 400,000,000 Negroes to claim Africa for themselves. . . . We are striking homewards toward Africa to make her the big black republic. . . . We are out to get what has belonged to us politically, socially, economically, and in every way. And what 15,000,000 of us cannot get, we will call 400,000,000 to help us get.[26]

Like the typical mass leader, Garvey had skill in portraying his dreams in symbolic language. The ability to use words is one of the indispensable means of power; it is characteristic of mass leaders, and Marcus Garvey had that ability not only in speaking but also in his writing. On this point Eric Hoffer observed that:

> The readying of the ground for a mass movement is done best by men whose chief claim to excellence is their skill in the use of the spoken and written word: that the hatching

of an actual movement requires the temperament and talents of the fanatic: and the final consolidation of the movement is largely the work of practical men of action.[27]

One of the main downfalls of the movement, as we will later see, was Garvey's effort to fulfill both roles, that of the visionary *and* the practical organizer. This was a mistake. Garvey was a dreamer, an idealist, a prophet, a man of charisma; the routinization of the movement needed more level-headed men to carry out those dreams. The prophet or the messianic leader, by nature, is scarcely prepared for day-to-day routine. But in the matter of *words,* it cannot be contested: Garvey had no equal until the time of Martin Luther King, Jr.

In the second great convention at Liberty Hall, New York City, Marcus Garvey's keynote speech contained some of his most classic statements:

The enemy may argue with you and show you the impossibility of a free and redeemed Africa, but I want you to take as your argument the thirteen colonies of America, that once owed their sovereignty to Great Britain, that sovereignty has been destroyed to make a United States of America. George Washington was not God Almighty. He was a man like any Negro in this building, and if he and his associates were able to make a free America, we too can make a free Africa. I prefer to die at this moment rather than not to work for the freedom of Africa. If liberty is good for certain sets of humanity it is good for all. Black men, colored men, Negroes have as much right to be free as any other race that God Almighty ever created . . .[28]

On another occasion he declared:

Our cause is based upon righteousness. And anything that is not righteous we have no respect for, because God Almighty is our leader and Jesus Christ our standard bearer. We rely on them on that kind leadership that will make us free, for it is the same God who inspired the Psalmist to write "Princes shall come out of Egypt and Ethiopia shall stretch out her hands unto God." At this moment . . . methinks I see the Angel of God taking up the standard of the Red, the Black and the Green, and saying "Men of the Negro Race, Men of Ethiopia, follow me. . . ."

It falls our lot to tear off the shackles that bind Mother

Africa. Can you do it? . . . You did it in the Civil War; you did it at the Battle of Marne and Verdun; You did it in Mesopotamia. You can do it marching up the battle heights of Africa. Let the world know that 400,000,000 Negroes are prepared to die or live as free men. Despise us as much as you care. Ignore us as much as you care. We are coming 400,000,000 strong. . . . My bulwark of strength in the conflict for freedom in Africa, will be of the three hundred years of persecution and hardship left behind in this Western Hemisphere. The more I remember the suffering of my forefathers, the more I remember the lynchings and burnings in the Southern States of America, the more I will fight on even though the battle seems doubtful. Tell me that I must turn back, and I laugh you to scorn. Go on! Go on! Climb ye the heights of liberty and cease not in well doing until you have planted the banner of the Red, the Black and the Green on the hilltops of Africa.[29]

In yet another speech delivered at Madison Square Garden, this one in March 1924, Garvey declared:

We should like to see a peaceful, prosperous and progressive white race in America and Europe; a peaceful, progressive and prosperous yellow race in Asia, and in like manner, we want and we demand, a peaceful, prosperous and progressive black race in Africa. . . .

Our desire is for a place in the world; not to disturb the tranquillity of other men, but to lay down our burden and rest our weary backs and feet by the banks of the Niger, and sing our songs and chant our hymns to the God of Ethiopia. Yes, we want to rest from the toil of centuries, rest of political freedom, rest of economic and industrial liberty, rest to be socially free and unmolested, rest from lynching and burning, rest from discrimination of all kinds.[30]

But words were not the only asset of Garveyism and Garvey himself was well aware of the fact that words alone could not hold his people together. He had to turn words into deeds. There had to be a practical program. In the prophetic moment of Garvey's dream, he asked himself these questions, "where is the Black man's government? where is his king and kingdom? . . . his army, his navy, his men of affairs?" Garvey wanted to make Negroes not only consumers, but producers. Thus the UNIA was intended not

just as another mass movement; it was actually a pilot project for
greater days in the Empire of Africa. Once the hope of repatriation
was firmly implanted, Garvey turned his attention to actually
creating a navy. In this "adventure" Garvey's daring as a mass
leader reached its zenith, for during that period, even a small nation hesitated to build up its maritime forces. But Garvey was not
an ordinary man: he was a man of dreams, fantastic dreams,
gigantic and spectacular dreams; a rare man indeed. Once committed to an idea, Garvey would not stop. No Black navy was sail-
ing the seas, so it seemed imperative to Garvey that the Black man
quickly find his place in the history books of maritime literature.
The Black Star Line became a reality in 1919, flying the Garveyite
colors of the red, black and green.[31] It was to be "a direct line
of steamships, owned, controlled and manned by Negroes to reach
the Negro peoples of the world." The plan was evident. The ships
were for the eventual repatriation of Negroes to their homeland.
The first of the line was the S.S. *Yarmouth,* later re-christened
S.S. *Frederick Douglass,* which was bought at the staggering sum
of $165,000. The second was an excursion ship, the S.S. *Shady-
side,* purchased at the cost of $35,000; the third was the S.S.
Kanawha, at the cost of $60,000, later re-christened S.S. *Antonio
Maceo*—after the Negro patriot of the Cuban struggle for independence. Garvey later began negotiations to add to his fleet a
much larger vessel, the S.S. *Phyliss Wheatley,* which was to "be
put on the African route and sail between America, Liberia and
Sierra Leone." This ship, however, marked the end of Garvey's
dream; financial embarrassment and sharp dealing on the part of
ship brokers coupled with Garvey's quarrels with the government
killed the Black Star Line. Nearly a million dollars were spent on
ships, but the end result was financial failure, and sadly enough
this was at least partially due to mismanagement and inefficiency on
the part of Black Star captains and crews. Yet even though the
venture failed, the fact that a Black had actually started a ship line
bolstered Black pride, especially among the members of the
Garvey movement. The enthusiasm with which they supported
the scheme attested to this fact.

The reclamation of Africa for the Black race was central to all
of Garvey's endeavors. The Black Star Line and most of Garvey's
UNIA projects were viewed as preludes to this one great event.
As early as 1920, a UNIA delegation was sent to Liberia to confer

with that government on the prospect of setting up the headquarters of the UNIA on African soil.[32] It seems to have been
Garvey's dream to establish his African beachhead in Liberia. The
delegation returned with the assurance of the Liberian Government that it would afford the movement every co-operation in
carrying out its proposed project. In that same year, Mayor
Gabriel Johnson of Monrovia, Liberia, was made a Supreme
Potentate of the UNIA and became the African liaison for the
movement, securing the necessary legislative backing for its in-
corporation in Liberia.[33] The Liberian Government was in every
way enthusiastic about American Blacks colonizing on its soil and
saw a great future in this project. Lands were set aside and the
work toward settlement began on a high level. Garvey saw that
specialists were sent to Liberia to prepare the land for the arrival
of the members of the UNIA. And by 1923, the plan was so near
realization that he began preparing for the first repatriation of some
thousands of families. In June of 1924, further shipments of machinery and other materials, said to have been worth $50,000,
were sent to Liberia, but by this time the opposition at home and
abroad, along with the growing doubt in Liberia itself, caused the
plan to abort.[34] The equipment was later confiscated by the
Liberian Government for various reasons, none of which seemed
an adequate explanation for such drastic behavior.

The Liberian Government, under the pressure of England,
France and America, soon moved to a position of total opposition
to the project. The Liberians even asked all steamship companies
to deny passage to members of the Garvey movement; they also
refused them visas. This brought to a full halt the greatest Black
repatriation movement in history. Although Garvey made heroic
attempts to renew his effort and to clear the records with the
Liberian Government, he was never successful. The land designated for Garvey's African project was later leased to the Firestone
Rubber Company of the United States.

C. The Aborted Dream:

The meteoric rise of Garvey created a widespread jealousy in
the ranks of the Black intellectuals, and soon plots of every kind
were devised for his overthrow. There was even an assassination
attempt. This having failed, the intellectuals sought to revive an
old indictment brought against Garvey by the state of New York

for allegedly using the mails to sell fraudulent stock in the Black
Star Line. Although there was but the slightest shred of evidence
in this case, the Black intellectuals, most of them members of the
NAACP, encouraged the attorney general of New York to press
charges. It was their firm conviction that "Garvey must go." Garvey
was indicted in 1924, and the story of his trial is one of the most
disgusting on the pages of legal history. It is a study in the miscar-
riage of justice. The details of the trial are so involved that we
must avoid discussing them here, but suffice it to say that he was
convicted on the most dubious evidence and was sent to prison,
January 1, 1925, for a five-year term. In 1927, his sentence was
commuted by President Calvin Coolidge, and since he was not an
American citizen, he was deported to Jamaica. He later went to
England, where he died in 1940.

It was not until Garvey was safely behind bars that the attitude
of the intellectuals emerged. W. E. B. Du Bois wrote in *Crisis,*
November 24, 1924:

> The American Negroes have endured this threat all too long
> with fine restraint and every effort to cooperation and under-
> standing. But the end has come. Every man who apologizes
> for or defends Marcus Garvey from this day forth writes
> himself down as unworthy of the countenance of decent
> Americans. As for Garvey himself, this open ally of the KKK
> should be locked up or sent home.

These were hard words for one Negro leader to use against another,
but the sentiments portrayed the depth of hatred that was en-
gendered among the intellectuals by the Garvey movement.
Garvey did not see his incarceration as the end of the struggle.
From jail he wrote numerous letters of hope to his followers, en-
couraging them to "keep the faith." On one occasion, he wrote:

> My work is just begun, and as I lay down my life for the cause
> of my people, so do I feel that succeeding generations shall
> be inspired by the sacrifice that I made for the rehabilitation
> of our race.[35]

How much has this prophecy come true? One must look at the
recent resurgence of the spirit of Garveyism for the answer. His
most dangerous enemy, W. E. B. Du Bois, who, ironically,
found refuge in the Africa Garvey had fought so hard for, finally

confessed that "Garvey was an extraordinary leader of men." In his last days in Africa Du Bois reflected on the Garvey movement:

> It was a grandiose and bombastic scheme, utterly impractica-
> ble as a whole, but was sincere and had some practical
> features; and Garvey proved not only an astonishingly popu-
> lar leader but a master propagandist. News of his movement
> and of his promise and his plans, reached Europe and Asia,
> and penetrated every corner of Africa.[36]

This was a complete turnabout for the man who sixteen years before saw Garvey as "a traitor," "a lunatic" and the greatest enemy of the Negro race. The Chicago *Defender,* which prided itself on being one of Garvey's most persistent slanderers, characterized him as the "patron saint of restless Africa" and at his death asserted that "Garvey was easily the most colorful figure to have appeared in America since the time of Frederick Douglass and Booker T. Washington." This was quite an honor indeed; but it came too late. In his book *Black Manhattan,* James Weldon Johnson of "Harlem Renaissance" fame both praised and damned Garvey:

> He had the energy and daring and Napoleonic personality
> —the personality that drew masses of followers. He stirred the
> imagination of the Negro masses as no Negro ever had. He
> raised more money in a few years than any other Negro or-
> ganization had and ever dreamed of. He had great power and
> great possibilities within his grasp. But his deficiencies as a
> leader out-weighed his abilities.[37]

A better way to assess his failing would be to say that he had the unusual ability to inspire other men, but this inspiration fell on poor soil. And so the assessment of Gunnar Myrdal seems more balanced.

> The response of the Negro masses [to Garvey] is even more
> interesting . . . for one thing, it proves that it is possible to
> reach the Negro masses if they are appealed to in an effective
> way. It testifies to the basic unrest in the Negro community.
> It tells of a dissatisfaction so deep that it mounts to hopeless-
> ness of ever gaining a full life in America. It suggests that
> the effective method of lining up American Negroes into a
> mass movement is a strongly emotional charismatic protest
> appeal. . . . The Garvey movement illustrates that the Negro

Movement in America is doomed to ultimate dissolution
and collapse if it cannot gain white support—This is a dilemma.
For white support will be denied to emotional Negro Chauvinism when it takes political form.[38]

If by chauvinism one means an exaggerated racial patriotism,
Garvey fits the mold. Yet it should also be noted that it was just
this kind of shock treatment that was needed to tear the blinders of
hopelessness from the eyes of oppressed Negroes in Garvey's
time. History has proven that this was an effective cure for the
ailment. It was not just chauvinism and emotional appeal that won
the masses to Garvey. Many leaders have appeared on the scene
since Garvey with more abrasive, emotional appeals, but their
following has been insignificant. In Garvey the people perceived a
peculiar power and vision. The success of a mass movement does
not only depend on the words and the emotional appeal of the
leader but also on the people's intuition of the true nature of the
man and his call. Archbishop George Alexander McGuire, one-
time chaplain to the Garvey movement wrote:

> Outsiders will never understand the psychology of those
> they call Garveyites. We doubt, if we who are thus nick-
> named, understand it ourselves. The binding spell, the inde-
> finable charm which Mr. Garvey exercises over us beggars
> description. But we find the reason for it in our conviction
> that no man has spoken to us like this man, inculcating pride,
> and nobility of race, and clearly pointing out the Star of Hope
> to a discouraged and down-trodden people.[39]

Malcolm X, the vibrant Muslim leader and one of the most influential Black nationalists, was greatly influenced by Garveyism.
His father, who was an active Garveyite, generally evangelized for
the movement between the duties of preaching in a Baptist church
in his Nebraska community. On these occasions, Malcolm accompanied him, and, reflecting on those days, he said:

> I remember seeing the big, shiny photographs of Marcus
> Garvey that were passed from hand to hand . . . and I re-
> member how the meetings always closed with my father saying
> several times, and the people chanting after him, "Up you
> mighty race, you can accomplish what you will!"[40]

Speaking to a news reporter, on his return from Africa, Malcolm X praised Garvey for his work:

> Every time you see another nation on the African continent become independent, you know that Marcus Garvey is alive. All the freedom movement that is taking place right here in America today was initiated by the philosophy and teachings of Garvey. The entire Black nationalist philosophy here in America is fed upon the seeds that were planted by Marcus Garvey.[41]

The "Messenger" of the Nation of Islam, Elijah Muhammad, in the foreword of his book *Message to the Black man in America,* said of Garvey:

> Garvey's "Back-to-Africa" slogan, based solely on vivid black nationalism, electrified Negroes to the point where more than 6 million joined his ranks and deified the pudgy black man whom they worshipped with their love and loyalty.[42]

Thousands of people in all walks of life all over the world are now assessing the works of Marcus Garvey. Not so long ago, the Harlem branch of the New York Public Library reported that there has been a steady reader demand for Garvey materials. And in Jamaica, where Garvey was born, he has now been elevated to the status of a national hero. In 1962, the Jamaican Government requested the return of his body from England and erected a monument in one of the city parks of Kingston as a national shrine. In 1965, the government of Jamaica established the Marcus Garvey Prize for Human Rights, a sum of $10,000 to be awarded to the person, "who in this generation has contributed most significantly to the field of Human Rights." In this same year, Martin Luther King, Jr. (who was awarded the prize posthumously in 1968), visited Jamaica and placed a wreath on the grave of Garvey. He said in part:

> Marcus Garvey was the first man of color in the history of the United States to lead and develop a mass movement. . . . He was the first man on a mass scale and level to give millions of Negroes a sense of dignity and destiny, and make the Negro feel he is somebody. . . . You gave Marcus Garvey to the United States of America, and gave to millions of Negroes in the United States a sense of personhood, a sense of manhood, and a sense of somebodiness.[43]

Garvey was possessed by a mission for his race that few men have been able to equal. In his message to the Negroes of the world from an Atlanta prison he wrote:

If I die in Atlanta my work shall then only begin, but I shall live, in the physical or spiritual to see the day of Africa's glory. When I am dead wrap the mantle of the Red, Black and Green around me, for in the new life I shall rise with God's grace and blessing to lead the millions up the heights of triumph with the colors that you well know. Look for me in the whirlwind or the storm, look for me all around you, for, with God's grace, I shall come and bring with me countless millions of black slaves who have died in America and the West Indies and the millions in Africa to aid you in the fight for Liberty, Freedom and Life.[44]

Here was the soul-force in action. Wherever Black men shall live in generations to come, Marcus Garvey's name shall be remembered, for it is certain that one can neither crucify a principle, nor nail the soul of a man to a cross, nor imprison or bury it. Garvey suggests that the soul will rise like the spirit of the Great Redeemer and men throughout the ages will take up the cry for which the principle was crucified.

CHAPTER 7

SOUL ASSERTING ITSELF:
The Rastafarians

Cults of revolution represent one extreme of the continuum of Black struggle. Keeping within the realm of religion, Black responses to oppression have varied from revivalistic movements whose goal is redemption from social pressure through supernatural means to the militant revolutionaries who seek, by any means available, the radical implementation of clearly defined goals: political and economic power, Black solidarity, dignity and self-determination. These revolutionary cults, in a sense, are extensions of the traditional African religion but with even more intensive religious commitment, in that these cultists offer up their lives in the cause of the revolution. Their techniques have less of an aura of "magic" than those of their ancestors, because the enemy's tactics have changed and this indicates a refinement of the old ways. However, the weapon of incantation still remains basic in the arsenal of the cults of Black revolution. The "word" is still the most formidable weapon of the Rastafarians, the Black Muslims and the Black Panthers. Modern society with all its scientific weapons still trembles at the imagery conjured up by Black revolutionary movements. The "word," then, is the cult weapon *par excellence*—the spell, the witchcraft, that conjures up in the mind of the enemy the "bogieman" of guilt and the threatening vision of revolution.

The other weapon which our ancestors employed successfully

and which still has potential in the cult of revolution is so-called "cultural judo," or the ability to keep the opposition guessing. The conflicting ideologies of the various revolutionary cults of the New World are an instance of cultural judo. There are those who preach a bodily return to Africa in mass repatriation; there are others who desire to stay in the West but in their own separate state; there are still others who desire to remain in their country of birth but with self-determination and cultural autonomy. Some are separatists, some are integrationists and some fall in between. There is no unanimity of voice, but all perceive a common goal which will eventually bring about total freedom for the Black man.

On the *nature* of Black cult movements, there is no single definition or theory which will account for all Black revolutionary cults. However, in their recent book *People, Power, Change: Movements of Social Transformation,*[1] Gerlach and Hine did provide an interesting identification scheme. They located three basic organizational tendencies in all radical cults: decentralization, segmentation and reticulation. Emphasis on the decentralized quality of such cults is certainly justified in relation to Black Power. The various leaders within the movement are autonomous in decision making. There is no authority above the level of the local community and even here the organization is quite diffused and flexible. The leaders are *primus inter pares,* or first among equals. The different so-called Black Power organizations do not agree on goals and methods and none of their leaders can make decisions binding on the membership. Such decentralization is characteristic of the Rastafarians in Jamaica and the Black Panthers in the United States; however, it should be noted that the idea is totally incorrect when applied to the Black Muslims. The Muslim organization is monolithic in structure due to the leadership of Elijah Muhammad, whose teachings and directives are followed to the letter. The local Black Muslim leader is under Elijah Muhammad's direct command and can be dismissed without warning.

The second characteristic of revolutionary cults cited by Gerlach and Hine is their segmented nature. Among Blacks these movements are composed of localized groups or cells which are essentially independent; but they can either combine to form larger units or divide into even smaller ones. This fission and fusion describe the dynamics of these movements. Each segment approaches its goal in its own way and each interprets the general ideology of the movement differently. Segmentation can be attributed to many things. First, it occurs because of new leaders who want more freedom and power; anyone is capable of receiving the charismatic gift from the divine leader. Second, it occurs through pre-existing social, personal or geographical cleavages. In this case segments of an older cell break away to form a new cell made up of special social groupings defined by education, financial status, or a certain urban-*v.*-rural outlook. A third cause of segmentation is ideological differences, or differences as to what methods should be used to achieve certain goals. Such clashes between conservatives, moderates and radicals in a cell often cause a three-way fission. Segmentation is a fact of life among the Rastafarians and Panthers and much of the above discussion can be applied to them. But again this does not fit the Black Muslims, at least not as yet. It is true that segmentation occurred in the early development of the Black Muslims and again to some extent with Malcolm X, but these splinter groups soon lost status and ceased to be effective parts of the movement.

The third descriptive term employed by Gerlach and Hine is "reticulation," which refers to the weblike configuration or criss-crossing of relationships characteristic of these movements. This intergroup linkage, not usually consciously contrived, is maintained through personal ties among members and leaders, ritual activities, national and regional associations, ideological linkages, extra-movement linkages and the mass media.

Now, all this reads well on the printed page, but in reality this is not so for all Black revolutionary cults. Among the Rastafarians, there is reticulation; members of one cell do maintain friendships with those of other cells. The leaders are well known throughout Jamaica, and all Rastafarians do have one ideological goal and they sometimes engage in co-operative ritual activity. But when this concept is applied to the Black Muslims almost every point is incorrect. The Black Muslims form an island unto themselves; they do not associate with "civil rights" activists. This is forbidden by the leader. Ideologically the Muslims and Black Power leaders are miles apart as to ends and methods. There is simply no inter-linkage between them and the other Black revolutionary groups. We may conclude, then, that there is no one definition under which all Black religious radicalism can be subsumed. Some of the most important cults, such as the Black Muslims and the Peace Mission movement of Father Divine, are not decentralized at all, but strongly monolithic. Similarly neither of these two is really segmented or reticulated.

The rest of this chapter will deal specifically and in detail with the Caribbean-based revolutionary cult which emerged in the 1930's. The cult[2] is a millenarian movement unique to Jamaica whose members believe that Haile Selassie, Emperor of Ethiopia, is God and that Ethiopia is the promised land of the Black man. The Blacks, they believe, are destined to return and live in Ethiopia through a wholesale repatriation from all Western countries where they have been in exile. This repatriation is believed to be inevitable, awaiting only the decision of Haile Selassie, who is at present working out the details. The emperor, it is thought, does not desire to put Western countries into any difficulty and therefore is giving the West enough time to work out their side of the project so that a smooth operation can be achieved. The details of the actual departure for Africa are somewhat vague in the minds of the Rastafarians. Some fantasies call for planes to the United States, then ships from the States to Africa. Others see the operation from the shores of Jamaica by British ships. Still others envision Ethiopian vessels operating at Jamaican expense. The place of destination is also vague in many minds, although the majority see Ethiopia as their homeland. For others, the whole continent of Africa is the homeland.

Rastafarians are found not only in Kingston, the major city of Jamaica, where they exist in the greatest numbers, but in country towns and remote mountain villages of the island as well. No census has been able to give an accurate count of the membership in the movement. Although some have said there are as many as 70,000 in the cult, a more conservative estimate would probably put the actual membership in the region of 20,000 with a considerable number of sympathizers and well-wishers. In addition, the membership is young. Up to 80 per cent of them are between the ages of seventeen and thirty-five; and the leading "brethren," as their leaders are called, are from thirty-five to forty years of age. The membership is predominantly male; women play a very minor role in Rastafarianism. They generally are in the background in the camps. In special meetings they may act as mistresses of songs or be used as recording secretaries, but in every other respect the male assumes the responsibilities of the movement. Members used to come almost exclusively from the peasant class, those who referred to themselves as "children of deprivation," but the movement has now penetrated the middle class. Rastafarians can now be found in the secondary schools, and among the university students who see no future for the island. They are almost 100 per cent people of African stock, Jamaicans who are proud of being called "Black men." There are, however, a few members of other ethnic groups, but these are either Afro-Chinese or Afro-East Indians, and are numerically of no significance. The membership is predominantly ex-Christian. About 90 per cent of those interviewed were formerly Protestant, Catholic or from other sect groups. The minority who said they had no previous church connection did in fact acknowledge that they came from Christian homes.

1. The cult's origin: The decade beginning in 1930 may well be called the "decade of despair" for the average Jamaican. The political situation was stagnant. The country was still in the hands of men who had little or no feeling for the hungry masses. The average wage for a full day of unskilled labor was twenty-five cents for men and fourteen cents for women. The island was the reserve of a few Englishmen who had the final word in all political and economic affairs. The men who invested in Jamaica did so only for monetary gain, and were unconcerned with human or cultural matters. None of the economic institutions were organized democratically. The typical institutional pattern was hierarchical, with decision and direction at the apex, submission and obedience at the bottom, and no machinery the masses could use to exert influence on the leaders. These were the years of the Great Depression, which saw lines of hungry people. These were also the years of violent hurricanes which left Jamaica and other West Indian islands devastated. Such a combination of natural and economic disaster brought only gloom and hopeless despair to thousands of Jamaicans. This feeling of futility finally came to a head in 1938, when violent labor disturbances broke out in Westmoreland, to be followed by grave disturbances in the city of Kingston, and the parishes of St. Mary, St. James and other parts of the island. These protests finally led the imperial government to send the West Indian Royal Commission to survey living conditions in Jamaica and other West Indian islands. This not only gave rise to the first

political parties in Jamaica, but also indirectly occasioned the birth
of the politico-religious movement known today as Rastafarianism.

Although a direct line cannot be traced from Garvey to the
Rastafarians,[3] cult leaders such as Sam Brown definitely see the
movement as a continuation of the struggle of the Black man begun by Garvey. In a pamphlet entitled *The Truth About the
Rastafarians,* Brown says:

> After the exodus of the great Garvey, cohesion among the
> black leadership was absent, simmering to almost purposeless
> effort. But in 1930 something new, yet nationalistic and black
> appeared, pioneered by Leonard P. Howell, who brought
> some order of centralization to all the elements of resistance
> who became stranded by the exodus of Garvey. He taught
> them the divinity of the black man, fostering the growing of
> the beard in direct imitation of the King. Howell, who mean-
> time carved out a tax-free state at Pinnacle in St. Catherine
> was subjected to numerous imprisonments and eventual inva-
> sion by the government which smashed the movement. The
> dismemberment of the movement eventually proved a bene-
> fit, for out of it came many leaders to spread the doctrine far
> and wide.[4]

Most scholars agree that the movement originated soon after the
coronation of Haile Selassie in Ethiopia.[5] In 1930, when Ras
Tafari, son of Ras Makonnen of Harar, from whom the movement
got its name, was crowned King of Ethiopia, he took as his title
Haile Selassie, King of Kings and Lord of Lords, Conquering Lion
of the tribe of Judah. (The name Haile Selassie means "Power of
the Trinity.") The newly crowned monarch asserted, and his faith-
ful subjects believed, that he was the only direct descendant of
David and the 225th of a line of Ethiopian kings stretching in unbroken succession from the time of the legendary Queen of Sheba
to the present.[6]

The coronation of this African king caused some Jamaicans of
African descent both on the island and in New York to study their
Bibles more closely. They remembered a pronouncement by
Marcus Garvey: "Look to Africa where a Black King shall arise—
this will be the day of your deliverance."[7] Prominent among the
Jamaicans inspired by Haile Selassie's coronation were Leonard
Howell, Joseph Hibbert, Archibald Dunkley, Paul Earlington,
Vernal Davis and Ferdinand Richetts. Those in Jamaica became

the pillars of the Rastafarian Movement, while their counterparts
in New York City became the founders of the Ethiopian World
Federation.[8] The latter will be discussed at greater length later.

At least three of these men are usually credited with founding
the Rastafarian Cult of Jamaica; they are Howell, Hibbert and
Dunkley. Leonard Howell, although a native Jamaican, had
traveled widely. He had been a soldier in the Ashanti War of 1896
and is said to have spoken several African languages.[9] He had
also traveled in the United States and while there had come into
contact with racism between whites and Blacks. It is Howell who
is reputed to be the first preacher of Rastafarianism.

Joseph Nathaniel Hibbert was born in 1894, and in 1911, he
went to Costa Rica, where he joined the Ancient Order of
Ethiopia, a Masonic Society. On his return to Jamaica in 1931,
Hibbert began to preach that Haile Selassie was "King of Kings,"
the "returned Messiah," and "Redeemer of Israel." Hibbert
started his preaching in the Benoah district of the parish of St.
Andrew, but later moved to Kingston, where he found Leonard
Howell already preaching about Ras Tafari at the Redemption
Market.[10]

H. Archibald Dunkley, also considered a founder, was a
Jamaican seaman employed by the Atlantic Fruit Company. Dis-
charged from their service, he returned to Jamaica on December
8, 1930, and devoted two and a half years to a study of the Bible,
trying to determine whether or not Haile Selassie was the Messiah
of whom Marcus Garvey spoke. Convinced by his study that he
was, Dunkley opened a mission in Kingston in 1933 and began
to preach that Ras Tafari was God, the "King of Kings" and "Root
of David."[11]

This group of Rastafarians soon began to attract the Garveyites,
who were by then without a leader; about 1934, they also accepted
Haile Selassie as the Living God, and as a result the Rastafarian
Movement was greatly strengthened. Many of Garvey's slogans
and ideas were taken over—a factor which gives a special flavor
to the movement to this day.

The Scripture which came to be most significant to these men
was the Revelation of St. John the Divine:

> And I saw a strong angel proclaiming with a great voice, Who
> is worthy to open the book and to loose the seals thereof?

And no man in heaven, nor in earth, was able to open the book neither to look thereon. . . . And one of the elders saith unto me, Weep not: behold, the Lion of the tribe of Judah, the Root of David, hath prevailed to open the book and to loose the seven seals thereof. . . . He hath on his vesture and on his thigh a name written, KING OF KINGS, AND LORD OF LORDS . . .[12]

a) *Howell* v. *the law:* The movement under Howell soon came into conflict with Jamaican law. In *The Daily Gleaner* of December 16, 1933, Howell is reported to have sold photographs of the Emperor Haile Selassie for a shilling each.[13] It is said that about five thousand of these were distributed with the understanding that they would serve as future passports to Ethiopia. Two years later, *The Gleaner* reported the arrest and trial of Howell at Port Morant. The following is an extract from *The Gleaner* of January 5, 1934, under the heading "ALLEGED SEDITION IN ST. THOMAS PARISH":

Crowds of people gathered at the court House Square, Morant Bay, on Wednesday to take a glimpse of the alleged seditionists and their followers, who were charged with less serious offences, who were brought before His Honour Mr. Ansel O. Thompson, Acting Resident Magistrate for St. Thomas . . . Robert Hinds, Leonard Howell who are alleged to be known as the representative of "Ras Tafari," King of the Ethiopians in this Island, were each charged on the accounts of sedition.

The case generated considerable interest and resulted in wide publicity for the Rastas.[14] Howell pleaded not guilty to the indictment which charged him with making a speech that attacked both the governments of Great Britain and of the island, and attempting to excite hatred and contempt for His Majesty the King and those responsible for the government of the island. Howell was further charged with disturbing the public peace and tranquillity. According to *The Daily Gleaner* of March 17, 1934, Howell was sentenced to prison for two years. *The Gleaner* reported that on sentencing Howell, the Chief Justice said:

"Howell, you have been convicted by the Jury for uttering seditious language; that is, such language as is calculated to cause disturbance and violence among ignorant people of this

country. . . . I consider you to be a fraud . . . but that unfortunately has no effect, because people take you for what
you say you are."

Robert Hinds, his deputy, who was also arrested with Howell,
received a twelve-month sentence. The editor, in the Kingston
Sunday Guardian, May 1, 1960, recalling the episode, sum-
marized the philosophy of Leonard Howell as follows:

1. Hatred for the white race.
2. Complete superiority of the Black race.
3. Revenge on white men for their wickedness.
4. The negation, persecution, and humiliation of the government and legal bodies.
5. Preparation to go "Back-to-Africa."
6. Acknowledgment of Emperor Haile Selassie as their supreme
   and only ruler and as their "god-emperor."

The arrest of Howell inaugurated a period of police surveillance
of the movement and soon Dunkley and Hibbert were also arrested and imprisoned; further details about them are obscure.

Following his release from prison, Howell reorganized his
movement. He seemed to have decided to "lay low" for a while,
for it was the year 1940 before we again find him in the news as
the head of a communal society at Pinnacle in the parish of St.
Catherine. The following extract is taken from *The Daily Gleaner:*

> In May 1940 he [Howell] purchased Pinnacle on behalf of
> the Society in America for the branch in Jamaica. Apart from
> himself, over five hundred members of the Society resided
> at Pinnacle. The members did not pay any rent for living there.
> They burnt coal and lime, and cultivated portions of the
> property, which was a large one. The proceeds of this, after
> the Manager had taken a portion for food allowance and
> clothing, went to the funds of the Society.[15]

b) Pinnacle enterprise: Pinnacle, near the country village of
Sligoville in St. Catherine, lies in the very mountainous terrain
visible to the west of Kingston, and is accessible only by foot, and
even this method is hazardous. Here, Howell developed the rudi-
ments of present-day Rastafarianism. One source has placed
the number of members that followed Howell to Pinnacle at
1,600.[16] Unfortunately, by the time the news of its existence became public, the police had already moved in to destroy the community.

Reports in *The Daily Gleaner,* which correspond closely with those of eyewitnesses, said that at Pinnacle Howell took the name of "Ganguru" or simply "the Gong." No explanation of the name is given. He is also said to have had thirteen wives or concubines and to have been in charge of all the activities carried on in the commune. The main food crops of the plantation were yams and other subsistence items, but the mainstay of the society was the cultivation of *ganja* or marijuana.[17]

In 1941, the police carried out systematic raids on Pinnacle. Issues of *The Daily Gleaner* of July through August gave extensive coverage to these operations. Seventy Rastas were arrested for growing ganja or for violence, and as a result of these raids twenty-eight were sent to prison. Howell, after evading the police for some time, was apprehended and sent to prison for another two years. *The Daily Gleaner* of July 13 reported that he had, among other things, threatened the neighbors of the community with lashings if they continued paying taxes to the Jamaican Government. He had also claimed all the lands of the Pinnacle area in the name of Haile Selassie.

However, by 1953, Howell was back at Pinnacle and continued operating there in much the same way he had before his arrest. He did seem to be paying more attention to security, however, because the brethren took on the fierce appearance that is now common among the "locksmen." These were the young men who grew beards and long hair, and called themselves "Ethiopian Warriors." Ferocious dogs were also used to assist the warriors in guarding Pinnacle. Strangers entering the compound were announced by the sounding of "gongs."

The university team who studied the Rastafarian movement in Kingston in 1960 said of the Pinnacle commune:

> By all accounts, Pinnacle seemed to have been rather more like an old maroon settlement than part of Jamaica. Its internal administration was Howell's business, not the government's. It is therefore understandable that the unit could have persisted as a state within a state for several years without the people or government of Jamaica being aware of it.[18]

The activities of Pinnacle were finally broken up in 1954, when 163 members of the group were arrested. Howell and his lieutenants were arrested but later acquitted. Eventually, however, he was discredited by his followers for claiming divinity for himself. He was committed to the Kingston Mental Hospital in 1960.[19]

The Pinnacle community is important to the development of Rastafarianism in Jamaica because many of the beliefs now current in the cult circles were discussed and refined in the free atmosphere of the St. Catherine Hills. The wearing of beards, a trademark of the Rastafarians, was developed at Pinnacle, as was the custom of plaiting the hair. Some believe that the Rastas began to wear these hair and beard styles in imitation of photographs they may have seen of Somali, Masai, Gulla or other tribesmen. Whatever the origin, the plaiting of hair by men, who came to be known as "dreadlocks" and "locksmen," certainly began at Pinnacle. According to informants, the "dreadlocks" began to appear in Kingston as early as 1947.

There is no record of the activities of the Rastafarians immediately after the breaking up of the Pinnacle enterprise, but reliable sources suggest that most of these returnees settled in the Back-O-Wall or Shanty-Town of Kingston. There, the most industrious of them engaged themselves in peddling fruits and brooms; some sold firewood and charcoal; others simply walked the streets and harangued about their social condition. The most eloquent of them began to preach the doctrine learned at Pinnacle, attracting followers to themselves. Several little groupings now began to emerge in different parts of the city. Nightly meetings, patterned after those of the Revivalists, soon began to take place on the streets of West Kingston. A new period of recruitment had begun; the movement became decentralized.

The period between 1947 and 1959 was one of reorganization and adaptation. It was a time of intense hatred for the established society. Rastafarians ran down the streets of Kingston, yelling, "Fire," "Brimstone," and "Babylon," using the most profane language ever heard in public. To the elite community they appeared to be madmen and several of them actually were apprehended by the law and sent to the asylum. Their language and behavior, however, also attracted the more favorable attention of many and soon wherever one of these "wildmen" appeared there was an audience. Their defiance of society was admired by many who secretly felt the urge to do the same, but did not have the boldness to exhibit their feelings. Meanwhile, the leading brethren continued to win converts until there were several separate camps all over the city, most in West Kingston.

In 1955, George E. Simpson reported that there were at least twelve Ras Tafari groups operating in West Kingston, with membership ranging from approximately twenty to one hundred and twenty.[20] Since then the number of camps has greatly increased and groups can be found not only in Kingston, but also in all major towns and villages of Jamaica.

2. The cult's development: At least five dramatic events brought the Rastafarian movement into prominence during the nineteen fifties and early nineteen sixties: (a) the Ethiopian World Federation, which became more active in Jamaica in 1953; (b) the Rastafarian Convention of 1958; (c) the Debacle of 1959; (d) the university team study and report of 1960 on the Rastafarian movement; and (e) the sending of two delegations to African countries in 1961 and 1962, as a result of this report.

a) The Ethiopian World Federation: In 1953, when George Simpson began his study of the Rastafarians, they had attracted little attention. Their peculiar habits and coarse language were diversions for the man in the streets, while the middle-class Jamaican considered them an "odd lot" or a mere nuisance. However, the Rastafarians were steadily gaining ground and within a short while their presence was felt throughout Jamaica.

In our previous discussion on the emergence of the Rastafarians, we noted that the revelation that Haile Selassie was God was given to two sets of Jamaicans: one in New York; the other on the island itself. The former became known as the Ethiopian World Federation, an organization which was a more culturally oriented body than the Rastas. It was incorporated in New York in 1937, with Dr. Melaku E. Bayen, an Ethiopian, as its president. The purpose of the organization is set forth in its preamble.

> We, the Black Peoples of the World, in order to effect Unity, Solidarity, Liberty, Freedom and Self-determination, to secure Justice and maintain the Integrity of Ethiopia, which is our divine heritage, do hereby establish and ordain this constitution for the Ethiopian World Federation, Inc.[21]

As early as 1938, a branch of the EWF was established in Jamaica. Its success, however, was limited due to constant internal tensions over leadership. Within the main group there seem to have been several splinter groups, each claiming to be the true branch of the Ethiopian World Federation, Inc. In 1955, Mrs. Mamie Richardson, one of the leading officials of the EWF, Inc., came to Jamaica to meet local leaders of the Federation. A large audience turned out to hear her message on Ethiopia, including many Rastafarians. Among the statements attributed to Mrs. Richardson, the one about the emperor's merchant navy and the possibility that ships from Addis Ababa would sail to American ports and possibly also to Jamaica, excited great interest among the brethren.[22] Mrs. Richardson's visit not only gave impetus to the rise of many local branches of the EWF, Inc., in towns all over Jamaica, but strengthened the millenarian tendencies of the Rastafarians. They thought that their redemption and repatriation to Ethiopia was at hand. Their hopes were fired even more by a letter from the Federation headquarters in New York stating that Emperor Haile Selassie had granted 500 acres of land to the Black peoples of the West who had aided Ethiopia during her war with Italy.[23] Despite the many conditions demanded of those who would migrate, conditions which would exclude most Rastafarians, the cry of the cultists was for immediate repatriation. This heightened expectation led to the Rastafarian Convention in Kingston.

b) The Rastafarian Convention of 1958: The second factor contributing to the sudden popularity of the Rastafarians in the fifties was their new strength gained from an attempt to organize all the various factions of the movement into one united body. This convention not only disclosed many aspects of the cult hitherto unknown to the public, but gave the Rastafarians unprecedented publicity. The newspapers in Jamaica, as evidenced by the following report, devoted considerable space to the convention.

> For the first time in local history members of the Rastafari Cult are having what they call a "universal convention" at their headquarters known as the Coptic Theocratic Temple in Kingston Pen. Some 300 cultists of both sexes from all over the island have been assembled at Back-O-Wall headquarters since Saturday, March 1. The Convention is scheduled to last until April 1. The Convention was said to be "The first and the last" in that they were expected to migrate to Africa their homeland.[24]

Although, little or nothing of the actual formal proceedings of the convention ever came to light, the publicity given to it resulted in an outpouring of "letters to the editor" and the city began to rock with gossip of every kind. There were reports of nightly rituals of drumming and singing, of abusive language directed at passing police, and that the Rastafarians planned to decapitate a police officer as a peace offering. At first the government paid little attention to the meeting at "Back-O-Wall," but as the days went by and the headlines became more lurid, police vigilance began to increase.

March 22, 1958, saw clashes between Rastafarians and the police, with the police on the worst end of the bargain. Perhaps as a result of this, the Rastafarians became bolder and tried to capture the city of Kingston. *The Star* printed the following:

> The City of Kingston was "captured" near dawn on Saturday by some 300 bearded men of the Rastafarian cult along with their women and children. About 3:30 A.M., early marketgoers saw members of the Rastafarian movement gathered in the center of Victoria Park, with towering poles, atop of which, fluttered black, green and red banners, and loudly proclaiming that they had captured the city. . . . When the police moved toward them, a leader of the group with hands raised issued a warning to the police: "touch not the Lord's anointed". . . . The police finally removed them . . . [25]

Later, in June of that year, the Rastafarians did take over Old King's House, the traditional residence of the governors of Jamaica.* Nine cult families, according to reports, held the house in the name of the king (*Negus*) for an entire week.[26] The police were called out and, as *The Tribune's* story went: "A business-like detachment of police mounted a counter-invasion. In a short time King's House was again liberated, not a shot fired, not a head broken."[27] The report of the university team to the government on the Rastafarians, said that the 1958 convention revealed the anti-social character of many of the cultists and thus created considerable opposition to the Rastas from the government as well as the public.

The months that followed the convention saw increased tension between the government and the Rastafarians. Under the Jamaican dangerous drug law, cultists were arrested for the use of ganja,[28] and subjected to search and harassment. Some even had their

* Located in Spanish Town.

heads shaven by the police, an act still remembered and discussed among the Rastafarians today. In 1959, the camp of Rastafarians led by Prince Edward on Spanish Town Road was raided by a squad of riot-ready policemen who took all the male members to jail and set the camp on fire. The men were defended by a lawyer named Evans, who also officiated in the "Mau Mau" trials in Kenya. The men were released.

Many prophetic voices were now raised among both the academicians and the Jamaican middle class beseeching the government to take a realistic look at the Rastafarian grievances. Among the academicians who spoke on behalf of the Rastafarians was Professor Gordon Lewis, who in an article entitled "The Apathy of the Masses Remains Untouched," saw the Rastafarian movement as a direct result of the social and economic neglect of that segment of the society. He concluded:

To speak with the Rastafari is to gain some insight into matters the historian of the region has avoided.

It is the business of the cultural anthropologist to study such sub-groups in a spirit of clinical detachment. But it is the business of the historian to recognise the historical roots of their universe of discourse.

And it is the business of the social moralist to insist that they dramatise in themselves, the disintegration and divisiveness of society and that society cannot, if only for moral reasons, pass by on the other side of the road, like the Pharisee in the Scriptures.[29]

A columnist, Clinton Parchment, writing in *The Daily Gleaner* just before one of the worst Rastafarian outbreaks, said: "If the problem of the Rastas is not faced now, it is liable to get so big that no one can deal with it and it will then become, perhaps very unpleasantly, yours and mine and the Ministers'."[30] These and many other voices were heard through the daily papers. But the storm broke nevertheless and the government was forced to declare a national emergency.

c) The Debacle of 1959: The third and most serious incident contributing to the Rastafarians' notoriety created a national emergency in 1959. The two figures in this fiasco were the Reverend Claudius Henry and his son, Ronald. The Reverend Claudius Henry, R.B. (Repairer of the Breach), a Jamaican by birth, lived in New York for many years. Returning to Jamaica

in the early part of 1959, he seems to have connected himself with
the Ethiopian World Federation, Inc., from which he later resigned
because of some differences over leadership. Subsequently, he became the founder of the African Reform Church at 78 Rosalie
Avenue in the western part of Kingston. During the summer of
1959, he distributed several thousand cards bearing the following
statement:

> Pioneering Israel's scattered children of African Origin back
> home to Africa. This year 1959, deadline date Oct. 5th, this
> new Government is God's Righteous Kingdom of Everlasting
> Peace on Earth, "Creations Second Birth." Holder of this
> Certificate is requested to visit the Headquarters at 78 Rosa-
> lie Ave., off Waltham Park Road, August 1st, 1959, for our
> Emancipation Jubilee, commencing removal. No passport
> will be necessary for those returning to Africa. Bring this
> Certificate with you on August 1st, for "Identification" We
> sincerely, "The Seventh Emanuel's Brethren" gathering Is-
> rael's scattered and annointed prophet, Rev. C. V. Henry,
> R. B. Given this 2nd day of March 1959, in the year of the
> reign of his Imperial Majesty, 1st Emperor of Ethiopia,
> "God's Elect," Haile Selassie, King of Kings and Lord of
> Lords. Israel's Returned Messiah.[31]

It is said that 1,500 of these "tickets" at one shilling each were
sold. Thousands of people among the rank and file of the Rastafarians as well as many other hopeful Jamaicans believed the
message of Claudius Henry and flocked to his banner. On October 5, hundreds of them from all over the country came by every
conveyance they could find to 78 Rosalie Avenue, ready to depart
immediately for Africa. *The Daily Gleaner* of October 6, carried
the following report:

> Hundreds of Rastafarians gathered at Headquarters of the
> African Reformed Church, 78 Rosalie Avenue, following ru-
> mours that members of the cult wishing to join the "Back-to-
> Africa" movement would leave the island by ship yesterday.
> No ships or plane had come for them, no passport arranged,
> nor passages booked, but they were going to Africa. . . .
> The cultists who came from all parts of the Island, started
> arriving at Rosalie Avenue from Sunday afternoon, and up
> to yesterday afternoon were still trickling in taxicabs, trucks,
> and afoot. Some with their belongings said that they were

ready to leave for the trip. It was learned that many of them, especially from the country parts, had sold out their belongings and were planning to leave for Africa yesterday. Many more were expected to arrive especially from Montego Bay area last night.

On October 7, *The Gleaner* reported:

Hundreds with no place to go lingered at 78 Rosalie Avenue; among these were women and children. Many from Kingston and St. Andrew, and St. Mary left for their homes, but others were ashamed to go home because they had sold their houses and lands. They lingered on the premises until told they could stay no longer.

As usual, the excitement created by this affair was almost ignored by government. *The Gleaner* reported that up to the eighth of the month no investigation had been made by the police. Under the caption "NEW MESSIAH," *The Gleaner* reported a visit of the Reverend Claudius Henry to the editor. During this interview the Reverend Henry is said to have explained that the deadline of October 5 was not a deadline to travel, but a deadline to see whether the white man would help the Black man. The people, he said, did not understand the meaning of his message. The police finally arrested Reverend Henry, but the court freed him and ordered him to keep the peace for a year. He paid 100 pounds sterling as surety to this end.[32]

It is quite possible that the political and social climate of Jamaica gave Henry the impression that repatriation could be carried out only if demands for it were made in a forceful way. He therefore seized the opportunity to become the leader and spokesman for the Rastafarians and set a "deadline" for the response which he hoped he could force the government to make.

However, after 1959, the activities of Henry became increasingly hostile. The movement, which had previously been benign, now took on a military dimension. This led to a second raid on Henry's headquarters in which 2,500 electrical detonators, 1,300 detonators, a shotgun, a caliber .32 revolver, a large quantity of machetes sharpened both sides like swords and placed in sheaths, cartridges, several sticks of dynamite, and other articles were seized.[33] Other things taken during the raid were conch shells filled with cement, and vegetable material believed to be ganja.

Similar raids were carried out in the parish of Clarendon, where the movement had branches.

Henry was convicted of treason and sentenced to prison for six years. His followers, however, received lighter sentences. Soon after Henry's imprisonment, a more serious outbreak took place under his son's leadership. The connection between the activities of the Reverend Claudius Henry and those of his son, Ronald, have never been officially verified, but many Jamaicans of Rastafarian connection believed that the operations of Claudius Henry and his son were part of the same plot to take Jamaica by force with the help of sympathizers from the United States and Cuba. Shortly after his father's arrest and trial, Ronald Henry was found in the Red Hills in the parish of St. Andrew, overlooking Kingston, with guns and ammunition, with hard-core Rastafarians under military training. This led to a clash between Ronald Henry and the Jamaican police and soldiers of the Royal Hampshire Regiment. Two of the soldiers were shot and killed by the cultists. A public manhunt was then undertaken by the Jamaican Government, employing every means available on the island, including helicopters, to bring the men to justice. After many days of searching in the jagged hills of Sligoville, Ronald Henry and four of his men were found, brought to trial and sentenced to death. Further investigation by the government in June of 1960 uncovered another tragedy. The bodies of three Rastafarians were found buried in a shallow grave near the Red Hills Camp, their death attributed to Ronald Henry, who was said to have mistrusted their loyalty.[34]

The activities of Claudius Henry and his son not only aroused the fear and concern of persons living in Jamaica, but in the United States as well. The following article appeared in *Time:*

Jamaica's whites and government officials were at first only amused last October when a self-anointed Negro holy man, the Rev. Claudius Henry, R.B. (for Repairer of the Breach) stirred an estimated 20,000 bearded cultists into a Back-to-Africa frenzy. No one paid much attention, even when Henry's Ras Tafarians pranced about holding aloft an empty platter they swore would hold Premier Norman Manley's head if he blocked their way. In April when raiding police found a cache of firearms and cement-packed conch shells (obviously intended as missiles) in the Ras Tafarian Church,

Jamaican authorities decided that the Rev. Claudius Henry
was no joke. He was jailed on a charge of treason. Even with
their leader in jail, violence broke out into the open last
week. Focus of the fighting was no longer Africa. Instead, the
new goal is to convert Jamaica itself into a Ras-Tafarian run
island republic. The leaders included Henry's son Ronald and
ten U.S. Negroes from Brooklyn when they turned up for
Henry's Back-to-Africa rallies last October. They got in again
three weeks ago under assumed names, went underground
in the remote Red Hills region seven miles northwest of
Kingston, and began breaking out smuggled weapons. Last
week 250 Jamaican policemen and rookies of Britain's Royal
Hampshire Regiment were sent out to reconnoiter the Red
Hills. The soldiers carried rifles, but no bullets (Jamaican law
forbids foreign troops to carry live ammunition without special permission). An unarmed patrol of British soldiers that
ran into an ambush laid by Ronald and his Brooklyn buddies,
surrendered after the first burst of machine gun fire. The Rastafarians then ordered the tommies to kneel, shot at them
from short range. Two were killed, the other two wounded.
The guerrillas commandeered a truck and headed deeper
into the hills. When news of the killing reached Kingston,
Premier Manley mobilized the island's forces. A force of
1,000 men, Jamaican cops, West Indian Regiment troops and
British soldiers of the Hampshire, were sent into action with
aircraft, police dogs, mortar and rocket crews . . . Manley
pleaded with Jamaica's hill dwellers who knew the fugitives'
whereabouts to cooperate in tracking them down, but for
fear of Ras Tafarian reprisal the answer was silence.[35]

Jamaicans in all walks of life were now afraid of the "bearded
ones." *The Sunday Guardian* carried a headline: "JAMAICANS
LIVE IN FEAR OF RASTA MEN."[36]

d) University team: In 1960, due to bad publicity and the de-
teriorating relationships between the Rastafarians and the public,
a group of Rastafarians in Kingston wrote to Dr. Arthur Lewis,
then principal of The University and Rex Nettleford of Extramural
Studies, asking that they assist the brethren by making a study of
their doctrine and demands. On July 4, 1960, the university sent
three men, Professor M. G. Smith, Professor Roy Augier and Professor Rex Nettleford, to study the Rastafari in Kingston. After
two weeks among the cultists they produced a most helpful docu-

ment which included a short history of the cult and its beliefs and ten recommendations for government actions. Among the recommendations of The University team were: (1) sending a mission to Africa, including Rastafarians, to arrange for immigration; (2) immediately discussing preparations for the mission with representatives of the brethren; (3) recognizing that the Rastafarians on a whole were peaceful people; (4) ceasing police harassment of Rastafarians; (5) initiating low-rent housing and self-help schemes; (6) arranging for water, light, sewerage disposal and collection of rubbish in the areas where they lived; (7) establishing centers for technical classes, youth clubs, child clinics, etc.; (8) inviting the Ethiopian Orthodox Coptic Church to establish a branch in West Kingston; (9) assisting in the establishment of co-operative workshops; (10) aiding the movement with press and radio communication.[37] These recommendations were well received by the government of Jamaica. The Premier praised the report as a real contribution to the knowledge of the problem, commending the university for its leadership in bringing to the government's attention a problem and, very likely, a threat to the well-being of the island.

The recommendations creating the greatest national stir were the first and second, requesting that the government send a mission to Africa and discuss preparations for this mission immediately. The government, through the Premier, responded to the recommendation immediately and proceeded to consider how and when all this might be carried out. When news of this came to the attention of several Rastafarian groups, it created quite a sensation. But the real question at issue was, who could rightfully be considered a leader of a movement which was so completely segmented? The question was settled when the Premier met with at least three groups of Rastafari leaders from the metropolitan area.

e) The delegations to Africa: As a result of these consultations, the government finally decided to send a fact-finding delegation to various African countries to discover how the heads of these governments would react to the idea of large-scale immigration to their lands. Members chosen for this delegation included Rastafarians and leaders of various Black nationalist groups in Jamaica.[38]

The mission was made up of the following men: Dr. L. G. Leslie, Advisor; Mr. V. S. Reid, Co-advisor; Hon. E. H. Lake (Antigua), Minister of Social Welfare; Dr. M. B. Douglas and Mr. Z. Monroe-Scarlett, Afro-West Indian Welfare Leagues; W. Blackwood, United Negro Improvement Association; Cecil Gordon, Ethiopian World Federation, Inc.; D. L. Mack and Filmore, Rastafarians from Eastern and Central Kingston; and Mortimo Planno (Togo Desta), also representing the Rastafarian Movement.

The mission left Jamaica on the fourth of April, 1961, and returned to the island on the second of June of the same year. Commencing in Ethiopia, where the mission remained for one week, it visited in turn Nigeria for two weeks, Ghana for one week, Liberia for six days and Sierra Leone for one week. Except in Liberia, where the delegation met up with some opposition, all the African heads of state were sympathetic to the project.

On the day of the mission's return to Jamaica, nationalists and cultists gathered at the airport. One of the delegates recalled the experience in the following words

> There was a tremendous welcome prepared for us by members of the Back-to-Africa Movements, including Rastafarian Brethren, UNIA, Ethiopian World's Federation and others. There were about 5,000 persons with banners, flags, singing, and shouting with joy as the mission members landed in their robes.[39]

The delegation reported to the government that almost all African countries visited were willing to accept Africans from abroad provided they were skilled artisans and willing to contribute to the country to which they emigrated.

In 1962, the Jamaican Government again sent a delegation to Africa, this time on a technical mission. The purpose of this mission was an attempt to explore the possibility of cultural exchange and trade. And, in 1964, a three-man team of Rastafarians—Messrs. Mack, Alvaranga and Clayton—left Jamaica for Ethiopia by way of New York. This team seems to have had no real success other than the prestige stature among their brethren in Jamaica, who now refer to them as ambassadors.

To date no plans for the repatriation of Jamaicans to Africa have been disclosed by the Jamaican Government. I have read many of the letters written to various so-called leaders of the cult from the Governor-General and other government ministers and all of them are noncommittal.

Since the outbreak in the Red Hills there has been only one

serious incident involving the Rastafari brethren, the Montego
Bay episode in which six men, three of them Rastas, were killed.
The problem, however, of a sudden outbreak of hostilities on the
part of some factions within the cult is an ever-present danger in
Jamaica.

3. Rastafarian beliefs: The Rastafarians have developed a body
of doctrine and myth which can be set out in some kind of systematic form, and we will look at the core of this. The content of
their ideology varies slightly from one group to the next, but the
following précis would probably be accepted by all. The material
contained in this section has been gleaned from public addresses,
interviews and short articles written by the leading brethren. At
least six basic beliefs can be identified as uniquely Rastafarian.
They are: (1) Haile Selassie is the living God; (2) Black men are
the reincarnations of ancient Israelites who have been in exile in
Jamaica; (3) the white man is inferior to the Black man; (4) the
Jamaican situation is a hopeless hell, Ethiopia is heaven; (5) the
invincible Emperor is now arranging for expatriated persons of
African origin to return to Ethiopia; (6) in the near future the
Black man shall rule the world. Let us examine these in detail.

1) Haile Selassie is the living God: All Rastafarians believe that
Haile Selassie, Emperor of Ethiopia, is the true and living God, at
least of the Black man. A member of the Rastafarian Repatriation Association explained it this way:

> We know before [sic] that when a King should be crowned
> in the land of David's throne, that individual would be Shiloh,
> the anointed one, the Messiah, the Christ returned in the
> personification of Rastafari. (On his vesture and on his thigh
> is a name written, "King of Kings and Lord of Lords".) He
> (Ras Tafari) is the "Ancient of Days" (the bearded God).
> The scripture declares that "the hair of whose head was like
> wool (matted hair), whose feet were like unto burning
> brass" (i.e., black skin). The scripture declares that God
> hangs in motionless space surrounded with thick darkness
> [hence a Black man].[40]

In his *Treatise on the Rastafarian Movement,* Samuel Brown
developed the idea as follows:

> Gods are the creation of the inner consciousness of nations'
> deification of an individual. Elders and parents beget proge-

nies who in turn carry on the perpetuation of such culture. Unlike all orders of religion, the culture of Rastafari was not handed down from father to son as the people of Christendom. We who have perused volumes of history know that in this 20th century a king would arise out of Jesse's root, who should be a God (Almighty) for his people, and a liberator to all the oppressed of earth. We the Rastafarians who are the true prophets of this age, the reincarnated Moseses, Joshuas, Isaiahs, Jeremiahs who are the battle-axes and weapons of war (a Jihad), we are those who are destined to free not only the scattered Ethiopians (Black men) but all people, animals, herbs and all life forms.

We are vanguard of 144,000 celestial selectees who shall in turn free 468,000 millions particularly, and the world at large. We are the disciples of Rastafari, who have walked with God from the time when the foundation of creation was laid through 71 bodies, to behold the 72nd house of power which shall reign forever. We now stand as the fulfillers of prophecy; we knew before that when a king should be crowned in the land of David's throne, that individual would be Shiloah, the anointed One, the Messiah, the Christ returned in the personification of Rastafari (on his vesture and on his thigh is a name written, "King of Kings and Lord of Lords"). We also know the significance of Daniel, declaring from that time to this time, "for I behold until all the thrones of Babylon were cast down and the ancient of days whose head was like unto wool, whose feet were like unto burning brass, and he treadeth the fierceness of the winepress of his wrath, to execute Justice and Judgement on the Gentiles." The scriptures declare God hangs in motionless space surrounded by thick darkness; hence black man. God came in many bodies to reign forever in Rastafari the Holy one of Israel whose ray of light shall finally dim the eyes of the dragon, and through whose power all those of many nations who embrace the faith and uphold its laws shall live forevermore with God. We are those who shall fight all wrongs and bring ease to the suffering bodies, and peace to all people.[41]

The cultists have not developed this idea of their divinity from idle dreams alone; they have been able to find numerous biblical passages supporting the doctrine, or at least they think they have. For instance, from Jeremiah 8:21 they are convinced that God

is Black: "For the hurt of the daughter of my people am I hurt;
I am black; astonishment hath taken hold of me." To the Rastafarians a Black God is of the greatest importance. "Blackness is
synonymous with holiness." The distinctiveness of Haile Selassie
lies therefore in the fact that he is Black. The color of their God
then is in accordance with Scripture. This belief is further strengthened because he was born in Ethiopia and the Bible made it clear
that their God would be born in that country. According to the
Rastafarians, Psalm 87:3–4 is unquestionable proof of that.
"Glorious things are spoken of thee, O City of God. Selah. I will
make mention of Rahab and Babylon to them that know me: behold Philistia, and Tyre, with Ethiopia; this man was born there."
The book of Revelation, containing the holy prophecy about the
emperor, has become the central text for the Rastas. This is the
book in which the great titles of the King are found, "King of
Kings and Lord of Lords, Conquering Lion of the tribe of Judah,
Elect of God and Light of the World."

The Rastafarians believe that the Jesus spoken about in the Bible
is Haile Selassie and that the white slave masters and the missionaries presented him as European for the express purpose of hiding
from their Black slaves their true dignity. The white man's God
is a different God from that of the Rastafarians. He is actually
the devil, the instigator of all evils that have come upon the world,
the God of hate, blood, oppression, and war; the Black God is
a God of "peace and love." The Christian preachers of the white
God, especially the Black clergymen, are the greatest deceivers and
represent the greatest evil to the Jamaican Black man. It is they
who are denying the Black man his true destiny by daily talking
to him about a God who expects him to be humble and bear suffering and shame in this life for the reward of an imaginary heaven
somewhere in the sky after death. To the Rastafarians, who believe
in life eternal in the here and now, this doctrine is a total farce.
Eternal life in Ethiopia is an imminent possibility which, furthermore, will be enjoyed under the leadership of a Black God among
Black people.

How does Haile Selassie see this development? And how does
he respond to the idea of being called God? No comment from
him has ever appeared in print. However, Dr. M. B. Douglas, a
delegate to Ethiopia in 1961, offered the writer this interesting
report. On their arrival in Addis Ababa, the delegates were met

by the Abuna, Archbishop of the Coptic Church of Ethiopia. Learning that the cult worshiped the emperor as God, he warned them that they should not make this known to him because such honor would cause him great discomfort. The emperor, he said, is a devout Christian, a regular worshiper at the cathedral. Douglas said that this did not discourage the Rastafarians; to the contrary, it only strengthened their belief. Their reply to the Abuna was, "If he does not believe he is God we know that he is God;" they further said, "He would never display his divinity for 'he that humbleth himself shall be exalted, but he that exalteth himself shall be abased.'" The Rastafarians left Ethiopia, Douglas observed, more convinced than ever that Haile Selassie is God.

The minority report to the government by the Rastafarian delegates reflected this belief and served to strengthen the Jamaican brethren in it. Similarly, Haile Selassie's recent visit to Jamaica (1966) did nothing to dampen belief either. The Rastafarians continue in their faith as they daily repeat the prayer, "So we hail our God, Selassie I, Eternal God, Ras Tafari; hear us and help us, and cause thy face to shine upon us thy children."[42]

2) The Black man is the reincarnation of ancient Israel: According to the Rastafarians, they, the true Israelites, were punished for their sins by God their father through slavery under the white man; thus it is as a result of their sin that they have been in exile in Jamaica. However, they were pardoned long ago and should have been returned to Ethiopia, but were prevented by the slave masters' trickery.

The Rastas are obviously strongly Old Testament-oriented. They will tell the investigator that all their laws governing food and drink are strictly Levitical and their hygienic laws are based on the Old Testament. As Samuel Brown has expressed it:

> The Rastafarian is he who bows the knee to God above, we are those who obey strict moral and divine laws based on the Mosaic tenet. 1) We strongly object to sharp implements used in the desecration of the figure of Man, e.g., trimming and shaving, tattooing of skin, cuttings of the flesh. 2) We are basically vegetarians, making scant use of certain animal flesh, yet out-lawing the use of swine's flesh in any form, shell fishes, scaleless fishes, snails, etc.[43]

Because of their unique relationship with Haile Selassie I, the believer, once he claims membership, also enters into a divine state of "sonship." However, to assume it, one does not, as in other organizations, merely "join" the cult. Membership in the cult is earned through a spiritual birth, through self-awareness; the Rastafarian religion is not simply adopted, it is a man's right by virtue of his sonship. The believer is therefore a son of "Jah Ras Tafari who is God" and, so, himself also a God.

I said ye are gods and all of you sons of the most high.[44]

Beloved now are we the sons of God, and it doth not yet appear what we shall be: but we know that when he shall appear we shall be like him [because he is black] for we shall see him as he is.[45]

On the subject of reincarnation the Rastafarians have a unique teaching. They believe that God revealed himself many ages ago in human form. To the Hebrews, God revealed himself in the person of Moses, who was the *first avatar* or savior, speaking God's word because he was God, revealing himself in the shape and form of a man. When his mission was fulfilled Moses disappeared from the earthly scene and "no man knoweth of his sepulchre unto this day." The *second avatar* was Elijah, who declared the will of God. But the rulers of earth paid him little attention. Elijah did not die as other men but "went up in a chariot of fire." The *third avatar* was Jesus Christ, who said quite emphatically, "Before Abraham was, I am;" and again "I and my father are one." Now the advent of Ras Tafari is the climax of God's revelation to man. Ras Tafari will therefore never die. He is eternal and all Rastafarians who believe in him are eternal and shall never see death.[46]

We who are Rastafarians are the disciples who have walked with god from the time when the foundation of creation was laid, through 71 bodies, to behold the 72nd house of power which shall reign forever.[47]

Although the Black man might have lapsed in his relationship with God at one time or another throughout this long existence, Rastafarians claim this is no longer possible because the age of theocracy has arrived. They therefore do not believe in death but in eternal life. "The wages of sin is death, but the gift of God is eternal life."[48] The brethren attribute the death of a member of the cult to a lack of proper self-preservation, to unfaithfulness to

"Jah." Because the dead is no longer one of them, they move away from the scene, justifying their behavior by the biblical injunctions which say:

> Leave the dead to bury their dead, but go thou and publish abroad the Kingdom of God.

> There shall none be defiled for the dead among his people . . . neither shall he go in to any dead body, nor defile himself for his father, or his mother . . . he shall not defile himself, being a chief man among his people, to profane himself.[49]

Pressing one Rastafarian leader for an explanation of the cult's view of eternal life, the writer was offered this theory:

> Even if a Rastafarian pass away because of old age he really is not dead. The atoms of his body pass back into the totality of things. These same atoms are again utilized into the formation of other newborn babes and life continues as before.[50]

Another leading Rastafarian explained it this way:

> Life is like a game of cricket. As long as the player makes the appropriate stroke that merits each ball, he can play on and on for centuries. The only way a good player can be bowled is when he makes an inappropriate stroke. The Rastafarian is the man who has acquired the appropriate spiritual way of dealing with life; he therefore is immortal.[51]

This emphasis on eternal life in this world is important for the Rastafarians, many of whom have never seen any of their members die of anything but police brutality.

3) The white man is inferior to the Black man: This idea of Black supremacy is largely an echo from the days of Garvey and remains a strong point in both the U.S. Black Muslim and the Jamaican Rastafarian movements. The Rastafarian leaders will quote at length the document known as "Fundamentalism" to prove the superiority of the Black man. We quote a portion of it:

> If others laugh at you, return the laughter to them; if they mimic you, return the compliment with equal force. They have no more right to dishonor, disrespect and disregard your feeling and manhood than you have in dealing with them. Honor them when they honor you; disrespect and disregard

them when they vilely treat you. Their arrogance is but skin
deep and an assumption that has no foundation in morals or
in law. They have sprung from the same family tree of ob-
scurity as we have; their history is as rude in its primitiveness
as ours; their ancestors ran wild, naked, lived in caves and in
branches of tree, like monkeys, as ours; they made human
sacrifices, ate the flesh of their own dead and the raw meat
of the wild beast for centuries even as they accuse us of doing; their cannibalism was more prolonged than ours; when
we were embracing the arts and sciences on the banks of the
Nile their ancestors were still drinking human blood and eating out of the skulls of their conquered dead; when our civilization had reached the noon-day of progress they were
still running naked and sleeping in holes and caves with rats,
bats, and other insects and animals. After we had already
unfathomed the mystery of the stars and reduced the heavenly
constellations to minute and regular calculus they were still
backwoodsmen, living in ignorance and blatant darkness.

The world today is indebted to us for the benefits of civilization. They stole our arts and sciences from Africa. Then
why should we be ashamed of ourselves? Their modern im-
provements are but duplicates of a grander civilization that
we reflected thousands of years ago, without the advantage of
what is buried and hidden, to be resurrected and reintro-
duced by the intelligence of our generation and our poster-
ity. Why should we be discouraged because somebody laughs
at us today? Who to tell what tomorrow will bring forth?
Did they not laugh at Moses, Christ and Mohammed? Was
there not a Carthage, Greece and Rome? We see and have
changes every day, so pray, work, be steadfast and be not
dismayed.[52]

Each night, on the streets of Kingston's West End, in typical
Rastafarian meetings, these ideas are echoed. A speaker will rise
and ask the question "How did we get here?" *Chorus:* "Slavery."
Who brought us here? *Chorus:* "The White man. The white man
tells us we are inferior, but we know that we are not inferior. We
are superior, and he is inferior. The time has come to go back
home."

This desire to separate themselves from all things having to do
with the white man has worked economic hardship on the cult
members. A Rastafarian usually will not work on any project
unless it is under the supervision of another Rastafarian or a Black

Jamaican with Rastafarian sympathies. This has the effect of virtually excluding the cultists from gainful employment.

4) The Jamaican situation is a hopeless hell, Ethiopia is heaven: Although a sprinkling of new recruits is now coming from the middle class, they have not come in sufficient numbers to change the character of the group, and it has already been shown that the Rastafarians represent the lowest of the Jamaican social classes. It is this level of Jamaican society which represents the largest section of the unemployed, underemployed and the greatest number of unemployables; consequently, the deprivation within this group is at the moment beyond description. The socioeconomic conditions at this general level of society have generated three observable social responses in Jamaica: aggression, acceptance and withdrawal. The first is exemplified by numerous instances of theft, usually petty in nature. The Rastafarians are aggressive, but on another level. They are against the ruling class, against Jamaica as a whole, but they will not steal, neither do they fight among themselves. Their motto is "peace and love" among the brethren, but "fire to Babylon." The second response is *acceptance;* segments of society may simply accept their hopeless condition. This attitude is well expressed in the Jamaicanism, "Wha fe do," which translates as, "One does not like it, but nothing can be done about it." The majority of the Jamaican peasants seem to settle in this attitude. They can scarcely make ends meet, but they can see no way out of their dilemma. The Rastafarians at least offer an alternative to such an attitude. The third reaction is *withdrawal.* This is the attitude of the separatists who see no good in society and see no hope of contributing any even if effort were exerted to this end. The Rastafarians fit in here. Seeing Jamaica as utterly hopeless for the Black man, they feel no stake in her future and therefore expect nothing from the society. They will point out that the Black man has given his labor to Jamaica's white rulers for three hundred years but has received nothing in return; the Black man does the work, the white man gets the profit. The Rastafarians are therefore united not to conserve Jamaica but to escape from it. As one of their leaders, Samuel Brown, expresses it:

> Because of the stand we have taken against white oppression, and the enforcement of their way of life on black people, we have become the target of abuse and murder, perpetuated

by the black mercenary policemen, white officered. Contrary
to the opinion formed abroad that Jamaica is a black man's
land, it is not true where power of rule is concerned, even
though we outnumber all races combined. A mulatto bour-
geois class holds the balance of power under remote control,
while the blacks are held as virtual slaves. The investiture
of a black governor-general who is continually reminded to
obey orders is the present fake. . .[53]

Thus the Rastafarians claim Africa or Ethiopia as their millenarian hope, their homeland, where they plan to "sit under their own
vine and figtree." According to Brown:

We are the people in Jamaica who are definitely opposed
to any form of integration or assimilation with the white
oppressor, or any non-African races and ourselves. We are
those who do not accept the name Jamaican, knowing we are
the Africans in exile. Our view is also to return to Africa
at any cost. We are also proud to be called Africans or Ethiopians, knowing creation owes to the black man its
paternity.[54]

To prepare the brethren for life in Africa, classes in what may
be called de-Jamaicanization have come into being. Instruction
in Amharic, the language of Ethiopia, is conducted twice weekly
in many camps. And in Eastern Kingston the Rastafarian Repatriation Association sponsors films on the culture of Ethiopia and
conducts a school at night for upgrading the group for leadership
in Africa.

5) The invincible Emperor of Ethiopia is now arranging for
expatriated persons of African origin to return to Ethiopia: Recently, the writer, on leaving a group of Rastafarians, promised
to return for a visit the following year. All the cultists expressed
uncertainty as to the possibility of this because of their belief in
the imminence of their repatriation. Their mode of behavior is
that of anxious waiting for the call to go. So convinced are they
of this event, that a visit of any sort of an African official to Jamaica can set off feverish speculation about immediate repatriation. For example, on July 27, 1966, a news item appeared in the
morning paper, announcing the arrival of the Ethiopian ambassador to Haiti for official talks with the Jamaican Prime Minister.
This gave rise to wild speculation that he had come to prepare
the way for repatriation. To this end, Ras Roy McDonald of the

Ethiopian African National Congress took himself to the streets of Kingston, informing all the brethren he happened to meet that they must prepare now, for the time had come for departure. Questioned by the writer about the source of his information on this urgent announcement, he replied that the spirit had revealed to him the mission of the ambassador.

Because of this mood of urgency the Rastafarians have time and again appeared fully dressed and ready for immediate departure at the Jamaican airport—all because of a dream. No advice to the contrary can persuade them that Ethiopia is unable to accept mass migration of unskilled or semi-skilled peoples. As recently as 1960, a representative to the United Nations from Ghana visited Jamaica to lecture at the Junior Library, Tom Redcam Avenue, Kingston. It is reported that the speaker, for the benefit of the gaudily robed Rastafarians in his audience, declared that African countries would not welcome unskilled people—not even strong nationalists like the Rastafarians, especially if the migrants planned to live without working. "A destitute and unskilled migrant," he said, "would have to be in position to trace his ancestors and have these ancestors support him if he were not to become a public charge." When the African official declared that "Africa is everywhere, Jamaica is Africa!" the Rastafarians all exploded in a shout, "Imperialist stooge!"[55] Disillusioned by the "absurdity" of the lecture of this so-called African official, they left the library in utter disgust.

The Rastafarians' utter disregard for reality was further underlined in a series of broadcasts conducted by the University Radio Service in 1965. This short dialogue taken from one of these interviews reads:

Morrison: What is your name?
Boa: Ras Boanerges.
Morrison: And what does Boanerges mean?
Boa: Interpretation, "Sons of Thunder."
Morrison: I was talking to some of the other brethren about the promised land for Rastafarians and they insist that it is Ethiopia and they want to leave Jamaica as soon as possible to go back to the land of Africa. Do you believe that too?
Boa: Truly. Africa.
Morrison: I was asking them whether there has been any

> special communication between the Ras Tafarians in Ja-
> maica and the Emperor of Ethiopia suggesting that they
> come there and settle in any particular place. Now what is
> your information on this?
>
> *Boa:*   Divinely we do operate ourselves and our communi-
> cation from our God Ja Ras Tafari is spiritual.[56]

Not only do these interviews show the tenacity of the brethren's
belief, they also provide good examples of Rastafarian logic and
mode of speech. It is a religious language, the language of myth.

Haile Selassie's 1966 visit to Jamaica has been interpreted as
the last step before repatriation. The Rastafarians are now anx-
iously awaiting the call recorded so long ago in the prophecy of
Isaiah: "I will say to the north, give up: and to the south, keep not
back; bring my sons from afar, and my daughters from the ends
of the earth."[57]

The Rastafarians constantly point to the glorious age of the
Black man in Africa before the coming of the European. Habitu-
ally they refer to the historical figures of Greece and Egypt as
Black men, who occupied intellectual and political positions far
superior in achievement to any that members of the white race
have had. Now the pendulum swings back and all signs point
once more to Africa, the richest of all continents in natural resources, and to Black men, the future elite of the world. This tendency to recall the past in support of the future has been noted
by Eric Lincoln, who writes:

> The black nationalist revives history (or corrects it, as he
> would say) to establish that today's black men are descended
> from glorious ancestors, from powerful and enlightened rulers
> and conquerors. This reconstruction of history may reach
> ridiculous extremes . . . But a history is essential to the
> black nationalist's self respect. Essential, too, is the certainty
> of a brilliant future, in which the inherent superiority of his
> race will triumph and he will again rule the world.[58]

6) In the near future the Black man shall rule the world: The
Rastafarians believe, based on their interpretation of the prophecy
of Daniel,[59] that the Black man is destined to be the ultimate ruler
of the world. In this prophecy, the Black man is "the stone cut out
of the mountain without hands." This stone represents the rising
African nations which have already smitten the great "image," the

European nations that once colonized the African continent. The head of the image, the "fine gold," is Great Britain; the "breast of silver," France; the "belly and thighs of brass," Belgium; and the "legs," part iron and part clay, represent Germany. All these nations have fallen because of the political blow dealt them by the rise of the Black man in Africa. Here is a typical exegesis of Scripture which lacks every semblance of scholarly or historical reality but is full of meaning and truth to the cultists. Along this same vein, the Rastafarians believe that the white man is destined to destroy himself with nuclear weapons, after which time only the Black man will survive on this planet.

4. The practice of Rastafarianism:

a) The organizational structure among Rastafarians: While Rastafarian groups differ from one another in organizational structure a general pattern is observable among them. Foremost in authority is the person referred to in this chapter as the "leading brother," or, in some groups, as the "priest." He functions as presiding officer at meetings and, in some groups, there may be more than one of these brethren. For example, in the Rastafarian Repatriation Association, the three delegates to Ethiopia are called "ambassadors" and share equal status; all are leading brethren. The leading brethren suggest plans and procedures to the group in business meetings, and in some cases call executive meetings. Generally, they are the ones who champion the causes of the movement with government officials. They keep the idea of repatriation alive in the minds of the brethren with speeches, movies and articles. They are usually the ones who explain the nature of the movement to visiting scholars. In official ceremonies they dress in special robes, which distinguish them from the rank and file.

Below the leading brethren, but still highly respected and sharing an elevated position, is the chaplain. His function is to open the meetings with a religious service and close them with songs, chants and benedictions. This position is sometimes filled by one of the leading brethren. After the chaplain comes the recording secretary, who generally is a man, although a woman may sometimes serve in this capacity. This individual takes the minutes of all meetings, presides over roll calls and records members' dues. A treasurer is usually in charge of the group's funds, and he is, in most cases, a trusted man. As a rule, there is no place for women, but a few are given the high-sounding name "leader of songs." Last on the scale of positions are sergeants-at-arms. These are men who guard the gates at meetings, keeping intruders out and watching for the police when ganja is being used heavily.

Despite this hierarchy of structure, the nature of the movement is highly democratic. Every member is given time for full and free debate on any subject under discussion, and may agree or disagree. Still, useful projects set forth by the leading brethren characteristically receive a high degree of co-operation. For example, when purchasing a truck, members of the Adastra Road group contributed money and the group now uses the truck to transport brethren to different parts of the island for "grounation" (a Rasta ceremony) and other special meetings.

Like other cult movements of this type, the Rastafarians have developed unique practices and taboos as instruments of identification and unification among their members. The following examples are the most outstanding ones.

b) The use of the Bible: The Bible is considered to be a holy book and the major prophets (Isaiah, Jeremiah, Ezekiel and Daniel) and the apocalyptic sections of Matthew, Mark and Revelations and Psalms are used constantly—although they are freely conflated with Rastafarian ideas as the occasion demands. Not all of the Bible is acceptable to the Rastafarians; it is their belief that due to the various translations from Amharic (which the Rastas believe to have been the original language of the Bible), many corruptions have occurred. These, they assert, enhance the philosophy of the white man. Therefore, to them the Bible is a book of symbols of contemporary significance, to which only the Rastafarians have the key.

However, some Rastafarian sects refuse to have anything to do with the Bible, even though they frequently repeat ideas and statements found in it. According to these cultists, such quotations come not from the Bible but from Rastafarian wisdom. Since man existed before the Bible was written, they say, the word of man is of greater significance than that of the Bible.

It is important to observe that in the development of their doctrine, the following process occurs. First, birth of an idea, then turning to the Scripture to prove it. Second, taking a text out of its context and discarding sections that may differ from accepted views. This is not considered intellectually dishonest, because it is the Rastafarians' opinion that the unadulterated word of God has come down to us neither in the translation of 1611 nor in any subsequent one. Certain sections of the Scriptures, they claim, were deliberately distorted by the translators to fit the religious ideas of the day and time. These glosses and interpolations are the very ones they claim they have the ability to detect through divine inspiration.

The main reason for the use of the Bible among the Rastafarians, however, lies in the fact that Haile Selassie himself has advocated its use. To substantiate this, Ras Douglas Mack produced a quotation of a speech delivered by the emperor in 1954:

> We in Ethiopia have one of the oldest versions of the Bible but however old the version may be, in whatever language it may be written, the words remain the same. It transcends all boundaries of empire and all conceptions of race, it is eternal. No doubt you all remember reading the Acts of the Apostles of how Philip baptized the Ethiopian official. He is the first Ethiopian to have followed Christ and from that day onwards, the word of God has continued to grow in the hearts of Ethiopians. And I might say for myself that from my early childhood I was taught to appreciate the Bible and my love for it increased with the passage of time. All through my troubles I have found it a cause of infinite comfort. "Come unto me all ye that labour and are heavy laden and I will give you rest." Who can resist an invitation so full of comfort?
>
> Because of this personal experience in this goodness of the Bible, I was resolved that all my countrymen should share its great blessing, and that by reading the Bible, they should find truth for themselves and therefore I caused a new translation to be made from an ancient language which the old and young understand and spoke. Today man sees all his hopes and aspirations crumbling before him, he is perplexed and knows not whither he is drifting. But he must realize that the Bible is his refuge and the rallying point of all humanity. In it man will find the solution of his present difficulties and guidance for his future actions, and unless he accepts with clear conscience, the Bible and its great message, he cannot hope for salvation. For my part I glory in the Bible.[60]

The above quotation contains much that is opposed to Rastafarian belief but they derive much consolation from it and strongly stress that line which says, "by reading the Bible, they should find truth for themselves." Thus the Rastafarians will accept no explanation of the Bible but that which they themselves have settled upon.

c) The beard: One of the chief marks of a Rastafarian is the way he keeps his hair. The popular belief is that long hair and beards are symbols of the authority of man, approved by God. Although some Rastafarians, such as the Grant's Pen Group and those of Adastra Road, groom the hair of their heads and their beards, they refuse to use a razor, supporting this custom with the biblical quotation: "They shall not make baldness upon their head, neither shall they shave off the corner of their beard, nor make any cuttings in their flesh."[61] According to Sam Brown, the unshaven man is a natural man who typifies the unencumbered life. Such a man, Brown thinks, is the true African. Brown said that among the "locksmen" not even the nails of the fingers and toes are cut.

The Rastafarians are very quick to defend their physical appearance against all critics. As a reply to a letter of criticism in *The Daily Gleaner,* one Rasta wrote:

> I will also attempt to set the records straight concerning the hair dressing Mr. Scotter spoke of (and Society believes too). The quaint curls of the Rastafarians, known as the locksmen, is not clay hardened ringlets as generally believed, but the wooly hair of the African, washed only with pure water and left undisturbed by comb etc., it will eventually curl to the consistency of the locks of its own volition . . . it is generally thought that the Rastafarians are unhigenic [sic]. The belief based upon the idea that we are unwashed, it is not true. The Rastafarian being a disciple of naturalism carries neither an over-perfumed body or an acrid odor. The same cannot be said of some sections of the society.[62]

To cut off a Rasta's beard against his will, something which has actually been done by the police, is very humiliating to him. The Rastafarian as "a disciple of naturalism" was the forerunner of the "hippie" movement. Their isolation from the wider world is due to the lack of publicity. In the last five years, American disciples of naturalism have discovered them and there is now a yearly pilgrimage from America to Jamaica.

At present, a new group of Rastafarians have appeared among the older segments of the cult. They are known as "clippies." These

are the young men from the middle-class section who are attracted
to the movement through frustration, yet are not ready fully to
identify with it. They clip their hair and shave their beards but
wear some identifying symbols of the cult such as the beret of
black, red and green, the Rastafarian colors. These "clippies" are
held in derision by the older Rastafarians, who accuse them of
conforming with "Babylon" to avoid the accusations of men.

New developments among the Rastafarians have been treated in
a recent play, "Unity or Bust," published by a Rastafarian in the
newsletter *Ethiopia Calls*. The play gives a good insight into how
the members view themselves. The characters are Ethiopians—
Yemane and Tesfoye. A section of the play is quoted here:

> *Yemane:*   From my source of information, the Rastafarians
> do not boast of many people with a formal education,
> however, the majority of them are skilled in farming, in-
> dustrial labour, brick masonry, carpentry, plumbing, auto-
> mechanics, electrical technology, the arts and crafts.
>
> *Tesfoye:*   Such people could be an asset to Ethiopia,
> especially in the field of agriculture, we have *goshis* of land
> that have not been touched by a spade. The Rastafarian
> could build new communities in conjunction with the Min-
> istry of Community Development.
>
> *Yemane:*   It all seems very simple but there are still prob-
> lems from the Ras Tafarians' side.
>
> *Tesfoye:*   What problems Ato-Yemane?
>
> *Yemane:*   I've been told that there is division among the
> Ras Tafari Brethren: the locksmen who wear their beards
> and hair natural; secondly, there are the combsome who
> comb their hair and beards. *Lastly,* there are clean-face
> men who trim and shave.
>
> *Tesfoye:*   It seems ridiculous to me for a group of people
> who have intention of coming to Ethiopia to help build
> our country to quarrel about personal appearance.
>
> *Yemane:*   When any group divides itself that group is prone
> to persecution and exploitation.
>
> *Tesfoye:*   A uniting of these factions could pave the way for
> great future accomplishments.
>
> *Yemane:*   Let us hope and pray that this unity can be accom-
> plished before it is too late.[63]

Here the Rastafarians are adopting one of the oldest methods of
education: Ethiopian names for authenticity; Ethiopian setting for

spiritual depth. Drama as a mass educational technique has often done its duty as an effective tactical weapon in shaping group conformity in social movements. This play is especially important because it indicates the current desire for unity of purpose within the cult itself.

d) The use of ganja among Rastafarians: One of the great concerns of the Jamaican Government is the Rastafarians' use of ganja, or marijuana. Its use, according to some informants, began with the Pinnacle community, where it was grown as one of the cash crops. Ganja is cultivated all over Jamaica but, for commercial purposes, large cultivation is carried on illegally in the high and inaccessible mountains. Rastafarians sometimes refer to ganja as the "herb" or "wisdom seed." Their tradition says the weed was found originally growing on the grave of King Solomon; hence the name "wisdom weed." A Rastafarian claims that smoking the "herb" or the "weed" gives him wisdom, keeps his mind steadily on higher things, and enables him to gain a clear insight into his problems. A follower once said to the author, "It calms you down and 'mek' you think straight." Its use among the brethren is widespread; in fact, it has become an inseparable part of the cult's ritual. And, despite its high cost and the poverty which prevails among this group of people, it is amazing how much of it is consumed. The local price of the herb is from two to five dollars per ounce, yet at any gathering of the brethren, a large amount of the ganja is available.

The brethren are not fond of the herb for its own sake. To them its use, based on biblical authority, is religious. Their reasoning is most emphatic: God, who created all things, made the herb for the use of men. Here is some of their biblical support:

> And the earth brought forth *grass,* and herb yielding seed after his kind . . . and God saw that it was good. . . . and God said, Behold, I have given you every *herb* bearing seed, which is upon the face of all the earth, and every tree, in the which is the fruit of the tree yielding seed, to you it shall be for meat.

> Better is a dinner of herbs where love is, than a stalled ox and hatred therewith.[64]

Biblical texts such as these referring to the "herb" are quoted by all cultists in defense of their practice.

Because of their constant use of it, Rastafarians are frequently in trouble with the law, and as a result regard the police as their greatest enemy. Thus ganja smoking is practiced in the presence of a visitor only after all doubts about his sincerity have been resolved. Then, at any point during an interview, a pipe may be produced and smoking may begin. First, a handful of the herb is produced, generally wrapped up in old newspapers or brown paper bags. The ganja may or may not be mixed with varying quantities of cigarette tobacco and minced. It is then placed in a pipe or made into a cigarette. Before lighting the pipe or the "spliff," the following benediction is pronounced:

> Glory be to the Father and to the Maker of
> creation. As it was in the beginning is now and
> ever shall be, world without end: Jah Rastafari![65]

Several strong pulls or deep inhalations are then made on the pipe or cigarette. The smoker goes into a trancelike state; exhales; repeats this two or three times; and then the pipe is passed on to someone else and from him to as many as desire to smoke. As a precaution to lessen the danger in the event of a raid, the pipe is periodically secreted away.

The brethren insist that ganja smoking is far less dangerous than cigarette smoking. Drinkers of Jamaican rum, they say, have created more serious social problems in Jamaica than all ganja smokers combined. Furthermore, the Rastas declare that, whereas rum makes one violent, ganja smoking makes one calm. Unfortunately for the Rastafarians, the university report takes exception to their assertions concerning the different effects of rum and ganja. This report includes the following statements:

> One difference between rum and ganja, which the brethren
> do not recognize, is that while an overdose of rum incapaci-
> tates, an overdose of ganja does not. Thus, when a man pre-
> disposed to violence drinks too much rum, he ceases to be
> dangerous. But such a man, on smoking ganja, becomes more
> dangerous the more he smokes.[66]

The controversy surrounding the effects of marijuana is academic and is outside the aims of this book. We prefer to allow the users to speak for themselves. Of the many Rastafarians questioned during this research on the effects of the use of ganja, the following

interview with Mortimo Planno (Togo Desta) will throw some
light on the question.

> *Question:* Mr. Planno, could you tell me why the herb is
> used by Brethren and what are its effects on the user?
>
> *Answer:* When smoking this herb for the first time, you
> would not be able to consume a great quantity. The herb
> is smoked in many different ways—it is made in cigarette
> form and smoked in pipes. You have more than one pipe.
> You smoke some with water in a vessel and the herb on
> top and a lighted coal over it. This is called a steam pipe.
> You also have a chillum pipe. When you become a pipe
> smoker that is the time you can consume plenty of the
> herb and it oftentimes gives the early smoker a kick or a
> blackout. At this time you have consumed too much, but
> to find out if you consume too much you will feel the dif-
> ferent changes of the body tendency like getting you a little
> shaky or nervous, then you know you must stop at that
> stage. But when you pass through a few stages like that,
> then you can consume a considerable amount for the day.
>
> As to the effects, functionally, you still have your proper
> function. It might only have that tendency on your nervous
> system like your getting up from a sitting position and then
> you just want to sit again because of weakness, but do
> not reach an incapacitated stage as when drinking alcohol.
>
> If we have a problem, for instance, say, something vex
> us, we have a row with someone, say your domestic life
> or someone from the outside—if you consume a dish of
> herb, you feel docile. You kind of forget that erratic atti-
> tude that possessed you in your ignorance. If I contemplate
> a fight with a man, it gives me a thought that I should not
> have a fight, because a fight will lead to death and death is
> murder and murder is trial and this can lead to hanging.
> It surprises me to hear that the Americans say that the
> Baluba tribesmen of the Congo smoke ganja when they go
> into battle—saying that it makes them brave. Well of a
> truth the bravery, I can understand, because ganja makes
> you feel more brave than timid. Smoking does not make
> one violent.
>
> But one thing I notice with the herb, Professor, in Ethi-
> opia we bought herb in the market. There is a law against
> smoking the herb in the streets of Ethiopia, but if you buy
> it in the market, the people who sell it have a pipe you can

use at that market, or at that residence. While I was in
Ethiopia I bought it and used it at the hotel. But in Jamaica if you use it at home it is against the law.[67]

Laws suppressing ganja in Jamaica have created a kind of survival system among the cultists. In the first place, they have developed an elaborate ideology justifying its use. The weed is biblical,
they say, and their only means of socializing among brethren and
friends. The weed, they claim, serves a much more useful function
than destructive alcohol because it contributes to sanity and peace
of mind. Second, they argue, the law has created more "pushers"
of the weed than there normally would be if there were no laws.
Consequently each Rastafarian, because he cannot afford the risk
of buying the drug from an outsider, is a distributor as well as
a smoker. Third, a defensive communication system has developed
among them, and Rastafarians are able to speak to each other in
words and gestures opaque to outsiders. The phrase "pass the
word" was often heard during this research. As one result of
this, a well-developed neighborhood warning system exists in
the Rastafarian communities to protect cultists from police inter-
ference. Finally, the dangers surrounding the use of the "weed"
serve a unifying function in fostering intense interpersonal relationships among the members of the group.

e) Property—land: Rastafarians do not think of themselves as
Jamaicans, but as Ethiopians awaiting repatriation. For this reason
a Rastafarian owns no property. He may rent land for farming or
business, but he does not buy property. Wherever a group of
Rastafarians needs a place to live, they "capture" a piece of land,
which, once captured, is difficult for the owner to regain. Sometimes police action and even an occasional loss of life are required
to get the land back in the hands of its rightful owner. The Rastafarian concept of property is summed up in the biblical assertion
that "the earth is the Lord's and the fullness thereof." As children
of God, Jah Rastafari, the brethren feel that they are free to take
whatever land they need. Therefore, while the Rastafarian may not
steal, he will take things if he needs them. Opposed to gifts motivated by pity, he rudely rejects any form of paternalism. Whatever
a Rastafarian needs he demands.

In many respects the Rastafarians reflect a biblical fundamentalism similar to the Holiness Churches which have established themselves among this class of people in Jamaica. Although the cultists

do not admit this, their behavior is a mixture of the severe Old Testament commandment, plus a pentecostal fervor and conservatism commonly seen in this area of Kingston. What seems to be taking place here is an attempt to copy that kind of religious life which these people traditionally think of as correct but with specific Rastafarian additions.

f) Peace and love: Wherever a Rastafarian meets another he is greeted with "Peace and love" or simply "Love." This salutation, in sharp contrast to the vile language frequently heard in Rastafarian camps, has an hypnotic effect in their assemblies. The writer attended meetings which, having become emotional and noisy with the introduction of a controversial item of business, were instantly quieted by the words "Peace and love, brethren!" The Rastafarians say that this salutation comes from an Ethiopian tradition. It is used both as a greeting between the brethren and as "a sword to the hearts of non-Rastafarians." Rastas insist that no non-Rastafarian can understand "Peace and love." One of the leaders put it this way: "We love and respect the brotherhood of mankind, yet our first love is to the sons of Ham."

g) Taboos: The Rastafarians make scant use of animal flesh, reject pork in any form, and refrain from eating shellfish, scaleless fish and snails. They do not drink cow's milk, alcohol or use vinegar or salt. They do, however, eat and are fond of fish with fins and scales. As a result, many Rastafarians are professional fishermen.

h) Method of indoctrination: The Rastafarians are firm in their belief that it is only a matter of time before 90 per cent of the Black Jamaicans will wake up to the fact that they are Africans. Until such time, however, Rastafarians believe that it is their duty to spread their doctrine so as many Black Jamaicans as possible may become aware of their true selves. They feel themselves called upon not only to redeem Jamaicans, but to extend their mission to the redemption of all Black men in the West.

The Rastas' method of spreading their ideas is patterned after the early revivalist movements. First and foremost, the brethren conduct street meetings in various parts of the city and in their camps. There are three types of meetings: business meetings, grievance meetings and religious meetings. In the first kind of meeting the members deal with matters of business affecting the cult's day-to-day operations: collecting dues, introducing new members and planning for a future "grounation" or dance. The grievance meeting resembles a business meeting but one item only is its central theme—perhaps a recent action of the government such as the destruction of Shanty-Town, the death of a cultist at the hands of the police or a tactical blunder of an activist endangering the existence of the cult as a whole. Here plans and strategy are agreed upon and ways and means of evasion or attack are planned. The third type of religious meeting is called either for the general edification of the members or for the purpose of winning new recruits. A typical meeting of this type was held at 24 D'Augilar Road in East Kingston; the writer was present and made a recording. It opened with the singing of a hymn "From Greenland's Icy Mountains to India's Coral Strand," followed by Psalm 42. Then a second hymn, "Negus Lover of my Soul, let me to thy bosom fly," was sung. Then a second lesson, this time from Matthew 24, followed by a verse-to-verse comment by the ambassadors as a particular verse brought a particular idea to mind. Ras Samuel Clayton then followed with a moving speech on "The Life and Customs of Ethiopia." Ras Moses next spoke on plans to be carried out when the brethren arrive in Ethiopia. Finally, Ras Mack appealed for membership. The meeting was concluded when the chaplain led the assembly in chanting and in singing the Ethiopian national anthem and then pronounced his benediction.

> Princes shall come out of Egypt, Ethiopia shall stretch forth her hand unto God. Oh, thou God of Ethiopia, thou God of thy Divine Majesty, thy spirit come within our hearts to dwell in righteousness. That the hungry be fed, the sick nourished, the aged protected, the infant cared for. Help us to forgive that we may be forgiven. Teach us love and loyalty as it is in Zion. Deliver us from the hand of our enemy that we may prove fruitful for the last day, when our enemy has passed, and decayed in the depth of the sea or in the belly of a beast. O give us a place in thy Kingdom for ever and ever. So we hail our God Selassie I, Jehovah God, Ras Tafari, Almighty God, Ras Tafari, Great and terrible God Ras Tafari who sitteth in Zion and reigneth in the hearts of men and women, hear and bless us and sanctify us, and cause thy loving face to shine upon us thy children that we may be saved. Selah.

There are many versions of this prayer and benediction, but the one given above is, perhaps, the most cogent. The word *selah* has an almost mystical connotation to the brethren and is always used in place of the traditional Amen.

5. The function of the movement: The Rastafarian movement has performed a function in Jamaica that no other movement has been able to perform since the days of Marcus Garvey. In speaking of the "function" of Rastafarianism, we mean that type of activity which has contributed to the adaptation or survival of the group in the existing social order. First of all, the revolutionary stance of the cultists has brought an important social awakening in Jamaica. They have stimulated a new sense of identity among the Black masses and indirectly influenced the ruling class by communicating to them a sense of urgency to redress the wrongs done to the underprivileged class of the society. The Rastas have also stimulated a revival of primitive art in the island and have thereby enhanced their own socio-economic status. They further serve a political function in trying to Africanize Jamaica, a process which began in slavery but lost its drive as the Blacks became more and more dependent upon the white ruling class. And finally they provide a viable religion for the oppressed class of Jamaica. We shall expand these points in some detail.

a) The function of identity: The movement provides a *sense of identity* to that large segment of the society which had lost all sense of social worth. Most of the members interviewed in this research reported that they became members in order to find identity. The cult provides a strong sense of "we-feeling," accentuated by the unique look, dress, speech, style and communal living of the Rastas. Their motto, "Peace and love," serves as a unification device. Members are known to one another as "brother," "Rasman," "Rasta," and no one feels any sense of inferiority in the brotherhood.

This feeling of personal identity is a unique factor in the appeal and impact which the cult now makes on the Jamaican society. Over against the Rastafarians stands Jamaican middle-class society, many of whose members are best described as pocket-sized Englishmen. Most members of the Jamaican elite have tried to a fault to copy the customs and mannerisms of the colonial administrators. The result is that the middle-class Jamaican has developed a Victorian outlook on life without the economic stability to bolster this sense of personal prestige. He will strain to dress like his English counterpart, in Scottish tweed in ninety-degree weather, or struggle to maintain a home with all the appearances of the Great Houses of the English barons with servants and yard boys. Each social stratum strains to appear like the one above it.

There are really three traditional classes in Jamaica: the upper class, the traditional owners of wealth and opportunity; the middle class, the near white and professional Blacks; and at the bottom, the lower class, which for generations has existed at little more than a subsistence level. In this last class are the people who, because of social and economic deprivation, have relied more and more on deliverance from "above." Katrin Norris, in her book *Jamaica: The Search for an Identity,* said of the so-called lower-class man:

> Having nothing in common with and no chance to express himself in the British oriented public life of Jamaica, which was until recently the exclusive reserve of an elite white and brown upper and middle class, he resigned himself to his own world, where religion became the outlet for his talents of leadership, oratory, music, poetry, or simply an escape from his hard life with the promise of divine salvation.[68]

The Rastafarians have sought to overcome this conflict by seeking to identify themselves with that aspect of their culture with which the middle class has had the greatest conflict. They prize the fact that they are Africans. They have deified Blackness. They emulate as many African customs as possible. They seek to buy authentic African clothing. From time to time they even change their western names where possible, as Mortimo Planno (now Togo Desta) did in Africa. He also gave his children African names, a practice which continues to gain strength among these people. Their belief in the supremacy of the Black man, specifically the "Ras man," gives them an ego boost which is portrayed in their walk, their talk and all their mannerisms.

Because of their strong sense of self-identity many Jamaicans see the Rastafarians as the only "real" Jamaicans. The result is that many Jamaicans loosely identify themselves with the cultists and imitate them in bodily appearance, and dress when possible. The Rastafarians have, therefore, become an unintended stimulus for that very self-identification which colonial administrations have unsuccessfully tried to stimulate for centuries.

The Rastafarians have thus created a society of Black men, men who want to buy Black, live Black and think Black. The Rasta rejects white values and claims the fullness of his own heritage. This has created a new climate of interest in the wider society and the unique ideology of the movement is now receiving attention in the press and from anthropologists and sociologists, consequently Rastafarians seem never to be out of the limelight. People of every walk of life are interested in finding out more and more about them. This gives a certain novelty to the position of the movement in Jamaica. Members are often solicited by schools and colleges to give lectures and speeches concerning their beliefs and practices. They make personal appearances on the Jamaican television station and are invited to dance and drum at many top-level receptions. The Rastafarians have received outstanding awards for dancing in the Jamaican Festivals. They were prominent in the reception given for Haile Selassie at King's House and at the Sheraton Hotel, privileges accorded to few of the Jamaican elite.

The movement has even given some of them the chance to visit Africa at government expense. They send numerous letters to all levels of government: to U Thant of the United Nations, to the Queen of England and above all to the Emperor of Ethiopia; and answers are forthcoming. Any Rastafarian group can produce letterheads from many of the greatest heads of government. Although these privileges are accorded only to the leading functionaries of the cult, the pride of their achievements is shared by the rank and file of the movement. Ras Graham now signs his name with the title "Honorable," because of his invitation to the King's House reception of Haile Selassie. Ras Hill expressed it as follows: "He lifted us from the dust of the earth and caused us to sit with princes of the land."

b) The movement's socio-economic function: An unintended function of the Rastafarian movement is the stimulus it has given to the Jamaican economy in the recent resurgence of arts and crafts. There have traditionally been only a handful of Jamaican native painters and the few that did emerge had no feeling for their own land. Their paintings have been of scenes from England, Scotland or perhaps abstracts of an academic nature. Today, there are scores of Rastafarian painters who engage in producing what may be termed "primitive art." These paintings are inspired by their deep religious consciousness and abound in symbolic animals, heads of cultists and other human figures. The figure of Haile Selassie is prominent and he is depicted both as a man or as the Lion of Judah. Rastafarian sculpture has also become popular. Their works can be seen in the art shops all over Kingston and are greatly sought after by collectors. These sculptures, which invariably portray the heads and faces of Rastafarians with their peculiar hairdo are carved from mahogany, mahoe and lignum vitae, the hardest woods in Jamaica. Along with these, are rugs made of goat skins, baskets, decorated seashells, calabashes and coconut shells and other craft objects. The Rastafarians find a thriving business for their work in the tourist market, thus indirectly contributing to the economy. Yet, despite this, they still see their work not as a contribution to the economy but solely as a means of getting money for their return to Ethiopia. So prolific is this growth of Rastafarian art, that the prestigious University of the West Indies recently sponsored a display of their things.

It will not be possible to enter into the music and dance of the Rastafarians here, but in these areas, the Rastas have contributed greatly. Their unique drumming, dancing and singing have become tourist attractions in the island. Many recordings of Rastafarian songs are now on the market.

c) Political function: The movement offers to its members opportunities for political consciousness. Rastafarian meetings often include lengthy denunciations of the leaders of government; their main theme of discussion on any meeting night usually is taken from the current debates in Parliament printed in the daily newspapers. The cultists will spend hours pointing out flaws in proposed projects. Even subjects such as birth control and the war in Vietnam are of personal concern to the Rastafarians and become topics of heated discussion in their meetings. In these meetings one hears constantly about the glaring contrast between the "Sodom of the West" (Jamaica) and the "land of promise" (Ethiopia). From the Rastas one can hear examples of true primitive philosophy on the one hand, and, on the other, hours of nonsense. Still, some Rastafarians display a knowledge of Jamaican politics and a knowledge of world trends far more sophisticated than their middle-class counterparts. Occasionally, one detects a hidden desire to take an active share in politics and a certain craving to be part of life in Jamaica.

d) Religious function: The religious function of a movement such as the one under discussion must not be underestimated. It should be remembered that the movement began on a strong religious note and that this has continued as its basic characteristic to the present day. Religious institutions embody in symbolic form some of the most profound insights of men. Far from being the unfortunate survival from man's primitive past, they are an integral and necessary element in any stable social system.

The Rastafarians have developed a religious dogma to fit their condition in life. They find no satisfaction in the belief in what they call a "European Jesus Christ"; therefore, they have turned their devotion to a Black God and a heaven among Black peoples. These to them are more satisfying symbols. They use the Bible and interpret it to suit Rastafarian beliefs. They use the hymns of the Christian Church in a revised form to bring out Rastafarian beliefs, and create new ones around their ideology. Along with these, they display flags and banners and paintings to keep the spirit of their ideas alive. Their prayers are recited with raised hands, facing Ethiopia, and they show a deep millenarian fervor.

Their meetings are characterized by *intense emotional experience,* at times close to spiritual possession. However, the Rastafarians differ in belief from the Pukumina and Revivalist cults when it comes to such things as obeah or witchcraft. They are officially opposed to obeah, yet it seems they share with these other Jamaican cults an emphasis on dreams and visions. And they too are steeped in the practice of bush remedies for every kind of illness. On the subject of witchcraft, several Rastafarians expressed the opinion that it was trickery and rubbish, and Ras Moses recalled for this researcher his confrontation with an obeahman who tried to practice obeah for his sister's protection. In this confrontation he recalled how he whipped the obeahman so severely that he ran away from the house and never returned. Although this attitude toward native folk belief may hold for the leading Rastafarians it cannot be applied indiscriminately to all the rank and file, for they undoubtedly still have a healthy fear of witchcraft. The truth probably is that the cultists have consciously tried to supplant the old folklore with a new ideology as a means of divesting themselves of all things Jamaican; and this includes obeah, which is practiced by the Christian-oriented cults of Jamaica.

From the discussion above we conclude that Rastafarianism provides a unique solution to the economic, political and religious problems of thousands of Jamaicans of the lower class. The cult provides a release from the drabness and drudgery and daily humiliation of life in an economically and socially deprived situation and, perhaps most important, a more satisfying religious alternative to Christianity.

e) Some conclusions: There remains only a final word to be said about the possible future of the Rastafarians in Jamaica. Here we are in the realm of prediction and this must be approached with caution. However, some broad guesses may be of interest.

1) The possibilities for repatriation: Up to 1961 repatriation seemed possible. The government then in power sent two delegations to Africa to study the possibility of mass migration. Since then, however, a new government has come into power in Jamaica and has until recently shown little interest in the project. The writer has read several letters written by the Premier, the Governor-General and ministers to Rastafarian leaders. These letters politely acknowledge the Rastas' correspondence about repatriation but give no indication that the government has any plans to help them achieve their goal. Furthermore, recent addresses and interviews by Africans coming to Jamaica seem to indicate that the African states would look very unfavorably on a mass immigration of Rastafarians at this stage of their development, especially if the immigrants were unskilled. Finally, those few people who have actually migrated to Ethiopia give no encouragement to the proposed repatriation movement and believe, firmly, that the Rastafarians would be at a serious disadvantage if their plans for mass migration were realized.

2) Changed economic situation could change outlook: There are, however, other possibilities for the movement in Jamaica as its economic condition improves. Many Rastafarian leaders now drive cars to their weekly meetings and so do some of the members. Some Rastafarians are running co-operatives in several parts of the island; others have set themselves up in a variety of small business enterprises such as running a grocery or vending fruit. We have already seen that there is a strong artistic revival in the movement which, if handled properly, could develop into a strong economic base. There are numerous examples of remarkable socio-economic developments generated within new religious

movements without outside help. We call to mind two examples: the Black Muslims of America, which is now a multimillion-dollar enterprise, and the Peace Mission movement of Father Divine which is entirely self-supporting and financially strong. These movements originated about the same time as the Rastafarians and they were reacting to the same type of socio-economic pressure. It is very obvious that these two movements have had a better chance to succeed because they were based in America, but the crucial advantage of these movements over the Rastafarians has been the quality of leadership. Should a charismatic leader arise within the Rastafarian movement who could channel its energies, we might see an exciting development in the coming decades.

CHAPTER 8

SOUL TRIUMPHING:
A Return to the Roots "At Home and Abroad"

1. Africa: When, over forty years ago, the Jamaican prophet Marcus Garvey pronounced, "Africa for the Africans at home and abroad," he envisioned the awakening of the sons and daughters of Africa on the continent as well as in the lands of exile. Although the intellectuals of his race scorned him, millions of his downtrodden brethren rallied to his messianic call. This call awakened millions of Black people from their slumber and they remembered the long-forgotten promise: "Princes shall come out of Egypt; Ethiopia shall soon stretch out her hands unto God" (Psalm 68:31). The rape of the Black race on a global scale did not go unnoticed by men like Edward Wilmot Blyden and Marcus Garvey, both sons of Africa and both of Caribbean origin.

Blyden lived most of his life in Africa and his missionary zeal did much to awaken the Africans to the deceit of imperialism, but it was the voice of Garvey that finally ignited the souls of Africa. We will call on a few Africans to testify to Garvey's influence. Peter Abrahams, a South African author writing in *Public Opinion,* November 3, 1956:

> And since the first stage in any kind of liberation is the liberation of the mind, Marcus Garvey can justly be regarded as a primary source of the great freedom movements in the colonial world—today.

Chief Nana Kobena Nketsia, Director of the Institute of African Studies, University of Ghana, on his visit to Jamaica, July 1965, on placing a wreath at Garvey's tomb, said:

"I sincerely believe our mission for freedom is not an accident of history, but the work of divine providence. . . . Thanks be to God and Marcus Garvey's teachings for the light that is shining over Africa today, and will always shine."

Dr. Kwame Nkrumah, speaking at the closing session of the All African People's Conference in Accra, December 13, 1958, stated in part: "Long before many of us were even conscious of our degradation, Marcus Garvey fought for African national and racial equality." We could go on with the testimonies of Africans across the continent but this is not our purpose here.

We began our study by reviewing our African heritage under the heading, "Source of Soul." In this discussion we established the fact that the sons and daughters of Africa did not come to the New World from a cultural wilderness but from a land with well-established cultural institutions, and that it was the transplantation of these culture dynamics in the New World that enabled the Africans in diaspora to preserve their sense of humanity in the face of the devastating assault of chattel slavery. In this closing chapter we return to the source—to Africa—to see how in the course of the centuries of exile, history has treated the motherland. But alas! What do we find? Devastation and ruin. The same hands that snatched the sons and daughters of Africa and sold them into slavery later returned with vengeance to destroy the source itself. The history of European imperialism in Africa is too complex for our present purposes. What we hope to show is that Africans, both at home and abroad, are only now putting the pieces of their lives back together again. It is a sad reflection on the history of Christianity when one considers that the main agent of African domination was clothed in the guise of Christian mission and that it was the agent of Christianity who, more than anyone else, sought to fetter the African soul. In his article on African religious movements, James Fernandez rightly observes:

The Christian missionaries, in most cases, then, were the first real agents of domination and deprecation, in reaction to which most religious movements arose. The thorough-going identification of the evangelical with the colonial and imperial

enterprise in the minds of Africans has been often re-
marked. Historically, however, Christian evangelization was
frequently the first term of this identification, colonial ad-
ministration second.[1]

At present, Africa is experiencing a religious ferment which has
resulted in schisms of no fewer than six thousand new separatists
movements on the continent, and the end of this fragmentation
is nowhere in sight.[2]

A cursory reading of the scholarly works on Africa suggests
that the failure of the Christian mission in Africa is due primarily
to the missionaries' lack of knowledge of African psychology. The
foundations of African society have for centuries been the home
and the extended family. All these features of tribal social structure, including polygamy, were the outcome of a long and complex history and are so closely knit that no change can be forced
in one area without it affecting all the others. The Africans' politics, law, religion, art, language, culture and society are so closely
interlocked in a self-balancing system, that when the missionaries
failed to take a proper appraisal of this they negated the possibility
of an effective Christian mission. The mentality of the nineteenth-
century missionary was ill fitted to this task.

At first, the coming of Christian missions to Africa aroused
widespread hope among a number of Africans. Large numbers of
them responded positively to the missions, both Protestant and
Catholic. But in the beginning of the Christian mission, few attempts were made to oppose the indigenous religions of Africa.
However, after the Berlin Conference of 1884, in which the African continent was divided up among the European powers, a
serious attempt was made to attack the traditional society of Africa. The early missionary attitude of courtesy toward African social and religious forms gave way during the period of 1885–1914,
and was replaced by a direct assault on "pagan superstition."

There were many reasons for this change of attitude. In the
first place, after 1885, missionary thinking shifted from a stance
of sympathy to one of paternalism. European colonial rule was
now considered the only hope for Africa's backwardness. By European comparison, African cultures seemed inferior, immoral
and doomed to collapse.

Second, with improved medical knowledge, Europeans were

able to live indefinitely in the tropics and an increasing number were brought out to run the missions at all levels, displacing the competent African converts. With the rise of communication, frequent furloughs were taken by the missionaries and this gave the impression that the missionaries were not totally committed to Africa. Along with this practice, families were brought to live in Africa and this resulted in less social mixing and increasing social distance between the two peoples. As a consequence, most of the European missionaries had little opportunity to gain a real knowledge of all these things of the African world view and they knew nothing of the social function of traditional religion.

While Africans appeared enthusiastically to accept European Christianity, a subconscious alarm at this new assault on their society was rung across the continent. Community structures were being demolished. Land, the life blood of the ancestors, was being absorbed, along with other African properties, to a foreign economy; laws and taboos were being destroyed; religious concepts were being discarded; magical concepts were termed superstitious; rituals and worship were attacked as pagan; and even the vernacular languages of the tribes were being proscribed.

The result of this situation was that Africans now realized with some bitterness that the hopes aroused by early missionary preaching would not materialize. They did not anticipate the consequences of the severe strain which was now being put on their traditional cultures and institutions. They had failed to augment their force vitale by the promised aid of the white man, either material, financial, cultural, spiritual or ecclesiastical.[3] Their societies' aspirations were not being fulfilled by the missionary religion. In place of the secure religion they had before, there was now only a religious void. A widespread sense of uncertainty and insecurity arose and hope was replaced by frustration and resentment as the Africans saw their traditional tribal complex disrupted by white expansion and the growth of urban communities from which they were generally barred.

All the new impinging forces consequent on European contact (economic, social, political and religious), led to widespread *anomie* and tension in African societies.[4] The result was a period of incubation in which a subliminal discontent grew slowly into a conscious awareness of disaffection.[5]

The publication of the Scriptures in the vernacular languages

of African tribes was an event of major importance. Africans
began reading the Bible, and again their hopes were raised by the
biblical vision of social renewal, power, prosperity, peace, love,
justice, brotherhood and equality. With the translation of the complete Bible, African societies gradually began to discern a serious
discrepancy between it and the teaching of the missionaries. They
soon discovered that the Bible gave its special blessing to family
life, land, fertility, the importance of women, polygamy and respect for family ancestors.

The Africans now realized that the missionaries had been
misrepresenting the biblical message and had added their own
cultural bias to it. A new wave crested of disaffection with the dis-
embodied doctrine, prefabricated dogma, formalized prayers, abstract theology, indigestible liturgy, complex regulations and harsh
ecclesiastical discipline all imported from Europe. Africans now
began to articulate the desire to manage their own affairs, free
from white political domination, and to desire to control their own
destiny by exercising the power promised to the people of God
through the Holy Spirit. The Africans were quick to point out
faults in the mission structure—the most important discrepancy
centering around the biblical concept of love. They accused the
missionaries of being remiss in the practice of agápē; their "paternalism" instead of "philadelphia."

At a certain point the limits of tolerance were reached and the
break came with the emergence of charismatic leaders, visionaries,
prophets and prophetesses, who tried to save the tribal religion—
indeed the society—from catastrophe. They often claimed an experience in the wilderness or some brush with death and resurrection and some said they had received messages from the gods and
ancestors telling them to drive out the Christians. The result was
the emergence of a new sort of religious movement generally
characterized as syncretistic and magico-religious. These movements retained some elements of Christian practice but were
strongly rooted in traditional African religious customs.

While it can be said that religion in its institutionalized form is
declining, it can be said without contradiction that, in new form
it is enjoying a period of renewed vitality in Africa. This is true
not only in West Africa but in the continent as a whole.

In Africa today one can distinguish various kinds of sects.
There are those that have been imported, such as the Jehovah's

Witnesses, the Seventh-Day Adventists, the Apostolic sects of the American Negro variety and the Pentecostals. And alongside of these there are the indigenous religious sects, of which South Africa has the most. The following are a few of the more prominent separatist churches in West Africa. *Sierra Leone:* The West African Methodist Church; The Nigerian Church of the Lord (Aladura), close to a quarter of a million in West Africa; The God is Our Light Church: all Methodist offshoots. *Ghana:* The Church of the Twelve Apostles; The Apostolic Revelation Society: mostly Ewe; The Eden Revival Church: mostly Methodist offshoots. *Nigeria:* United Native African Church: an Anglical offshoot; The Cherubim and Seraphim Church; The Church of the Lord (Aladura). *Dahomey:* Mission d'union Africaine; The Native African Church; Si C'est Bien, Viens (If We Are Right, Join Us); Elija (Fishmongers). *Ivory Coast:* The Eglise Harriste; Eglise Deimatiste (Church of Ashes Purification). *Togo:* Wovenu's Apostolic Revelation Society.[6]

It is important to note that all these new sects are associated with problems of African identity; only in this light can the new religions of Africa be understood. They are mechanisms for adjustment to the rapidly emerging urbanism in Africa.[7]

In Ghana, in particular, as in Africa as a whole, various types of religious movements have emerged. Most of these appear to be a blend of Christianity and traditional religious systems. These indigenous religions are trying to recreate new social communities, communities in which social relationships are patterned on the tribal-kinship structure. To orthodox Christians, religious separatism is regarded as a sort of religious delinquency, but this is not the way it is viewed by the separatists. On the contrary, they must be understood as people who are trying to relate their day-to-day experience with what they understand as supernatural forces.

a) Women as leaders: One of the new phenomena in African protest movements is the emerging leadership of women.[8] This is a new avenue of social mobility for the African woman.

Perhaps the most powerful of the sects under female leadership is to be found in Zambia and is led by Alice Lenshina. At one point her movement clashed head on with the Zambian Government, and people were killed as a result of it. What is especially interesting about this is that it was a woman who led the revolt, something which is rare in African traditional societies.

The history of Alice Lenshina is typical of most of the religious leaders of this type in Africa.[9] Alice was an illiterate middle-aged housewife, whose unique claim was that she had actually been dead for a period of three days. According to her, on her way to heaven, she was stopped by Peter, who asked her to return and to preach to her people against witchcraft. Returning to earth, she began preaching. First she went to the pastor of her church and told him about her return from heaven, but like all pastors of established religions, he considered this type of vision awkward. Alice persisted, now believing that her type of vision could not be contained in the church. Alice soon began to gather around her a band of enthusiastic followers. She was later expelled from her denomination and, as a result, many left along with her. For a time, peace prevailed in the new church, which was given the name of The Lumpa Church. (Lumpa is a Bemba word meaning "above all things," signifying the level of religious purity which was associated with the movement.) Many people flocked to the movement because of the reported ability of the leader to cleanse witchcraft. Alice later surrounded herself with her own apostles and deacons and all the trappings of an institutionalized church.

In Africa, religion and politics have traditionally avoided clashing with each other. This was not to be so with the Lumpa sect. On her second visit to heaven, Alice was advised that membership in a political party is incompatible with membership in the Body of Christ. And that anybody holding a party card was automatically denied admission to heaven. She revealed this new vision to her followers. In Zambia, where the one party system was considered sacred, this type of anti-political teaching was to meet with immediate opposition. The followers began to burn their party cards. Later they came to regard the Zambian secular society as sinful, and so they withdrew from the Zambian society and built their own village. They were attempting to create not only a new religious community but a new secular polity. This was regarded by the government of Zambia as treason. The conflict worsened when Alice Lenshina's people withdrew their children from the secular schools. The government stepped in and began to try to coerce the Lumpa sect to drop their anti-social behavior. An open conflict resulted between the Zambian security police and the Lumpa sect, in which conflict 850 people died.

Now, the Lenshina religious movement may serve as a model of all the new movements. They pass through various stages. First, comes the vision; this is one of the main factors by which African religious leaders legitimate their authority. Later, there is a period of development in which the movement draws heavily on African mythology. For example, Alice offered protection against witchcraft, one of the perennial fears of Africans. Anyone who sets up a movement on this basis has a chance of succeeding. In a continent where the religious and the secular blend into one another, sects such as this command a large following, especially if the content is congruent with the aspirations of the Africans. This is especially true in urban communities, where we find that the people who belong to the newer religious movements are those who live on the margins of society. They are people who have been uprooted from their traditional cultural background and yet are not fully integrated into the newer value system of the industrial urban community in which they live. These are the people who need a new type of socialization.

A summary view of the new religious movements yields the following broad points: (1) There is a *centrality of the historical Jesus* as *Lord* and *Savior,* although considerable differences exist in belief and practice. (2) There is a complexity of new religious forms which seeks to incorporate traditional customs with selective drawings from Western culture, mission theology and practice. (3) Religious leaders are most often prophets and prophetesses who undergo various religious transformations such as death and resurrection, trances, visions and revelations. (4) Religious symbolism consists of various meaning-charged colors revealed in dreams. The colors most favored are blue, red and white. Along with the colors are symbolic staffs, banners and flags. (5) Rituals consist of the blessing of medicines, newly bought articles, dancing in circles, the ritual use of holy water, purification rites, baptism in the "Jordan," exorcism of devils, release from witchcraft and sorcery. (6) Worship includes special spirit language, religious gruntings, religious joy and ecstasy, handclapping, vernacular hymns set to indigenous tunes, and vernacular Scripture reading in a multi-tribal context.

F. B. Welbourn, referring to this new type of movement, said:

The whole complex may be regarded as a focus of a new type
of community, a restructuring of society which replaces the
old tribe by the new church often with its own closely-
integrated institutions, customs, belief and laws, in which the
mass of innovatory ideas and practices serves to bring
about a quite new social cohesion in a disintegrating society.
The new society, then, becomes a place to feel at home, capable of fulfilling the same mediating role in the new secular
world as the traditional tribal complex played in the old.[10]

In the wake of the Western evangelizing mission, Europe gave
Africa the Bible (with all pacifying influences that this implies)
while stealing its lands and resources. It took centuries for Africans to see what was really taking place, but when they finally
awakened, they found themselves robbed of their heritage. Like
an organic reaction to invading disease, the process of revitalization begins slowly. The Africans in crisis, like their brothers in
exile, appropriated aspects of the Christian religion to use as
weapons in their fight for freedom and dignity. Thus the prophetic movements in Africa are direct counterparts of Black freedom movements which are taking place in the New World.
They are reactions to the deprivation of their possession, their
status and their worth as a people. As we have seen throughout
this book, a people in situations of this type often returns to aspects of its remembered culture. And, in most cases, this takes
the form of a religious return. It is generally at a later period that
the emerging intellectuals are drawn into the battle. In our day,
the problem of African identity has surfaced in the minds of her
intellectuals, and those who once were proud of their French and
English education have now returned to draw inspiration from
their roots.[11] Thus from the pens of Senghor in Senegal, to Cyp-
rian Ekwensi and Chinua Achebe in Nigeria, to Ezekiel Mphahlele
in South Africa, we read loud and clear that Africa and its heritage
have not been destroyed. The novels and poetry of these literary
greats announce to the world that the cultural roots of Africa are
deep. The theologians have also joined in the defense of African
religion and the works of John S. Mbiti of Kenya and E. Bolaji
Idowu of Nigeria are now well known. These men, though
trained in the Christian creed, have now returned to their cradle

of religious inspiration and are finding out that the spirituality of
their African heritage is not only alive but essential to their lives
and the lives of their people.

2. The Americas: The meaning of Black struggle must be discovered in the ethos of the people. Ethos is here defined as the
fundamental attitudes and values of a group, which distinguish
that group from all others. Black life-force has been characterized
by many as basically supernatural; hence to speak of Black ethos
is, inevitably, to speak of religion. We have seen that the traditional African world view is primarily concerned with man's relation to his power sources and the discussion of the previous
chapters indicates that the New World experience did not completely erase this attitude from Black consciousness. If anything,
it has been reinforced under New World conditions, since the
Black man's only consolation has been his firm belief in the power
of a God who gives him strength in weakness and comforts him
in sorrow. Consequently, his entire life has been an unceasing
evocation of this divine power. Divine power became his one all-
absorbing concern because it was the only source of help open
to him. Similarly for traditional Africans, today, God is no mere
intellectual pastime. In God, the traditional African lives, moves
and has his being. God is the axis around which the world of men
and created things move. So also for the African in "exile": the
concept God was in the past, and to a great degree is, still today,
the center of his existential concern.

As was said before, the Black world had produced no great
theologians. This is not to say that Blacks have no theology. It is
simply the case that the black man has neither had the time nor
felt any need to write his theology because he lives it. Theology
is the science of thinking about God and as such can only be indulged in by people who have time for reflection and an atmosphere of relative security. The Black man in the New World has
had no such luxuries. Unlike white Christians, who have a God
who is a reflection of their own high esteem for riches and plenty,
the Black man's religion has been, from the beginning of his New
World experience, a religion of suffering. And so Black theology,
although unwritten (like the oral tradition of the African ancestors)
finds expression in the myths, stories and songs of suffering.
Nevertheless, it was not until recently that a new, evocative and
revolutionary theology of "Blackness" emerged. The new young

Black theologians, if we may call them so, were born out of the struggle of the Civil Rights movement. As products of conflict, they have tried to resolve their inner turmoil not only in poetry and novels, but in wrestling with thoughts of God and destiny. Although their writings are not yet well known, they represent an *avant-garde* of radical theological thinking which can be favorably compared with the work of Dietrich Bonhoeffer during the Second World War.[12]

The African *Zeitgeist* in exile emerged much earlier than it did on the continent. It was this *Zeitgeist* that led to the flowering of such movements as Negrism in Cuba, Indigenismo in Haiti, the Back-to-Africa movement in Jamaica and Négritude in Martinique. It was from the Caribbean that African descendants such as Edward Wilmot Blyden, Marcus Garvey, Claude McKay, Jean Price-Mars, Aimé Césaire, Alexandré Dumas, George Padmore and Franz Fanon burst upon the scene with their praise of their African heritage—even though some of them had never seen the shores of Africa. It was these carriers of the Black ethos who inoculated others with the germ of their peculiar heritage, that germ which was later to break out in a worldwide cultural epidemic, a return to Black roots.

Although the African ethos still persists in the Caribbean in the various movements discussed in the preceding chapters, no real cult leader has done any writing of consequence. The writings of such scholars as Rex Nettleford, Orlando Patterson and Edward Brathwaite in Jamaica and René Piquion in Haiti are examples of Caribbeanists whose writings continue to throw light on the African identity of the region.[13] Although Santeria in Cuba is experiencing a mild revolution very little has been published recently. The spirit of Africa has now swung to North America, where the sentiment finds its most fervent advocates in men and movements. African-Americans now lead the New World in the cultural return. It is here that we find the great writers on Black values who are prepared both emotionally and intellectually to defend the Black ethos. No one stands out more than Martin Luther King, Jr., whose writings and devotion to Black betterment have inspired a whole generation of men and women of all races. His life and dreams will illumine the pages of Black history for generations to come.

In the field of religion, where Black scholars have established themselves, the writings of C. Eric Lincoln of Fisk University, Deotis Roberts of Howard, Joseph R. Washington of Virginia University and Gayrand Wilmore of Boston University have all contributed much to the ongoing quest for Black identity.

Alongside of the above scholars and leaders, a new theological literature is being developed which may revolutionize Black thinking. This is called Ethnic or Black theology. Among the foremost in this field is Albert B. Cleage, Jr., whose radical pronouncement that Jehovah and Jesus were Black,[14] has had overwhelming acceptance in the Black community.

But the most important of these men is James H. Cone of Union Theological Seminary.[15] Cone is by far the most perceptive religious thinker in Black America in this decade. His writing centers around the theological implications of Black Power. He sees the "symbol of Blackness" as a potent synthesis of the Black experience in the United States and therefore as a concept loaded with revitalizing possibilities for Black and white alike. Blackness, for Cone, involves an ontological restructuring of the traditional force-vitale. "Blackness" is holiness. As a concept, it is emotive and evocative; its mood is anger; it is "soul." Thus, at its deepest level, Black Power shows itself to be nothing but "Black soul-force"— life reacting to overcome white racism and its attendant slow death. Perhaps the most interesting thing is that it represents a reversal of traditional Christian symbolism. Black Power asserts the power of darkness which is righteous, over against the power of light which is evil. Deep down in the white American psyche, "Blackness" equals evil. Thus the devil is black, sin is black, all that is polluted is black; and as such, Blackness is the negation of goodness or whiteness. But Black Power, as a theological concept, reverses this symbol. Now "Blackness" becomes the archetypal symbol of righteousness; it is beauty, and thus, instead of being a negation of good, Blackness heralds the redemption of all that is pure and sacred. In similar fashion white comes to represent all that is evil and repressive. In fact, white is the very essence of satan himself. Now, the polarity of "Blackness" over against "whiteness" is obviously a myth created for white oppressors; but a myth, once internalized, becomes the basis for a people's action. And so the only way to steal its power is to break the symbols, turn the myth upside down, and thus make it work for the new cause of freedom.

Black Power also is the assertion of *being* in the midst of forces which threaten *non-being*. This rather interesting insight comes straight out of traditional African thought. Father Tempels, in his book *Bantu Philosophy*, throws light on this ontological emphasis in traditional African thinking.[16] He observes that the African divides the cosmos into three levels. (1) Above man are the higher forces of being, including God (the source of all power and the giver and sustainer of life); the spirits (who carry out the injunctions of God); and the spiritual ancestors of men (who also share in the power). (2) On the second level is man, who, having supreme control over created things, is the embodiment of power on earth. The forces above him are not only his source of power, but are also strangely dependent on him for their subsistence. (3) Below man are the created things both animate and inanimate. These are the agencies of life and they are for the use of man. Man has a symbiotic relationship with them and if he makes proper use of them, he can augment his force-vitale. Thus man lives his life in a force field in which every being is force and every force is being. Beings are always in interaction and so each man's chief aim in life is to keep his being from destruction by other forces or beings. Thus to live strongly, to reinforce being, has always been the greatest drive in the African personality. It is to this end the African prays, offers sacrifice and maintains a proper relationship with the forces above him, with man, and with the agencies of life below him. The African man seeks, above all things, to maintain ritual neutrality with his cosmos in order that the channels of power be open to his being. Any sign of a diminution of his being gives rise to the quest for reinforcement. Thus the idea that Black Power is the assertion of Black being strongly suggests that present-day trends are best seen as revitalizations of a traditional African world view. And that, in fact, is the main thesis of this book. Black Power, as the assertion of Black being, is a return to the ancestral ontology. How valid is this hypothesis? The answer can be found in a review of Black experience.

The Black man in New World societies was reduced to the status of a thing—and a disposable thing at that, one to be used and abused at will. The well-known spiritual represents Black humanity as a heap of "dry bones," without life, the scrap heap of oppression. But how much potential life is there in a "thing"? The concept of "thingness" has a special place in the traditional African world view. The word in the Bantu language is *kintu*, "thing."[17] But kintu also represents what we have just referred to as "agencies of life." Now, in African thought, kintu, or "things," are not merely inert; they have latent powers. These powers can be actuated by God or by the medicine man. This is done by incantation, the releasing of power through words. "Things" thus empowered become forces for good or evil. We recall our reference to W. E. B. Du Bois's observation that on the plantation the forerunner of the Black preacher was the medicine man. Is it too farfetched to suggest that Black Power is itself an incantation, a miraculous call to being and life where there had only been death, hopelessness, and "dry bones"? In African thought the "Word," is the instrument of incantation and as such it is power. It is creative force. In the Bantu language it is *nommo* and is similar to the Greek *logos*.[18] From the Word comes being. The New Testament states: "And the Word became flesh . . ."[19] This idea becomes crystal clear when set within the context of African theology. Thus it was the incantation of Black magicians such as Frederick Douglass, Marcus Garvey, Malcolm X and a host of other visionaries that brought a psychological resurrection to Black men. It was the power called forth that has enabled Blacks everywhere to tear off the "graveclothes of inferiority" and to reassert their Black identity, their Black personality and their Black sacred destiny.

Black Power is Black incantation (magic) pronouncing a curse on the witchcraft of white racism, and it is African theology. In African thought magic is nothing but the setting loose of powers contained in the world, either for protection against evil, or for the destruction of it. Magic is needed because of the existence of a ritual pollution, an evil counterforce which is undermining the proper ordering of the cosmos and of mankind.

Contemporary Black theology, then, is rightfully understood as primarily a reconstruction of the collective unconscious of African peoples. As such it is revolutionary. It is revolutionary because an awakened Black consciousness can no longer be at ease in the status quo.

Black theology claims to have biblical support. It states that the essence of theology is God's creative action in history, the repeated redemption of suffering humanity.[20] After all, the biblical God first made himself known to man in a suffering community; it was Israel's oppression in Egypt that motivated God to reveal himself. Therefore, if God is concerned with the suffering of the oppressed, this God is today most especially the God of the Black man, for Blackness is the most potent modern symbol of suffering and oppression. According to Black theologians, God's deliverance of Israel was only symbolic of his concern for all the downtrodden. Theology, then, is not the truth about God unless it is a statement about God's redemptive activity. God is a God of justice, only if he is moved by injustice. He is a God of righteousness only if he opposes unrighteousness.[21]

And it was Jesus who announced his redemptive mission by saying, "The spirit of the Lord is upon me because He has anointed me to preach good news to the poor; He has sent me to proclaim release to the captives, the recovery of sight to the blind, to set at liberty those who are oppressed, to proclaim the acceptable year of the Lord."[22] Thus the Judaeo-Christian tradition is permeated with the theme of God's stand against oppression, but the Christian Church in its Western expression has never championed "Black liberation." On the contrary, it has all too often been the staunch advocate of the status quo, continually promoting the exploitation of Blacks. The white Christian conscience has been slow to respond to the cries of oppressed Blacks. And thus, according to Black theology, is the direct result of a deliberate failure on the part of Christianity to carry out the command of God. Thus, while Black theology is cast in the thought forms of Christianity, it is really anti-Christian in thrust. It reaches back to the world view of African humanistic philosophy and simply reinterprets it in Christian terms. As a revolutionary theology, it is saying to Christianity: "The Black world which you have persisted in oppressing has returned to the humanizing ideologies of its racial heritage. We will no longer suffer the indignities of your theology based on a white God, a God in your own image; we will return to the source of power, the God of our fathers, the God who has upheld our people for millennia past. He made us 'Black' and so he must be 'Black.' "

Finally, Black theology and Black Power are not only revolutionary, but also redemptive. They evoke the power that enables Black people to say "yes" to *being,* and "no" to *non-being.* It is this Black "power" that enabled Martin Luther King, Jr., to glimpse the fulfillment of his dreams in what most others took to be a hopeless situation: "I have been to the mountaintop." What King saw on that mountaintop, we on the plains of struggle have not yet been privileged to see, but the spiritual and psychological emancipation of the Black man is inevitable now. It may be that the days are yet far away when the leaven of traditional Black religion, with its positive vision of human and social integration, will be realized. It may be that the white world will persist a while longer in its myth of white superiority and Black inferiority. But as an Akan proverb says: "The beginning and the end of the great panoramas of creation no man knows except God." Still, the African soul is naturally an optimistic one. The African personality is grounded on the tenacity of a faith in the ultimate decency of things, a strong belief that there is a God somewhere in the universe who has tomorrow in his hands.

CHAPTER 1—*SOUL-FORCE: Introduction*

1. Rex Nettleford, *Mirror Mirror: Identity, Race and Protest in Jamaica* (Kingston/New York: Collins, 1970), p. 174.

2. Lerone Bennett, Jr., "The First Generation: The Birth of Black America," *Ebony,* June 1969, p. 32.

3. Placide Tempels, *Bantu Philosophy: Présence Africaine* (Paris: Rue des Écoles, 1959). This book is the best analysis of African world view yet written.

4. To get a broader view on the reaction of primary society to Western intrusion, one should read John V. Taylor, *The Primal Vision* (Philadelphia: Fortress Press, 1963); David B. Barrett, *Schism and Renewal in Africa* (New York: Oxford, 1968); Sylvia Strupp, ed., *Millenarian Dreams in Action* (The Hague: Mouton and Co., 1962) especially the article by David Aberle on "Relative Deprivation." See additional materials in the Bibliography.

5. See Eric Hoffer, *The True Believer* (New York: New American Library, 1951); also Luther P. Gerlach and Virginia H. Hine, *People, Power, Change: Movements of Social Transformation* (New York: Bobbs, 1970).

6. William E. B. Du Bois, "The Soul of Black Folk," *Three Negro Classics* (New York: Avon Books, 1965).

7. Ralph Linton, "Nativistic Movements," *American Anthropologists,* 45 (1943).

8. Anthony F. C. Wallace, "Revitalization Movements," *American Anthropologists,* 58 (1956).

9. Keorapetse Kgositsile, "Spirits Unchained," *My Name Is Afrika* (New York: Doubleday/Anchor, 1971), p. 85.

CHAPTER 2—*SOURCE OF SOUL: Our African Heritage*

1. Melville J. Herskovits, *The Myth of the Negro Past* (Boston: Beacon Press, 1969), chap. 2; Orlando Patterson, *The Sociology of Slavery* (London: Maggibon and Kee, 1967); Basil Davidson, *Black Mother* (London: Gollancz, 1968).

2. Melville J. Herskovits, *The New World Negro: Selected Papers in Afro-American Studies* (Bloomington: Ind. Univ. Press, 1966).

3. Sir Edward Burnett Tylor, *The Origin of Culture* (London: Harper Torchbooks, 1958), p. 1.

4. An elaborate discussion of this concept is found in *African Worlds,* ed. Daryll Forde (London/New York: Oxford, 1954). See the article "The Fon People of Dahomey" by P. Mercur; also, Melville J. Herskovits' elaborate study of *Dahomey, An Ancient West African Kingdom,* Vols. I and II (Evanston, Ill.: Northwestern Univ. Press, 1967).

5. E. Bolaji Idowu, *Olòdúmaré: God in Yoruba Belief* (London: Longmans, 1962), pp. 18–48. This book is the most definitive study of Yoruba religion to date.

6. J. B. Danquah, *The Akan Doctrine of God* (London: Cass, 1968) (1st ed., 1944), Sec. II, chap. 1, pp. 30–77.

7. R. S. Rattray, *Religion and Art in Ashanti* (Oxford, 1927). Also see Bibliography for works by E. B. Idowu, John S. Mbiti, Kwesi Dickson and Paul Ellingworth.

8. John S. Mbiti, *African Religions and Philosophy* (New York: Praeger, 1969), chap. 3, pp. 15–47; especially his concept of the *sasa* and *zamani* periods.

9. William Abraham, *The Mind of Africa* (Chicago: Univ. of Chicago Press, 1963).

10. K. A. Busia, "The Ashanti," in *Forde,* op. cit.

11. For a good study on sacrifice in African traditional religion, see E. E. Evans-Pritchard, *Nuer Religion* (New York: Oxford, 1956). For West Africa, two excellent articles by C. R. Gaba, "Sacrifice in Anlo Religion," Pts. I and II, *The Ghana Bulletin of Theology,* 3, no. 5 (December 1968), 3, no. 7 (December 1969). Harry Sawyer, "Sacrifice," in *Biblical Revelation and African Beliefs,* Kwesi Dickson and Paul Ellingworth, eds. (Maryknoll, N.Y.: Obis Books, 1969).

12. Gaba, op. cit., pp. 13–19.

13. See biblical references: Genesis 22:1–10; Judges 11:19; and Micah 6:7.

14. W. J. Goode, *Religion Among the Primitives* (Glencoe, Ill.: Free Press, 1951).

15. Placide Tempels' discussion on the subject, op. cit.

16. Mbiti, op. cit., chaps. 15–16.

17. Ibid., pp. 217–18.

18. Claude Levi-Strauss, *The Savage Mind* (Chicago: Univ. of Chicago Press, 1969), p. 13.

19. According to a survey made in 1938, only five thousand African tales have been collected out of an estimated quarter of a million existing on the continent. See *African Myths and Tales,* ed. Susan Feldmann (New York: Dell, 1961). Among the important sources in myths and proverbs are: Geoffrey Parrinder, *African Mythology* (London: Paul Hamlyn Pub., 1967); Paul Radin, *African Folklore* (Princeton, N.J.: Princeton Univ. Press, 1970); Rattray, *Ashanti Proverbs* (London: Clarendon Press, 1916); and *Akan-Ashanti Folktales,* 1930.

20. Richard F. Burton, *The Proverbs: Wit and Wisdom from Africa* (New York: Negro Univ. Press, 1969—originally published, 1865), p. 25.

21. Ibid.

22. Daniel F. McCall, *Africa: In Time-Perspective: A Discussion of Historical Reconstruction from Unwritten Sources* (New York: Oxford, 1969), pp. 38–61.

23. Edward Wilmot Blyden, *African Life and Customs* (London: African Publication Society, New Impression, 1969), p. 62; Blyden quotes "The Hibbert Lectures," 1878, p. 195.

24. Quoted in ibid., pp. 64–65.

CHAPTER 3—*SOUL IN CAPTIVITY: Africa in the Americas*

1. Eric Williams, *Capitalism and Slavery* (Chapel Hill, N.C., 1938), chap. 1.

2. St. George Tucker, *Blackstone's Commentaries . . . with an appendix to each volume,* 4 vols. (Philadelphia: W. Y. Birch and A. Small, 1803), Bk. I, Pt. II, in an appendix on Slavery (H), p. 55.

3. Urlich Bonnell Phillips, *American Negro Slavery, A Survey of the Supply, Employment and Control of Negro Labor as Deter-*

mined by the Plantation Regime (New York: Appleton, 1936), p. 495.

4. Herbert S. Klein, *Slavery in the Americas: A Comparative Study of Virginia and Cuba* (Chicago: Univ. of Chicago Press, 1967), p. 40.

5. Ibid., p. 38.

6. William Waller Hening, ed., *The Statutes at Large: being a collection of All the Laws of Virginia from the first session of the Legislature in the year 1619,* 13 vols. (Richmond: Samuel Pleasents, Jr., 1819–23), II, 270.

7. Ibid., II, 299.

8. Ibid., III, 87–88.

9. Charles Colcock Jones, *Religious Instruction of the Negroes in the United States, 1842* (reprinted from an original edition in Fisk University Library).

10. Ibid., p. 14 ff.

11. Ibid.

12. Ibid., p. 21.

13. Ibid.

14. Ibid.

15. Ibid., p. 22.

16. Ibid., chap. 1.

17. Ibid., p. 44.

18. Ibid., p. 45.

19. Quoted in William James Gardner, *A History of Jamaica from Its Discovery by Christopher Columbus to the Present Time* (London, 1873), p. 331.

20. *Recopilación de leyes de los reynos de las indias,* 3 vols. (Madrid: D. Joaquin Abarra, 1791), I, 234–36, Libro II, Título II, Ley XIII. My translation.

21. Ibid.

22. *Las Siete Partidas del rey Alfonso el sabio, cotejadas con varios codices antiguos, por la Real Academia de la Historia,* 3 vols. (Madrid: La Imprenta Real, 1807), III, 30, Partida IV, Título V, introducción. My translation.

23. Ibid., III, 570, Partida VII, Título VIII, Ley IX.

24. Ibid., III, 381, Partida VI, Título III, Ley III.

25. Klein, op. cit., p. 60.

26. Ibid., p. 66.

27. Antonio Dominguez Ortiz, "La esclavitud en Castilla durante

la edad moderna," *Estudios de Historia Social de España* (Madrid: C.S.I.C., 1952), II, 369–428.

28. Ibid., pp. 376–77.

29. Frédéric Mauro, *Le Portugal et l'Atlantique au XVIIᵉ siècle (1570–1670)* (Paris: S.E.V.P.E.V., 1960), p. 147.

30. Quoted in Fernando Ortiz, *Hampa afro-cubana: los negros esclavos, estudio sociológico y de derecho publico* (Havana: Revista Bimestre Cubana, 1916), pp. 350–51. My translation.

31. Klein, op. cit., p. 78.

32. The code, divided into fourteen chapters, is found reprinted in "Real Cédula de Su Magestad sobre la educacíon, trato y ocupaciones de los esclavos, en todos sus dominios de Indias, c islas Filipinas," *Revista de Historia de América*, 3 (September 1938): 50–59.

33. Klein, op. cit., p. 80.

34. Quoted in Klein, op. cit., p. 95.

35. Ibid., p. 98.

36. Robert Francis Jameson, *Letters from Havana During the Year 1820* (London: John Miller, 1821), pp. 21–22.

37. Klein, op. cit., p. 100.

38. Ibid., p. 105.

CHAPTER 4—*SOUL IN CAPTIVITY: The African Reaction to Slavery*

1. A very readable study in "Black slave rebellion" is that edited by Joanne Grant entitled *Black Protest: History, Documents, and Analyses, 1619 to the Present* (New York: Fawcett, 1968). The most recent researches on slavery contain chapters on "black rebellion." A good study is Herbert Aptheker's, *American Negro Slave Revolts* (New York: Int. Pubs., 1970); also, Gary Robinson, *The Fighting Maroons of Jamaica* (Kingston: Collins, 1969).

2. Bryan Edwards, in his *History, Civil and Commercial of the British Colonies in the West Indies* (London, 1793), pp. 88–89, reported that Jamaican planters were especially opposed to buying Nigerian Negroes and especially the "Ibos" because they possessed a relatively high tendency toward suicide.

3. Sir Spencer St. John in his book *Haiti or The Black Republic* (London, 1884), p. 215, spoke about sorcery in that island and stated: "During thirteen years [in the island] I had the best op-

portunities of hearing of the opinions of presidents, intelligent secretaries of states, the principal members of the medical profession, lawyers, merchants, both foreign and native, as well as other residents, who had passed a lifetime in the Republic, and the testimony was more or less unanimous as to the profound knowledge of the use of herbs possessed by the *Papaloi*."

4. Robinson, op. cit.

5. Hurbert Herring, *A History of Latin America* (New York, 1965), p. 113.

6. Mary Reckford, "The Slave Rebellion of 1831," *Jamaica Journal*, June 1969, pp. 25–31; Esteban Montejo, *The Autobiography of a Runaway Slave*, ed. Miguel Barnet, trans. Jocasta Innes (New York: Pantheon Bks., 1968).

7. For example, see James G. Leyburn, *The Haitian People* (New Haven: Yale Univ. Press, 1966); and Montejo, op. cit.

8. St. John, op. cit. This is by far one of the worst books on Haiti, but yet worth reading. A better book on Haitian history is Leyburn, op. cit.

9. Stanley M. Elkins, *Slavery: A Problem in American Institutional and Intellectual Life* (New York: Grosset, 1963), p. 98.

10. Ibid., p. 98 ff.

11. Wallace, op. cit.

12. Patterson, op. cit.; and Edwards, op. cit. Both men seem to agree with this latter opinion.

13. Gardner, op. cit., Preface, p. 4.

14. Edward Long, *The History of Jamaica* (London, 1774), II, 472; John Joseph Williams, S.J., *Psychic Phenomena of Jamaica* (New York: Dial Press, 1934), pp. 48–49, also came to a similar conclusion when he wrote:

. . . the Ashanti exercised a paramount influence in the development of the present cultural complex in Jamaica. In consequence we are justified in assuming, that when there is no evidence to the contrary, in the case of Jamaican traits and practices that are not in themselves fully intelligible, in all probability the true explanation is to be sought among the manners and customs of the Ashanti. . . .

15. Danquah, op. cit., p. 464.

16. R. C. Dallas, *The History of the Maroons* (London, 1803), I, 24 ff.

17. James Murcel Phillippo, *Jamaica: Its Past and Present State* (London, 1843), p. 75.

18. Ibid., p. 76.

19. H. G. DeLisser, *Twentieth Century Jamaica* (Kingston, 1913), p. 108.

20. Mary Douglas, *Purity and Danger: An Analysis of Concepts of Pollution and Taboo* (London: Routledge, 1966), comes closest to the function of witchcraft in a society. Sorcery generally occurs when a society is in disarray. Sorcery can be the cause of this disarray or it can use the disorder in the society to its profit.

21. DeLisser, op. cit., p. 108.

22. *Acts of Assembly,* passed in the Island of Jamaica, from 1681 to 1737, inclusive (London, 1743), p. 35.

23. The word "Taky" as it appears in the history of Jamaica has raised many questions about the origin of the name. The name appears in Danquah's book as *"Kwatakye"* and simply means a brave person, a valiant man. It was the name given to the Maroon leader of the Jamaican Rebellion of 1760.

24. Edwards, op. cit., p. 64.

25. "Records of the Colonial Office 139/21," quoted from Williams, op. cit., p. 18.

26. J. Banbury, *Jamaica Superstitions, The Obeah Book* (Kingston, 1894), p. 5.

27. J. J. Williams, op. cit., p. 72.

28. Long, op. cit., p. 146.

29. Rev. T. G. Christaller, Dictionary of the Asante and Fante Language, 2d ed. (Basel, 1933).

30. A verbatim report by a Cumina queen in the parish of St. Thomas, Jamaica, July 1971.

31. "Governor Codrington to the Council of Trade and Plantations (December 30), 1701"; also "Calendar of State Papers," *Colonial Series,* ed. Cecil Headlam, America and West Indies, Vol. XIX, No. 1132, pp. 720–21, quoted in *Savacou,* Vol. 1, No. 1, 1970.

32. In a recent article in *Savacou* (published at the University of the West Indies by the Caribbean Artists' Movement), an erudite discussion on the Ashanti leadership during slavery can be found. It is written by Monica Schuler and is entitled "Akan Slave Rebellion in the British Caribbean," June 1970.

33. Mrs. Carmichael, *Domestic Manners and Social Conditions*

of the White, Coloured and Negro Population of the West Indies,
Vol. II (London, 1833).

34. Phillippo, op. cit., p. 85.

35. The dance of the Fon people of Dahomey is more fluid. Especially the *Yanvalo* dance, which depicts the snake movement, where the head, hand and back move with snakelike ripple. The Akan dance was more martial, with a stiff posture and much stamping of the feet.

36. Albert Mawere-Opoku's article on *The African Dance* (unpublished), pp. 1–3.

37. J. J. Williams, op. cit., p. 71.

38. Quoted in ibid.

39. Phillippo, op. cit., p. 101.

40. Various estimates have been given on this subject. Robert Rotberg puts the figure at 25 million for the slaves who arrived in the New World. He estimated that 10 million slaves died in transit and another 10 million slaves were taken to the Asian and Arabian markets. See Robert Rotberg, *A Political History of Tropical Africa* (New York: Harcourt, 1968), p. 152. Donald L. Weldner, *A History of Africa South of the Sahara* (New York: Vintage, 1962), gave the conservative estimate of 4 and 6.5 millions, and suggested that of this number 3.5 and 5.5 millions arrived in the New World. Phillip D. Curtin, *The Atlantic Slave Trade* (Madison: Univ. of Wis. Press, 1969), concludes that the number was approximately 9,566,100.

41. Sylvia Winters' article in *Jamaica Journal*, June 1970, quotes John Taylor, writing from Port Royal, Jamaica, 1685.

42. Charles Leslie, *New History of Jamaica* (London, 1740), p. 308.

43. Gardner, op. cit., p. 386 ff.

44. Ibid.

45. *Cultures and Societies of Africa,* eds. Simon and Phoebe Ottenberg (New York: Random House, 1963), p. 3 ff.

46. For a definitive statement of the influence of African religious dance on the New World, see Janheinz Jahn, *Muntu: The New African Culture* (New York: Grove Press, Inc., 1961), pp. 29–95.

47. This research study was carried out in 1971.

48. St. John, op. cit., p. 216.

49. Herbert M. Morais, *The History of The Negro in Medicine* (New York: 1967), p. 15.

50. Michael Kraus, "American and European Medicine in the 18th Century," *Bulletin of the History of Medicine,* 8 (May 1940): 690.

51. Geoffrey Parrinder, *West African Religion* (London: Epworth, 1949), p. 203; see also A. P. Ellis, *The Yoruba Speaking Peoples of the Slave Coast of West Africa* (Chicago, Benin Press, 1964), p. 402.

52. Morais, op. cit., p. 12.

53. "The Negro Caesar's Cure for Poison," *Massachusetts Magazine,* 4 (1792), 103–4.

54. Ibid.

55. Ibid.

CHAPTER 5—*SOUL UNDER STRESS: Redemption Cults— Caribbean*

1. Vittorio Lanternari, *The Religion of the Oppressed: A Study of Modern Messianic Cults* (New York: Mentor Books, 1965).

2. Moreau de Saint-Méry, *Description topographique physique, civile et historique de la partie française de L'Isle de Saint-Dominique* (Philadelphia, 1797), I, 44–59.

3. Leyburn, op. cit., p. 141.

4. Quoted in Alfred Metraux, *Voodoo in Haiti* (New York: Schocken, 1972), p. 26.

5. Ibid.

6. Ralph Korngold, *Citizen Toussaint* (New York: Macmillan Press, 1943), p. 33. This quotation, no doubt, is slightly biased, but it is the least biased of the many sources that could be used in this context.

7. Leyburn, loc. cit.

8. Jean Price-Mars, *Ainsi Parla L'Oncle* (Port-au-Prince, 1928), chap. 2.

9. Maya Deren, *Divine Horsemen: The Voodoo Gods of Haiti* (New York: Chelsea House, 1970), p. 116.

10. Ibid., p. 96.

11. Ibid., p. 62.

12. Ibid.

13. Price-Mars, op. cit., p. 46.

14. Harold Courlander and Rémy Bastien, *Religion and Politics in Haiti* (Washington: Institute for Cross Cultural Research, 1966), p. 2.

15. Metraux, op. cit., p. 165.

16. Michelson Paul Hyppolite, *A Study of Haitian Folklore,* trans. Edgar Laforest and Mrs. Pansy Hart (Port-au-Prince, n.p. 1954), p. 27.

17. Ibid.

18. Quoted by William Seabrook, *The Voodoo Island* (New York: Lancer Bks., 1929), pp. 319.

19. Ibid., pp. 319–20.

20. Ibid., p. 20.

21. Deren, op. cit., p. 62.

22. Seabrook, op. cit., p. 318.

23. See Leyburn, op. cit.; Courlander and Bastien, op. cit.; and others.

24. Metraux, op. cit., p. 42.

25. C. L. R. James, *The Black Jacobins: Toussaint L'Ouverture and the San Domingo Revolution,* 2d rev. ed. (New York: Vintage, 1963), p. 87.

26. Quoted in Hyppolite, op. cit., pp. 21–22.

27. Quoted in Gardner, op. cit., p. 331.

28. Curtin, op. cit., p. 32. See also *The Baptist Register* (London, 1790–93), pp. 332–37.

29. Letters showing the "Rise and Progress of Early Negro Churches of Georgia and the West Indies," *Journal of Negro History,* 7, no. 1 (June 1923).

30. Ibid., p. 84.

31. Warrant Carlile, *Thirty-eight Years of Mission Life in Jamaica* (London, 1884), p. 121.

32. Gardner, op. cit., p. 464.

33. J. H. Buchner, *The Moravians In Jamaica* (London, 1853), pp. 139–40.

34. Martha Warren Beckwith, *Black Roadways: A Study of Jamaican Folk Life* (Chapel Hill: Univ. of N.C. Press, 1929), pp. 168–69.

35. *The Daily Gleaner,* Kingston, Jamaica, December 26, 1920.

36. Beckwith, op. cit., p. 170.

37. *The Daily Gleaner,* December 31, 1920.

CHAPTER 6—*SOUL AWAKENING: The Garvey Movement*

1. Marcus Garvey, *The Philosophy and Opinions of Marcus Garvey* or *Africa for the Africans,* compiled by Amy Jacques Garvey, 2 vols., 2d ed. (London: Cass, 1967), Pt. II, pt. 1, p. 121.

2. Ibid., p. 124.

3. Ibid., p. 126.

4. Ibid.

5. Ibid.

6. Ibid.

7. Ibid., p. 128.

8. Ibid.

9. Edmund David Cronon, *Black Moses, The Story of Marcus Garvey and the Universal Negro Improvement Association* (Madison: Univ. of Wis. Press, 1966), chap. 2, p. 21 ff.

10. Garvey, op. cit., Pt. II, pt. 1, p. 128.

11. Ibid., p. 128 ff.

12. There is still a great difference of opinion about the number of people who were actually Garveyites. Garvey often spoke of six millions, his enemies spoke of a few thousand. The exact number is hard to calculate.

13. Garvey, op. cit., Pt. II, pt. 1, p. 38.

14. Ibid., p. 81.

15. Theodor Herzl, *The Jewish State* (New York: American Zionist Emergency Council, 1946), pp. 85–86.

16. Ibid.

17. Ibid.

18. Ibid.

19. Garvey, op. cit., Pt. II, pt. 1, pp. 135–40.

20. Ibid.

21. Cronon, op. cit., p. 62.

22. Ibid., pp. 62–63.

23. Taken from "Program of International Convention of the U.N.I.A. and African Community's League," August 1920.

24. Ibid.

25. John Hope Franklin, *From Slavery to Freedom* (New York: Knopf, 1947), p. 452.

26. Cronon, op. cit., pp. 65–66.

27. Hoffer, op. cit., p. 20.

28. Garvey, op. cit., Pt. I, pp. 72–73.

29. Ibid., pp. 73–74.

30. Ibid., Pt. II, pt. 1, pp. 119–20.

31. For further information on the Black Star Line and Garvey's trial and imprisonment, see Garvey, op. cit., Pt. III; also, Cronon, op. cit., chap. 4.

32. Garvey, op. cit., Pt. III, pp. 362 ff.

33. Ibid.

34. Ibid., p. 396.

35. Ibid., p. 238.

36. W. E. B. Du Bois, Dusk of Dawn (New York: Harcourt, 1940), pp. 277–78.

37. James Weldon Johnson, Black Manhattan (New York: Knopf, 1930), p. 285.

38. Gunnar Myrdal, An American Dilemma: The Negro Problem and Modern Democracy (New York: Harper, 1944), p. 749.

39. The Negro Churchman, September–October 1923.

40. The Autobiography of Malcolm X (New York: Grove, 1968), pp. 6–7.

41. Ibid.

42. Elijah Muhammad, Message to the Black man in America (Chicago, Muhammad Mosque of Islam, No. 2, 1965).

43. Quoted from an address by Dr. Martin Luther King, Jr., delivered in Kingston, Jamaica, August 1965.

44. Garvey, op. cit., Pt. III, p. 239.

CHAPTER 7—SOUL ASSERTING ITSELF: The Rastafarians

1. Gerlach and Hine, op. cit.

2. For a more detailed study of the Rastafarian Cult, see the author's "The Rastafarians: Messianic Cultism in Jamaica," published by the Institute of Caribbean Studies (Puerto Rico, 1968). The author is grateful to the Institute for the permission to summarize the movement's beliefs and practices in the present book. New materials have been added which do not appear in the original.

3. Ibid., chap. 4, "The Garvey Movement."

4. Quoted from field study materials gathered in 1965 from Samuel Elisha Brown.

5. G. E. Simpson, "Political Cultism in West Kingston, Jamaica," Social and Economic Studies, 3, no. 4 (1955); (Jamaica:

University of the West Indies); also, M. G. Smith, Roy Augier and Rex Nettleford, "The Ras Tafari Movement in Kingston, Jamaica," *Social and Economic Studies* (University of the West Indies, 1960).

6. *The Daily Gleaner* (Kingston: November 11, 1930) has a very well written historical article on the life of Haile Selassie.

7. Many such prophetic statements are attributed to Marcus Garvey. No written source for this statement has been found.

8. Smith, et al., op. cit., pp. 9–11.

9. Ibid.

10. Ibid.

11. Ibid.

12. Revelation, chaps. 5 and 19.

13. A shilling was the equivalent of twenty-five cents.

14. The cultists are called by many names, such as Rastafarians, Rastas, Rasman and Brethren.

15. *The Daily Gleaner,* August 25, 1941.

16. Ibid.

17. Ibid.

18. Smith, et al., op. cit., p. 12.

19. Ibid.

20. Simpson, op. cit.

21. *The Constitution and By-Laws of The Ethiopian World Federation.* Exists only in pamphlet form.

22. *The Daily Gleaner,* September 30, 1955, p. 1.

23. Letter to the Jamaican Ethiopian World Federation by George Bryan, Executive Secretary, September 24, 1955. The text of the letter can be found in my monograph on the Rastafarians. See Bibliography.

24. *The Star,* Kingston, March 6, 1958.

25. *The Star,* March 22, 1958, p. 1.

26. *Negus* is a name similar to "his majesty" and is Rastafarian praise name.

27. *The Tribune,* Kingston, June 30, 1958.

28. Ganja is another name for marijuana.

29. *The Daily Gleaner,* March 15, 1958.

30. *The Daily Gleaner,* March 2, 1958.

31. Collected from field research, 1965.

32. *The Daily Gleaner,* October 7, 1959, p. 1.

33. *The Daily Gleaner,* April 7, 1960.

34. *The Daily Gleaner,* June 22, 1960, p. 1.

35. *Time,* July 4, 1960, p. 1.

36. *The Sunday Guardian,* Kingston, May 1, 1960.

37. Smith, et al., op. cit., p. 38.

38. "Report of the Mission to Africa" (Kingston: The Government Printing Office, 1961). There were two reports: one by the non-Rastafarians, entitled the "Majority Report," the other by the Rastafarians, entitled the "Minority Report."

39. *The Daily Gleaner,* July 31, 1961.

40. Excerpt from a taped interview with a leader of the Rastafarian Repatriation Association, July 11, 1965.

41. Samuel Elisha Brown, *Treatise on the Rastafarian Movement* (unpublished manuscript), collected on field research, Jamaica, July 1965.

42. The effect of this prayer is not conveyed accurately in its printed form. In speech, Selassie *I* rhymes with Ras Tafar*i*.

43. Brown, op. cit.

44. This is evidently a Rastafarian exegesis of I John 4:4.

45. I John 3:2.

46. Quoted from research notes. The term "avatar" is added by the author.

47. Brown, op. cit.

48. Romans 6:23.

49. Matthew 8:22 and Leviticus, chap. 21. Rastafarians' usage of the Bible is rather erratic—they most often quote from memory.

50. Ras Moses, an informant. Taped interview, August 1966.

51. Ras Samuel Clayton. Taped interview, August 8, 1966.

52. Marcus Garvey, "African Fundamentalism: A Racial Hierarchy and Empire for Negroes" (unpublished manuscript, 1925).

53. Brown, op. cit.

54. Ibid.

55. From field notes of August 1966.

56. A transcribed text of the University Radio Service program, 1965, over the facilities of Jamaica Broadcasting Company.

57. Isaiah 43:6.

58. C. Eric Lincoln, *The Black Muslims in America* (Boston: Beacon Press, 1961), p. 44.

59. Daniel 2:31–42.

60. A verbatim transcription from a taped interview, August 11, 1966.

61. Leviticus 21:5.
62. Notes taken from the files of Samuel E. Brown, July 1965.
63. Gladstone Robertson, "Unity or Bust," *Ethiopia Calls,* n.d.
64. Genesis 1:12 and 29; and Proverbs 15:17. See also Genesis 3:18, 9:3 and Psalm 104:14.
65. Rastafarian Benediction, transcribed from field notes.
66. Smith, et al., op. cit.
67. Transcribed from field interview.
68. Katrin Norris, *Jamaica: The Search for an Identity* (London: Oxford, 1962), p. 17.

CHAPTER 8—*SOUL TRIUMPHING: A Return to the Roots "At Home and Abroad"*

1. James Fernandez, "African Religious Movements: Types and Dynamics," *The Journal of Modern African Studies,* 2, no. 4 (London: Cambridge, 1964), 533.

2. An extensive body of literature on the origin, nature and extent of schisms in Africa is steadily being produced. These works are of great value to the scholars of culture change phenomena but most important to the missionologist and to the student of comparative religion. Many of these works provide a much needed insight into what takes place in society when Western Christendom confronts African and Asian world view. Among the most important are David B. Barrett, op. cit.; F. B. Welbourn, *East African Rebels: A Study of Some Independent Churches* (London: MacGibbon, 1957); B. G. M. Sundkler, *Bantu Prophets of South Africa* (London: Oxford, 1961). For a study of the same phenomenon on the Asian scene see Peter Worsley, *The Trumpet Shall Sound* (London: MacGibbon, 1957); and Sylvia L. Thrupp, *Millenial Dreams in Action: Essay in Comparative Study* (The Hague: Mouton, 1962).

3. For a study of the term *force-vitale* as it refers to African traditional religion, see P. Tempels, op. cit. Tempels believed that the key concept to African religions and philosophy is what he calls "the vital force." He isolates this as "the essence of being: force is being and being is force." See also John S. Mbiti, op. cit., for a critical comment on Tempels' concept.

4. For a discussion on the term "anomie," see Robert K. Merton, *Social Theory and Social Structure,* rev. ed. (Glencoe, Ill.:

Free Press, 1957), p. 162. "Anomie . . . is a breakdown in the cultural structure, occurring particularly when there is an acute disfunction between the cultural norms and goals and the socially structured capacities of members of the group to act in accord with them."

5. According to Barrett, op. cit., African awakening conscious-ness is based on a "Zeitgeist" which builds up momentum over several years, which inevitably ends in a schism. The Zeitgeist consists of eighteen variables such as the extent of white occupa-tion of lands, the length of time since missionary activities started in the tribe, the number of white missionaries residing in the tribal unit, what portion of the Bible has been translated in the vernacular and so on. Barrett's scale of variables shows that whenever seven of these variables are present in a tribe, there begins what is called marginal separation. If twelve of these variables are present a medium high pressure for separation is present, but whenever eighteen of these variables are present, there will be inevitable separation. See Barrett, p. 111.

6. Barrett, op. cit., pp. 18–32. See also Welbourn, op. cit., for information on East Africa and Sundkler, op. cit., for information on South Africa.

7. Mbiti, op. cit., p. 2; see also F. B. Welbourn and B. A. Ogot, *A Place to Feel at Home: A Study of Two Independent Churches in Western Kenya* (London: Oxford, 1966), p. 13. This study is one of the most sympathetic introductions to the problem of African alienation.

8. Barrett, op. cit., pp. 146–50.

9. For a discussion of the Lenshina movement, see ibid., p. 149.

10. Welbourn, op. cit.

11. For some examples, see Léopold S. Senghor, especially his poems "Black Women" and "Night in Senegal"; Aimé Césaire, especially his poems "Cahier d'un retour au pays Natal"; *Kwame Nkrumah's Autobiography* is also an excellent study of Africans returning to their roots.

12. Dietrich Bonhoeffer, a young German theologian, born in 1906, was martyred by the Nazis in 1945. As a radical theologian, he questioned the traditional religion of his time and found it ir-relevant to the rapid social change which emerged after the Second World War.

13. See Nettleford, op. cit.; Patterson, op. cit.; and René Piquion, *Manuel de Négritude* (Port-au-Prince: Editions Henri Deschamps, 1965).

14. Albert B. Cleage, Jr., *Black Messiah* (New York: Sheed, 1968).

15. James Cone is at present Professor of Black Theology, Union Theological Seminary, New York City; a Ph.D. of Northwestern University. He is a prolific writer and a spellbinding lecturer. His ability to portray the "Black experience" in a theological perspective makes him the most relevant Black thinker in religion today. His best-known book is *Black Theology and Black Power* (New York: Seabury, 1969). Among the other Black writers are J. Deotis Roberts of Howard University and Albert B. Cleage, Jr., of the Shrine of the Black Madonna in Detroit.

16. Tempels, op. cit., chap. 2.

17. For a discussion on the word *kintu,* see Jahn, op. cit., chap. 4.

18. Ibid., chap. 5.

19. John 1:14.

20. Cone, op. cit., chap. 2.

21. Ibid.

22. Luke 4:18–19; see Cone, op. cit., p. 35.

A SELECT BIBLIOGRAPHY

1. AFRICA:

Abrahams, William. *The Mind of Africa.* New York, 1963.

Barrett, David B. *Schism and Renewal in Africa.* New York, 1968.

Bohannan, Paul, and Curtin, Phillip. *Africa and Africans.* New York, 1971.

Danquah, J. B. *The Akan Doctrine of God.* London, 1968.

Debrunner, H. *Witchcraft in Ghana.* West Africa, 1959.

Deschamps, H. *Les Religions de L'Afrique Noire.* Paris, 1960.

Dickson, Kwesi, and Ellingworth, Paul. *Biblical Revelation and African Belief.* Maryknoll, New York, 1969.

Evans-Pritchard, E. E. *Witchcraft, Oracles and Magic among the Azande.* Oxford, 1937.

——. *Nuer Religion.* Oxford, 1956.

——. *Theories of Primitive Religion.* Oxford, 1965.

Field, M. J. *Religion and Medicine of the Ga People.* Oxford, 1937.

Forde, D., ed. *African Worlds.* Oxford, 1954.

Fortes, M. *Oedipus and Job in West African Religion.* Oxford, 1959.

Frobenius, Leo. *The Voices of Africa.* London, 1913.

Herskovits, Melville J. *Dahomey,* Vols. I and II. Evanston, Ill., 1967.

Idowu, E. B. *Olòdúmaré: God in Yoruba Belief.* London, 1962.

Jahn, Janheinz. *Muntu.* New York: Grove Press, Inc., 1961.

Kenyatta, J. *Facing Mount Kenya.* London, 1938.

Mbiti, John S. *African Religions and Philosophy.* New York, 1969.

——. *Concepts of God in Africa.* New York, 1970.

Rattray, R. S. *Religion and Art in Ashanti.* Oxford, 1927.

Rotberg, Robert I. *Rebellion in Black Africa.* Oxford/New York, 1970.

Smith, E. W., ed. *African Ideas of God*. London, 1950.

Sundkler, B. G. M. *Bantu Prophets of South Africa*. London, 1961.

Taylor, J. V. *The Primal Vision*. Philadelphia: Fortress Press, 1963.

Tempels, P. *Bantu Philosophy*. Paris, 1959.

2. CARIBBEAN:

A. Cuba

Bascom, William R. "The Focus of Cuban Santeria," *Southwestern Journal of Anthropology* (1950).

Klein, Herbert S. *Slavery in the Americas: A Comparative Study of Virginia and Cuba*. Chicago, 1967.

Ortiz, Fernando. *Hampa Afro-Cubana: Los Negros Esclavos*. Havana, 1916.

——. "Los Cabildos Afro-Cubanos," *Revista Bimestre*, 41 (1921).

——. "La Fiesta Afro-Cubana del día de Reyes," *Revista Bimestre Cubana*, 40 (1920).

——. *Hampa Afro-Cubana: Los Negros Brujus*. Madrid, 1906.

Saco, José Antonio. *Historia de la esclavitud de la raza Africana en el Nuevo Mundo*. Barcelona, 1879.

Wright, Irene Aloha. *The Early History of Cuba, 1492–1586*. New York, 1916.

Wurdemann, J. G. F. *Notes on Cuba*. Boston, 1844.

B. Haiti

Antonio, Louis-Jean. *La Crise de Possession et la Possession Dramatique*. Port-au-Prince, 1956.

Courlander, Harold. *The Drum and the Hoe*. Los Angeles, 1960.

—— and Bastien, Rémy, *Religion and Politics in Haiti*. Washington, 1966.

Deren, Maya. *Divine Horsemen: The Voodoo Gods of Haiti*. New York, 1970.

Dérose, Rodolphe. *Caractère Culture Vodou*. n.p., 1961.

Dorsainvil, J. C. *Vodou et Névrose*. Port-au-Prince, 1931.

Duvalier, François. *Éléments d'une Doctrine*, Vol. 1. Port-au-Prince, 1968.

Gayot, Gerard. *Clergé Indigène*. Port-au-Prince, 1956.

Leyburn, James G. *The Haitian People*. New Haven, 1966.

Madou, Thomas. *Histoire d'Haïti*. Port-au-Prince, 1904.

Marcelin, Milo. *Mythologie Vodou*. Port-au-Prince, n.d.

Metraux, Alfred. *Voodoo in Haiti*. New York, 1972.

Price-Mars, Jean. *Ainsi Parla L'Oncle.* Port-au-Prince, 1928.

St. John, Sir Spencer. *Haiti or The Black Republic.* London, 1884.

C. Jamaica

Banbury, R. Thomas. *Jamaica Superstitioner, The Obeah Book.* Kingston, 1894.

Barclay, Alexander. *A Practical View of the Present Slave State in the West Indies.* London, 1828.

Barrett, Leonard E. *The Rastafarians: Messianic Cultism in Jamaica.* Puerto Rico, 1969.

Beckwith, Martha Warren. *Jamaica Anansi Stories.* New York, 1924.

——. *Jamaica Folklore.* New York, 1929.

——. *Black Roadways: A Study of Jamaican Folk Life.* Chapel Hill, N.C., 1928.

Cundall, Frank. *Studies in Jamaica History.* London, 1927.

Curtin, P. D. *Two Jamaicas: The Role of Ideas in a Tropical Colony, 1830–1865.* Cambridge, Mass., 1955.

Dallas, Robert Charles. *The History of the Maroons.* London, 1803.

DeLisser, Herbert G. *Twentieth Century Jamaica.* Kingston, 1913.

Edwards, Bryan. *History, Civil and Commercial of the British Colonies in the West Indies.* London, 1793.

——. *Proceedings of the Governor and Assembly of Jamaica in Regards to the Maroon Negroes.* London, 1796.

Emerick, Abraham J. *Obeah and Duppyism in Jamaica.* (Printed privately.) Woodstock, Mass., 1915.

——. *Jamaica Myalism.* Woodstock, Mass., 1916.

——. *Jamaica Duppies.* Woodstock, Mass., 1916.

Gardner, William James. *A History of Jamaica from its Discovery by Christopher Columbus to the Present Time.* London, 1873.

Hogg, Donald. *Jamaican Religions.* (Unpublished dissertation.) Yale, 1964.

Knibb, William. *Facts and Documents Connected with the Late Insurrection in Jamaica . . . etc.* London, 1832.

Long, Edward. *The History of Jamaica.* London, 1774.

Moore, Joseph G. *Religion of Jamaican Negroes: A Study in Afro-Caribbean Acculturation.* (Doctoral dissertation series.) Ann Arbor, Mich., 1954.

Nettleford, Rex M. *Mirror Mirror: Identity, Race and Protest in Jamaica.* Kingston/New York, 1970.

Patterson, Orlando. *The Sociology of Slavery.* London, 1967.

Phillippo, James Murcel. *Jamaica: Its Past and Present State.* London, 1834.

Seaga, Edward. "Cults in Jamaica," *Jamaica Journal,* June 1969.

Simpson, George E. "Political Cultism in West Kingston, Jamaica," *Social and Economic Studies,* 3, no. 4 (1955).

———. "The Ras Tafari Movement in Jamaica: A Study of Race and Class Conflict," *Social Forces,* December 24, 1955.

———. "Jamaican Revivalist Cults," *Social and Economic Studies,* no. 5 (1956).

Smith M. G., Augier, Roy, and Nettleford, Rex. "The Ras Tafarian Movement in Kingston, Jamaica," *Social and Economic Studies,* University of the West Indies, 1962.

Williams, J. J. *Psychic Phenomena of Jamaica.* New York, 1934.

Abosom (Akan deity representatives), 22
Abrahams, Peter, quoted on Garvey's influence, 203–4
Accompong (Akan deity), 62–63
Achebe, Chinua, 211
Adjas (Haitian people from West Central Africa), 99
Africa, 13–39, 41 ff. (*see also* Afro-Americans; specific aspects, countries, people, places); for Africans (repatriation movements), 129–52, 154, 156–201 (*see also* specific individuals, movements); and new religious sects, 208–18; religious beliefs and, 4 ff., 16–39, 78 ff., 95–127, 208–13 (*see also* specific aspects, movements, people, religions); slavery and, 41–56 (*see also* Slaves); as source of "soul," 13–39
Africanization (indigenization), New World slavery and, 75–93
African Religions and Philosophy (Mbiti), 29
Afro-Americans (Blackamericans), 1–11 ff., 41–56, 57 ff. (*see also* specific aspects, developments, individuals, movements, people, places); and African heritage, 13–39, 213; inferiority myth and, 14–16; and new religious sects, 203–18; reaction to slavery among, 41–56, 57–93, 95–127 (*see also* Slaves; specific aspects, individuals, movements); redemption cults and, 95–127; religious beliefs and, 4–11, 16–39, 60–72, 78–93, 95–127, 208 ff. (*see also* specific beliefs, cults, movements, peo-

ple); and return-to-Africa movements, 129–52, 154, 156–201; and slavery, 3–4, 6, 13 ff., 41–56, 75–93 (*see also* Slaves); and soul, 1–11 ff.
Afro-Christian cults, 95–127. *See also* specific aspects, beliefs, cults, religions
Agonas (Haitian people from West Central Africa), 99
Agwé (Vodun water deity), 103
Akan people, 14, 18, 21–22, 24–25, 33–34, 36, 62–63, 68, 71–72, 73, 76, 83, 116; cultural and religious influences of, 18, 21–22, 24–25, 33–34; and slave revolts, 72
Allada, 102
All African People's Conference (Accra, December 13, 1958), 204
Amulets, use of, 86
Ananse, in New World folklore, 36–37
Ancestor beliefs (ancestor cults), 17, 22–24, 61, 70, 71, 80, 84
Angels, 121–22, 123
Angola, 13, 99
Animal sacrifice, 26, 70, 110, 117–18, 120
Animal stories, folklore and, 35, 36–37
Animism, 37
Anomie, African society and, 206, 233
Antonio Maceo, S.S., 146
"Apathy of the Masses Remains Untouched, The" (Lewis), 167
Aradas (Haitian people from West Central Africa), 61, 99, 103